RETHINKING AFRICA SERIES

WHOSE HISTORY COUNTS

Decolonising African Pre-colonial Historiography

JUNE BAM
LUNGISILE NTSEBEZA
ALLAN ZINN
EDITORS

Whose History Counts? Decolonising African Pre-colonial Historiography

Published by AFRICAN SUN MeDIA under the Conference-RAP imprint

All rights reserved

Copyright © 2018 AFRICAN SUN MeDIA and the editors

Conference papers published in this volume were approved by the editorial board of the conference and peer reviewed after the conference took place. Thereafter these proceedings were subjected to an independent double-blind peer evaluation by the publisher.

The editors and publisher have made every effort to obtain permission for and acknowledge the use of copyrighted material. Refer all enquiries to the publisher.

This publication is Volume III in the CAS Papers from the Pre-Colonial Catalytic Project, published under the auspices of the Rethinking Africa series. The Pre-Colonial Catalytic Project is funded by the National Institute for Humanities and Social Science.

No part of this book may be reproduced or transmitted in any form or by any electronic, photographic or mechanical means, including photocopying and recording on record, tape or laser disk, on microfilm, via the Internet, by e-mail, or by any other information storage and retrieval system, without prior written permission by the publisher.

First edition 2018

ISBN 978-1-928314-11-0
ISBN 978-1-928314-12-7 (e-book)
https://doi.org/10.18820/9781928314127

Set in Cambria 10/15
Cover design, typesetting and production by AFRICAN SUN MeDIA

Conference-RAP is a licensed imprint of AFRICAN SUN MeDIA. Conference proceedings are published under this imprint in print and electronic format.

This publication can be ordered directly from:
www.sun-e-shop.co.za
africansunmedia.snapplify.com (e-book)
www.store.it.si (e-book)
www.africansunmedia.co.za

CONTENTS

Abbreviations & Acronyms	iii
Contributors	v

Chapter 1 — 1
Introduction
Lungisile Ntsebeza

Section I | Decolonising Historiography

Chapter 2 — 15
Of Definitions and Naming:
"I am the earth itself. God made me a chief on the very first day of creation."
Nomathamsanqa C. Tisani

Chapter 3 — 35
Language as Source of Revitalisation and Reclamation of Indigenous Epistemologies: Contesting Assumptions and Re-imagining Women Identities in (African) Xhosa Society
Pamela Maseko

Chapter 4 — 57
The Missing Idiom of African Historiography: African Historical Writing in Walter Rubusana's Zemk'inkomo Magwalandini
Nomalanga Mkhize

Chapter 5 — 75
Repositioning uMakhulu as an Institution of Knowledge: Beyond 'Biologism' towards uMakhulu as the body of Indigenous Knowledge
Babalwa Magoqwana

Chapter 6 | **91**

The long southern African past:
Enfolded time and the challenges of archive
Carolyn Hamilton

SECTION II | **The Challenges of Praxis**

Chapter 7 | **119**

The study of earlier African societies before colonial contact in the former Xhalanga magisterial district, Eastern Cape: A case study of three villages in the district
Fani Ncapayi & Mlingani Mayongo

Chapter 8 | **139**

The Home of Legends Project: The Potential and Challenges of Using Heritage Sites to Tell the Pre-colonial Stories of the Eastern Cape
Denver A. Webb & Mcebisi Ndletyana

Chapter 9 | **155**

Considerations towards establishing equitable stakeholder partnerships for transformation in higher education in South Africa: A review of the challenges, constraints and possibilities in working on pre-colonial history
June Bam, Bradley Van Sitters & Bongani Ndhlovu

Chapter 10 | **179**

Allegorical Critiques and National Narratives: Mapungubwe in South African history education
Himal Ramji

Chapter 11 | **199**

Conclusion
June Bam & Allan Zinn

Appendix 1 | **205**

Conference Closing Remarks and Acknowledgements (transcribed)
Denise Zinn

Index | **209**

ABBREVIATIONS & ACRONYMS

ADM	Amathole District Municipality
ANC	African National Congress
APC	Archive and Public Culture Research Initiative
CALUSA	Cala University Students Association
CANRAD	Centre for the Advancement of Non-Racialism and Democracy
CAPS	Curriculum Assessment Policy Statements
CAS	Centre for African Studies
CSIR	Council for Scientific Research
DBE	Department of Basic Education
DEIC	Dutch East India Company
FET	Further Education and Training
FHYA	Five Hundred Year Archive
FMF	#FeesMustFall
GET	General Education and Training
HoL	Home of Legends Project
IKS	Indigenous Knowledge System
ILO	International Labour Organisation
KZN	KwaZulu-Natal
LTSM	Learning & Teaching Support Materials
NCS	National Curriculum Statement
NEUM	Non-European Unity Movement
NGO	Non-Governmental Organisation
NHC	National Heritage Council

NIHSS	National Institute for Humanities and Social Sciences
NMMU	Nelson Mandela Metropolitan University
NMU	Nelson Mandela University (previously NMMU)
NRF	National Research Foundation
PAC	Pan Africanist Congress
PAR	Participatory Action Research
RMF	#RhodesMustFall
SADET	South African Democracy Education Trust
SAHP	South African History Project
TK	Traditional Knowledge
TRC	Truth and Reconciliation Commission
UCT	University of Cape Town
UNESCO	United Nations Educational, Scientific and Cultural Organisation
UNISA	University of South Africa
Wits	University of the Witwatersrand

CONTRIBUTORS

Editors

Lungisile Ntsebeza
(Editor and Author of Chapter 1)

Lungisile Ntsebeza (email lungisile.ntsebeza@uct.ac.za and lntsebeza@gmail.com) is Professor of Sociology and African Studies at the University of Cape Town. He also holds two Research Chairs: the NRF Research Chair in Land Reform and Democracy in South Africa: State and Civil Society Dynamics, as well as the AC Jordan Chair in African Studies, both located in the Centre for African Studies at UCT. He has conducted extensive published research on the land question in South Africa around themes such as land rights, democratisation in rural areas under the jurisdiction of traditional authorities and social movements in the land sector. He is currently working on the intellectual and political legacy of the world-renowned engaged scholar, Archie Mafeje.

June Bam
(Editor and Co-author of Chapter 9 and Chapter 11)

June Bam, PhD. M.Ed (email: june.hutchison@gmail.com and june.bam-hutchison@uct.ac.za) has worked widely in her research field in all provinces of South Africa, and also within African Diaspora scholarship networks (West African, East African and Caribbean communities) abroad. As the former head of South Africa's History Project (curriculum, policy, teacher training, knowledge production, and research), she engaged in a number of local community history and heritage partnership projects. More recently, she worked on the digital Five Hundred Year Archive at the University of Cape Town and is a key member of the Pre-Colonial Catalytic History Project at the Centre for African Studies. She has held Visiting Research Fellowships at the Institute for the Public Understanding of the Past (York University, UK) and in Human Rights at Kingston University (London). Bam is a Visiting Professor with Stanford University.

Allan Zinn
(Editor and Co-author of Chapter 11)

Allan Zinn (email: allan.zinn@mandela.ac.za) is the Director of the Centre for the Advancement of Non-Racialism and Democracy [CANRAD] at Nelson Mandela University. A Fulbright Scholarship enabled post-graduate studies at Columbia University, USA. He has taught at Columbia, Clark and Rhodes universities. He has had extensive experience in the NGO and donor-funded sectors, working for the Educational Support Services Trust (ESST) and the IMBEWU II Programme in the Eastern Cape. Zinn has published and edited materials in the Education, Gender Equity and Sports arenas.

Authors

Nomathamsanqa C. Tisani
(Chapter 2)

Dr Nomathamsanqa Tisani (email: thami.tisani@gmail.com) has worked in Higher Education Institutions – Rhodes University, Cape Technikon, Cape Peninsula University of Technology and the College of Transfiguration – in various capacities as a tutor, lecturer and academic manager, as well as a member of the Executive Management. Her research in history covers 18th and 19th century writings on African historiography, as well as women in Mission Stations and 20th century women at Nokholeji (Fort Hare). She founded Eyethu Imbali, a Community History Project, which sought to redefine history with community members, teachers and school children. She was also a member of Prof Kader Asmal's National History Project that focussed on the revision of the history curriculum.

Pamela Maseko
(Chapter 3)

Pamela Maseko (email: p.maseko@gmail.com) is the Executive Dean of the Faculty of Humanities at the North West University, South Africa and a Visiting Professor at Rhodes University, South Africa. She has also worked as Professor of Linguistics at the University of the Western Cape. Her research interests are on Sociolinguistics and Literary Studies. She is the Principal Investigator in the *"African Languages Literary Research Hub"*, a Project funded by the National Institute for Humanities and Social Sciences, and the Andrew Mellon funded project, *"Ulwimi njengovimba wolwazi*: Language as a reservoir of knowledge".

Nomalanga Mkhize
(Chapter 4)

Nomalanga Mkhize (email: nomalanga.mkhize@mandela.ac.za) is a historian with a Master of Arts degree in History from Rhodes University and a PhD in Sociology from the University of Cape Town. Her teaching interests include themes in ancient African history, 19th century intellectuals, and South African economic history. She is developing research expertise in the historiographical traditions and contributions of 19th century African writers.

Babalwa Magoqwana
(Chapter 5)

Babalwa Magoqwana (email: babalwa.magoqwana@mandela.ac.za) is a senior lecturer in the Sociology, Anthropology and History Department at Nelson Mandela University. She holds a post-doctoral fellowship with the American Council of Learned Societies (ACLS) – as an African Humanities Programme Fellow in association with UNISA – where she is the Social Policy Chair of the South African Research Chair Initiative (SARCHI). She is also the president of the South African Sociological Association (SASA). She is the recipient of the National Research Foundation/First Rand Foundation Sabbatical Grant for her project on "Woman-centred Vernacular Sociology of the Eastern Cape".

Carolyn Hamilton
(Chapter 6)

Carolyn Hamilton (email: carolyn.hamilton@uct.ac.za) holds the National Research Foundation (NRF) Chair in Archive and Public Culture at the University of Cape Town. Her research encompasses the pre-industrial history of southern Africa, the nature of the archive, the constitution of evidence and the public life of ideas. Her publications include the co-edited *Tribing and Untribing the Archive* (2016), *Uncertain Curature* (2014), *Cambridge History of South Africa, From Early Times to 1885* (2010), *Refiguring the Archive* (2002), as well as her *Terrific Majesty* (1998) and *The Mfecane Aftermath* (1995).

Mlingani Mayongo
(Chapter 7)

Mr Mlingani Mayongo (email: yongos@gmail.com) is a research assistant at Cala University Students Association (CALUSA), a land-based rural non-governmental organisation in Cala, Eastern Cape. He also works on youth matters.

Fani Ncapayi
(Chapter 7)

Fani Ncapayi (email: f.ncapayi@gmail.com) holds a PhD in Sociology from the University of Cape Town (UCT) and is an Honorary Research Associate of the Centre for African Studies (CAS) at UCT. He is the Senior Researcher for the Inyanda National Land Movement and also the Director of CALUSA, a land-based rural non-governmental organisation in Cala, Eastern Cape.

Mcebisi Ndletyana
(Chapter 8)

Mcebisi Ndletyana (email: nmcebisi@uj.ac.za or mcebisin@hotmail.com) holds a PhD in Political Science from the University of the Witwatersrand, Johannesburg. He is currently an Associate Professor of Political Science at the University of Johannesburg. Before joining the University of Johannesburg, he held senior research positions at several research institutions including the Mapungubwe Institute and the Human Sciences Research Council, and taught at the City University of New York and Marymount Manhattan College. His latest publication is a book entitled, *Institutionalising Democracy: The Story of the Independent Electoral Commission of South Africa, 1993 to 2014* (Pretoria: HSRC, 2015).

Denver A. Webb
(Chapter 8)

Denver A. Webb (email: denver.webb@nelsonmandela.ac.za) is an historian and heritage practitioner working at Nelson Mandela University. He holds a Master of Arts degree in History from Rhodes University and a D Litt et. Phil from the University of Fort Hare. His doctoral dissertation examined military conflict and the extension of colonial hegemony over African polities in what is now the Eastern Cape in the 18th and 19th centuries. He has published on different aspects of the nature of colonial power and military conquest in the Cape Colony and *emaXhoseni* in the *South African Historical Journal, African Historical Review, Journal of African History, Scientia Militaria* and *South African Journal of Art History*.

Bongani Ndhlovu
(Chapter 9)

Bongani Ndhlovu (PhD in History) (email: ndhlovubc@gmail.com) is the Executive Director: Core Functions at Iziko Museums of South Africa and a former Research Fellow at UWC's CHR. He has been extensively involved in heritage for the past 22 years and has served museums and tourism bodies in various capacities. His interest is in the interface between the museum, the collections and communities.

Bradley Van Sitters
(Chapter 9)

Bradley Van Sitters (email: bradlox@gmail.com) was a student at the University of Namibia where he studied GOWAB (KhoikhoiGowab). He also worked in partnership on indigenous knowledge with Professor Catherine A.O. Hoppers, Research Chair in Development Education at the University of South Africa. Bradley is also a member of the Khoi Revivalist Movement and has participated in marches from the Northern Cape to Parliament, and from Mossel Bay to Cape Town, as forms of protest to highlight contemporary battles of the Khoi with the late David Kruiper. Like Bam, Van Sitters grew up around the Cape Flats wetlands, considered 'sacred sites' by the Khoi Revivalists.

Himal Ramji
(Chapter 10)

Himal Ramji (email: himalramji@gmail.com) is a PhD student with the Andrew Mellon Foundation's History Access programme at the University of Cape Town's Historical Studies department. His current work is towards the delineation of the relationship between past, present and future in (the production of) political discourses. His Master's thesis, titled *Producing the Precolonial: Professional and Popular Lives of Mapungubwe, 1932-2017*, assessed the movement of knowledge associated with the southern African past before colonial times, from archaeology, to education, to the creative arts.

Denise Zinn
Appendix 1

Denise Zinn (email: denise.zinn@mandela.ac.za) is the Deputy Vice Chancellor: Teaching and Learning at Nelson Mandela University. She holds Master's and Doctoral degrees in Education from Harvard University Graduate School of Education, which she undertook after having been a high school teacher in Port Elizabeth for 12 years. Prior to taking up the position of DVC TL, she was the Executive Dean of Education at NMU after serving in the same position at University of Fort Hare. Her teaching and research interests are in humanising pedagogies, teacher education, language and literacy, and social justice in education.

CHAPTER 1

Whose History Counts?

An Introduction

Lungisile Ntsebeza[1]

Background

This book is the third volume published under the "Rethinking Africa" series of the Centre for African Studies (CAS), University of Cape Town (UCT). Its focus is the catalytic project on the pre-colonial historiography of southern Africa, an initiative of the National Institute for Humanities and Social Sciences (NIHSS).[2] The NIHSS defines catalytic projects as "primarily research-based" programmes which aim "to catalyse and open up new avenues" for Humanities and Social Sciences (HSS) scholarship, "and to assist in and promote the development of research in the HSS".[3] Established in 2012, the overarching aim of the pre-colonial historiography project was to create a platform that would support and nurture research over the long term, and promote the development of methodologies that would take forward the study of the pre-colonial eras in southern Africa.

The book is the outcome of a conference that was held at the then Nelson Mandela Metropolitan University (now Nelson Mandela University) from 15 to 17 March 2017. The conference was organised by CAS in collaboration with the Centre for

---

[1] lungisile.ntsebeza@uct.ac.za and ntsebeza@gmail.com
[2] The NIHSS was itself the outcome of a Humanities Initiative by the then Minister of Higher Education, Blade Nzimande. See www.nihss.ac.za
[3] See www.nihss.ac.za

the Advancement of Non-Racialism & Democracy (CANRAD) at Nelson Mandela University. Volume 1 (Ntsebeza & Saunders 2014) of the project was published, following a conference held in the CAS Gallery on 28 and 29 March 2014. A second 352-page volume (De Prada-Samper 2016) on stories from the Karoo in the Northern Cape was published at the end of 2016. This was the result of research done by Professors Simon Hall of UCT and Jose Manuel de Prada, Honorary Research Associate in the UCT Humanities Faculty.

Evolution of the project

A key objective of the pre-colonial history project, when it was conceived in 2012, was to coordinate a network of researchers from institutions located in different provinces in order to construct a history of broader South Africa from the 11th to 16th centuries. At the time, the title of the project was "Pre-1652 historiography". However, this title was changed in favour of the generic title "pre-colonial historiography" in order to challenge the widely-accepted notion that the arrival of Jan van Riebeeck in 1652 marks the point of departure in studying and understanding the history of southern Africa. Further, how far back the research would go was left open, rather than restricting the period to the 11th to 16th centuries. The geographic scope of the project was also modified to broaden the scope beyond the current borders of South Africa and to make this a southern African project. This modification was effected to make the point that the notion of a nation-state, such as South Africa, is a colonial construct and a project such as this one should be questioning these conceptions rather than taking them as a given.

Great strides have been made in the project. Firstly, at the level of coordinating a network of researchers from institutions located in different provinces in South Africa, participation has broadened from the initial group of academics from the universities of Cape Town, KwaZulu-Natal, Witwatersrand and Fort Hare who pledged their interest in the project and participated in the first conference in 2014. At the 2017 conference, participants were drawn from more South African universities, including Nelson Mandela University, the University of South Africa (UNISA) and Rhodes University. Furthermore, we took the first vital step of extending our activities beyond the boundaries of South Africa. To this end, we were joined by a colleague from the Institute of Arts & Culture in Mozambique, who is also curator of the Maputo Fortress National Historical Monument.

The focus of the book

The conference on which this book is based was initially informed by an observation that the Eastern Cape was conspicuous by its absence in the two earlier volumes of the project. We wondered why and how, in the context of pre-colonial historiography, the Eastern Cape would be in the margins. There is little doubt that the history of colonialism in South Africa would be incomplete if it omitted the Eastern Cape. For almost a century, between 1779 and 1878, the indigenous people in this part of South Africa witnessed a British onslaught in what is often referred to as the "frontier wars" (Peires 1981, 1989; Davenport 1986). These major wars were fought over land which British colonialists were using to divide Africans, by, for example, granting land under a quitrent title system to some blacks, in an attempt to create a class of black farmers (Bundy 1988). It is also in this province that missionaries established mission schools that were key to the colonial civilising mission and produced African nationalist leaders and academics of note such as Nelson Mandela, Robert Sobukwe and AC Jordan, to cite a few.

With the above concerns in mind, we in CAS took a decision that the next conference would focus on the Eastern Cape. We embarked on a diligent search for academics and public intellectuals in the province who were doing work on the history of the Eastern Cape. In the Xhalanga area, which falls under the Chris Hani District municipal area in the Eastern Cape, CAS set up a research group whose objective was to conduct research on life in this area, before the arrival of colonialists. Most of the above took place during the course of 2014 and early 2015 and the conference was planned for 2017 at a university in the Eastern Cape, which ended up being, as already stated, Nelson Mandela University.

The 2017 conference turned out to be path-breaking. There was a major shift from the white and male-dominated 2014 conference in Cape Town, with the bulk of the presenters being black women. Furthermore, contrary to our expectation that the conference would be fact-based in the true tradition of history, foundational and searching questions were raised about the writing of history and whose history counts. Additionally, questions on the methodologies on researching and writing history were also raised and hotly debated.

In other words, what was originally planned as a conference on the pre-colonial history of the Eastern Cape, ended up focusing on epistemological and methodological issues, including challenging the very concept 'pre-colonial'. This book is thus not about a factual account of the Eastern Cape, or a pre-colonial history of *amaNguni*.

The extent to which reference is made to the Eastern Cape is in the context of using the province to draw examples that would elucidate conceptual and methodological matters. What accounts for this dramatic turn of events?

De-colonisation re-visited

A question that dominated presentations and discussions throughout the conference revolved around the reconstruction of the past, including a close questioning of the credentials of those who wrote/write history. Some presenters, as already indicated, even questioned the use of the term 'pre-colonial', associating it with a particular form of history-writing, with deep roots in colonialism. How history is researched and written, and who writes the history of the indigenous African people, were issues that were debated and discussed. This is something that was missing at the 2014 conference. So, why this change then in 2017?

The 2017 conference took place in a context that was, I would argue, fundamentally different from 2014. It was held at a critical moment that was characterised by a student-led rebellion against what students dubbed 'colonial' education and a clamour for, among others, a 'decolonised curriculum'. The student-led campaign manifested itself in the open when, on 9 March 2015, a UCT student activist, Chumani Maxwele, defamed the imposing statue of Cecil John Rhodes on UCT grounds. Soon thereafter, his student supporters, who organised themselves under the #RhodesMustFall movement, demanded the removal of the statue. They alleged that the statue signified deep-rooted links between the University of Cape Town and colonialism or, in the words of Emeritus Associate Professor Dave Cooper, "colonial capitalism" (Cooper 2015). The students occupied the administrative block of the university and announced that they would not leave until the statue was removed. Within a month, the statue was removed – a major victory for the student-led effort. By this time, a number of universities in South Africa and beyond had pledged support for the campaign. At the same time, students had added more demands, notably the decolonisation of the curriculum, as they called it, and the insourcing of former university workers.

The announcement by various universities in South Africa that fees would be increased in 2016 set the proverbial cat among the pigeons and led to an unprecedented student-led campaign against the increase, called #FeesMustFall. This campaign drew wide support, including parents and workers who bore the brunt of paying the fees. The student-worker-parent alliance was no doubt the climax of the activities of the student-led campaign, forcing a complete shutdown of all South African universities, and spurring marches to Parliament in Cape Town, the African National Congress (ANC) headquarters in Johannesburg and the Union Buildings in Pretoria, the very seat of government administration. In the end, the ANC-led government was forced to make an announcement that there would be no fee increases in 2016. Furthermore, the campaign forced universities to reverse their policies of outsourcing workers. The "decolonisation of the curriculum" and the #FeesMustFall campaigns dominated debates and discussions in South African higher education institutions, especially towards the end of 2016, often leading to violent clashes with university and private security guards.[4]

A feature of the 2015/2016 student campaign is that it took place mainly in historically-white, advantaged universities such as UCT, Witwatersrand (Wits), Rhodes and Stellenbosch. Crucially, it is mainly towards these institutions that the demand for curriculum reform was directed. What is important to note is that historically, the quality of education that was offered at these universities was, in many ways, seen as a model of good education. For example, when he left Fort Hare and joined UCT in 1945 as its first black scholar, AC Jordan, the politically-engaged linguist, novelist and musician, defended himself against those who criticised him for leaving Fort Hare, a university for African students, for a white-dominated UCT, by saying that he wanted "to open that [UCT's] door, and keep it ajar" (Ntsebeza 2012:9). This was seen as a firm commitment on his part to make UCT accessible to black academics and students. Furthermore, when the so-called Extension of Universities Act was promulgated in 1959 (creating racially and ethnically exclusive institutions), the outcry was that this paved the way for the introduction of Bantu Education in higher education (Alexander 1990; Kallaway 1984, 1988, 2002; Hartshorne 1995). There seems to have been a sense that places like UCT and Wits offered a model of quality education and that the University Act of 1959 was meant to lower the quality of education offered to Africans.

The student rebellion of 2015/2016 brought to the fore that there were deep problems with the curriculum of the historically-white and privileged universities of South Africa. What the students have told us is that the kind of education delivered at these universities is not beyond criticism. Students have exposed it as colonial in its origin and in urgent need of transformation. This is an important message to take from the protests. In many ways, students have given academics and the wider

---

4   For an interesting analysis of the student led rebellion, see Nyamnjoh 2017, 2016.

society legitimate research questions which should be added to research agendas on higher education in South Africa and other former colonies.

A question that arises is: what would a transformed curriculum look like? What can we glean about this from the student protests? It seems possible to identify a couple of issues: the material that is prescribed, how it is taught, and who teaches it. Students complain that the books prescribed to them are authored by non-Africans and are written from a 'Eurocentric' point of view, which ignores the realities of the African continent and its people. Students are exerting pressure for the development of materials that are written by Africans and speak to African conditions and experiences. There is also pressure for an 'Afrocentric' approach to research and teaching which takes, as its point of departure, African conditions and the experiences of Africans.[5]

It is worth noting that the debate on decolonising higher education institutions in South Africa is not new. The issue was a subject of fierce and acrimonious debate at UCT in the late 1990s. The issue revolved around the establishment of a foundation course in teaching first-year students about Africa. CAS was entrusted with the task of setting up this course. A planning committee was set up to oversee the process of designing and implementing the teaching of the course. However, a dispute about the design of the course, its content and how it should be taught could not be resolved, leading to Mahmood Mamdani – the then Director of CAS and inaugural holder of the AC Jordan Chair in African Studies – making the unfortunate decision of leaving UCT (Mamdani 1996, 1998; Graaff 1998; Hall 1998.).[6] His departure left a huge gap in CAS and had a serious negative impact on debates on 'decolonising' the curriculum not only at UCT, but at higher education institutions across South Africa. Nearly 20 years later, it would take the students of UCT to put the issue of decolonising the curriculum back on the agenda.

Further on in this chapter, in the section on the outline of the book, I have described how the presenters at the conference (and subsequent authors of this book), while not directly addressing the issues raised by the student protest, showed great awareness of the current context surrounding higher education in South Africa, and the need to address the question: Whose history counts?

---

5   See Mafeje 1981, 1994 for an elaboration of this approach. Also see Ntsebeza 1996 for an analysis of Mafeje's theory.
6   The debates on this matter were extensively covered by the Centre for African Studies journal, *Social Dynamics*.

Finally, the role of 'organic' intellectuals outside the academy has also been acknowledged and recognised in this book. The example of Isaac Bongani Tabata (Tabata 1950, 1952) of the Unity Movement and his contribution in the political history of South Africa has been highlighted. In addition, there is a strongly held view that, as part of decolonising higher education, if not education in general, the Pre-colonial Historiography project should aim at drawing the greater participation of broader society, especially poets, artists and organic intellectuals who are researching and writing their own history, focusing on their clans and/or family histories. Were these texts to be prescribed in schools, they would contribute to the transformation of education at primary and secondary levels. Several chapters written by organic intellectuals address the issue of developing materials for primary and secondary schools (see also Mafeje 1994; Mamdani 2016).

Outline of the book

This book is divided into two sections: Decolonising Historiography (chapters 2-6); and the Challenges of Praxis (chapters 7-10). This is followed by a brief concluding chapter, summarising the key aspects of the book and outlining an agenda for future research in preparation for the third conference.

Section I Decolonising historiography

This section, comprising only women authors, deals with the epistemological issues highlighted above. The women's approaches are truly foundational and highly questioning of prevailing and seemingly accepted concepts such as 'pre-colonial'. They also question the assumption that the contributions by Africans in scholarship be restricted to providing primary data that gets analysed by European scholars. The essential point made is that Africans should write history from their vantage point and that African writers of the 19th century, for example, should be seen as making a contribution to South African historiography as historians in their own right. The roles of language and *uMakhulu* (grandmother in isiXhosa) are highlighted as crucial in our quest to reconstruct life before colonial intrusion.

In chapter 2, Nomathamsanqa Tisani pursues research questions on how Africans defined and named themselves in the face of creeping colonialism and incipient Christian religion. The departure point in this chapter is a discussion of how Africans defined themselves as examples of self-framing, which should be one of the undergirding approaches in researching the African world in the past and present. The author argues that at a broader level, Africans cannot frame and shape themselves in line with the charts of the coloniser.

Pamela Maseko, in chapter 3, seeks to reconstruct the experiences of a pre-colonial isiXhosa-speaking Nguni society to understand society's ways of knowing, in relation to social roles. She examines, through linguistic evidence, the manner in which social roles are constructed within amaXhosa society. She specifically considers whether 'gender' is a key factor in organising relationships and roles. Through the lens of the #FeesMustFall student protests, Maseko presents language as a possible source of essential evidence not only in the reconstruction of social roles in pre-colonial isiXhosa-speaking Nguni society, but also in the efforts of centring African experiences in knowledge production and dissemination in the academy. She concludes by arguing that if we have to develop knowledge about African society, it makes sense that we listen to what African languages are saying about their societies.

In chapter 4, Nomalanga Mkhize argues that South African historiography has been a white record of black actions. What is missing is the recognition of the many scattered writings by black South Africans. Mkhize goes on to explore some historical puzzles through the clan genealogies compiled by Walter Rubusana in his edited volume *Zemk'inkomo Magwalandini*. Her point is that African versions of history have yet to be acknowledged formally as South African historiography even though it is through African accounts that many pre-colonial narratives can be excavated; and that the idiomatic layers of African language are central to the reconstruction of the missing African historiography in South Africa's history scholarship.

Babalwa Magoqwana, in chapter 5, seeks to challenge some of the narrow conceptions that define *uMakhulu* purely in economic and seniority terms in African households. The chapter positions *uMakhulu* as an institution of knowledge that transfers not only 'history' through *iintsomi* (folktales), but also as a body of indigenous knowledge that stores, transfers and disseminates knowledge and values. In other words, her chapter goes beyond the narrative of *uMakhulu* as a 'safety net' and 'caregiver' under harsh socio-economic conditions in the rural households. In using *uMakhulu* as the institution of knowledge, she argues, society can move beyond the gendered and binary nature of institutions of learning (public versus private spaces of learning) and integrate the local language and values carried by our grandmothers in dealing with social, political and economic challenges in societies.

Carolyn Hamilton argues in chapter 6 that the long southern African past, before the advent of European colonialism, remains neglected despite powerful post-apartheid impulses of various kinds for its recovery and celebration. Her contention is that, in the last 20 years or so, outside of the specialist discipline of archaeology, there has been relatively little research undertaken to support those impulses. She goes on to offer her understanding of some of the things that have given distinctive shape to this field, attempting to account for its stalled aspect, identifying key challenges, and indicating some of the directions of new research currently being inaugurated.

Section II | Challenges of Praxis

This section builds on the previous one and grapples with methodological issues on how a decolonised history can be written. At the heart of this section is an attempt to critically look at the relationship between researchers in the academy and the host community against the backdrop of a perception that academic research is extractive and sees the host community merely as a source of primary data. The strong message here is that the gap between the academy and the host community must be bridged, with community members who participate in research seen as collaborators. Furthermore, this section considers ways of ensuring that the new materials are made widely accessible, especially in educational institutions.

Fani Ncapayi and Mlingani Mayongo's original contribution in chapter 7 provides a powerful illustrative case. Both operate in the non-governmental organisation (NGO) sector and collaborate in their research with CAS at UCT. In this groundbreaking chapter, the authors not only participated on an equal basis with academic researchers in CAS, but, working with the youth in their research sites, they actually drove the research and became the authors, with CAS researchers providing support. Their chapter investigates the lives and living conditions of people in early African societies, before colonial contact, in the former Xhalanga magisterial district. Through a combination of qualitative and participatory research techniques, the chapter details the lives and living conditions of families in three villages of the former Xhalanga magisterial district to get a sense of life in these villages before contact with colonialists. As much as the research provides knowledge about early African societies, its participatory approach empowered the participating local youth with research techniques as well as report-writing skills.

In chapter 8, Denver Webb and Mcebisi Ndletyana write about their project – The Home of Legends – which originated as an Eastern Cape branding and marketing exercise, launched in 2012. While it elicited considerable public interest, commentators highlighted a number of problems. Subsequently, the Eastern Cape Office of the Premier and the National Heritage Council (NHC) entered into a partnership to commission research that would provide a firmer academic basis for a revitalised Home of Legends project. One of the key aspects was how heritage sites in the Eastern Cape could be used to tell the stories of the province, stretching from the geological and palaeontological eras to the recent past. The palaeontological and pre-colonial periods were initially included in the project, then dropped and have subsequently been re-instated.

Chapter 9, co-authored by June Bam, Bradley Van Sitters and Bongani Ndhlovu, outlines the authors' engagement with museums, heritage agencies and various communities over many years. They each bring a particular set of knowledge, perspectives, experiences and interactions to the pre-colonial project, which they have woven into five key emerging research themes. This chapter discusses these themes and attempts to identify possible ways for working on the pre-colonial project with higher education institutions in the future, and considers the possible impact on higher education transformation, should these recommendations be considered. Of special mention to this chapter's 'triangulation' research method (systematic triangulation of perspectives as a conversation analysis and validation strategy) (Flick 1992) in the three-way conversation and collaboration, is the working relationship between Bam (a university-based scholar) and Van Sitters as the 'keeper of pre-colonial knowledge' and as an 'organic intellectual' over the past three years.

The last chapter in this section, by Himal Ramji, addresses the aims of the prescribed Curriculum and Assessment Policy Statement (CAPS) in schools, with specific focus on the 'pre-colonial' sections of CAPS and the topic of Mapungubwe, as prescribed in grade 6 in South African schools. This chapter compares the interpretations provided in the CAPS curriculum and prescribed school textbooks, to the interpretations of the novel – in this case, Zakes Mda's *The Sculptors of Mapungubwe*. Essentially, this paper asks: what might the creative interpretation of the distant past offer to improve or expand our history education?

In conclusion, this third volume of the pre-colonial historiography project has taken a significant step in fulfilling the overarching aim of the pre-colonial historiography project, which, as indicated at the outset, is to create a platform that would support and nurture research over the long term, and promote the development of methodologies that would take forward the study of the pre-colonial eras in southern Africa. Although initially planned as a volume that would focus on the pre-colonial history of the people of the Eastern Cape province, the student-led protests manifesting themselves in the open in 2015 compelled academics and intellectuals more broadly to confront foundational issues around epistemology and methodology that had been off the radar for more than a decade since the Mamdani debacle at UCT.

References

Alexander, N. 1990. Education and the struggle for national liberation in South Africa. *Essays and speeches by Neville Alexander, 1985–1989*. Braamfontein: Skotaville Publishers.

Bundy, C. 1988. *The Rise and Fall of the South African Peasantry*. Cape Town: David Philip.

Cooper, D. 2015. *Thieves' Role in Tainted History*. Cape Times, 7 April.

Davenport, T.R.H. 1986. *South Africa: A modern history*. London: Macmillan Press Ltd.

De Prada-Samper, J.M. (ed.). 2016. *The man who cursed the wind and other stories from the Karoo*. Volume II of the Pre-Colonial Catalytic Project. Cape Town: African Sun Press and the Centre for African Studies, University of Cape Town.

Gordon, L.R. 2014. Disciplinary decadence and the decolonisation of knowledge. *Africa Development*, 39(1): 81-92.

Graaff, J. 1998. Pandering to pedagogy or consumed by content: Brief thoughts on Mahmood Mamdani's "teaching Africa at the post-apartheid university of Cape Town". *Social Dynamics*, 24: 76-85. https://doi.org/10.1080/02533959808458650

Hartshorne, K. 1995. Language policy in African education: a background to the future. In: R. Mesthrie, *Language and social history*, 306–318. Cape Town and Johannesburg: David Philip.

Flick, U. 1992. Triangulation revisited: strategy of validation or alternative? *Journal for the theory of social behaviour*, 22(2), 175-197.

Hall, M. 1998. "Bantu education"? A reply to Mahmood Mamdani. *Social Dynamics*, 24: 86-92.

Hartshorne, K.B. 1992. *Crisis and challenge: Black education 1910-1990*. Oxford: Oxford University Press.

Kallaway, P. (ed.). 2002. *The history of education under apartheid, 1948-1994: the doors of learning and culture shall be opened*. Pinelands: Pearson.

Kallaway, P. 1988. From Bantu education to people's education in South Africa. In: N. Entwisle. *Handbook of educational ideas and practices*. London: Routledge.

Kallaway, P. (ed.). 1984. *Apartheid and education: The education of black South Africans*. Johannesburg: Ravan Press of South Africa.

Luckett, K. 2016. Curriculum contestation in a post-colonial context: a view from the South. *Teaching in Higher Education*, 21(4): 415-428. https://doi.org/10.1080/13562517.2016.1155547

Mafeje, A. 1994. African intellectuals: an inquiry into their genesis and social options. In: M. Diouf & M. Mamdani (eds.). *Academic Freedom in Africa*. Dakar: CODESRIA Book Series, 95-211.

Mafeje, A. 1981. On the articulation of modes of production. *Journal of Southern African Studies*, 8(1), 123-138. https://doi.org/10.1080/03057078108708037

Mamdani, M. 2016. Between the public intellectual and the scholar: Decolonization and some post-independence initiatives in African higher education. *Inter-Asia Cultural Studies*, 17(1): 68-83. https://doi.org/10.1080/14649373.2016.1140260

Mamdani, M. 1998. Teaching Africa at the post-apartheid University of Cape Town: A response. *Social Dynamics*, 24: 40-62.

Mamdani, M. 1996. Centre for African Studies: Some preliminary thoughts. *Social Dynamics*, 22: 1-14. https://doi.org/10.1080/02533959608458607

Ntsebeza, L. 2016. What Can We Learn from Archie Mafeje about the Road to Democracy in South Africa? *Development and Change*, 47(4), 918-936. https://doi.org/10.1111/dech.12244

Ntsebeza, L. 2012. African studies at UCT. In: R.T. Nhlapo and H. Garuba (eds.). *African Studies in the Post-colonial University*. Cape Town: University of Cape Town Press, 1-20.

Ntsebeza, L.& Saunders, C. (eds.). 2014. *Papers from the Pre-Colonial Catalytic Project, Volume I*. Cape Town: Centre for African Studies, University of Cape Town.

Nyamnjoh, A. 2017. The phenomenology of Rhodes Must Fall: Student activism and the experience of alienation at the University of Cape Town. *Strategic Review for Southern Africa*, 39(1): 256.

Nyamnjoh, F.B. 2016. *#RhodesMustFall: Nibbling at Resilient Colonialism in South Africa*. Langaa: RPCIG.

Peires, J. 1989. *The Dead Will Arise: Nongqawuse and the Great Xhosa Cattle-killing Movement of 1856-7*. Johannesburg: Ravan Press.

Peires, J. 1981. *The House of Phalo*. Johannesburg: Ravan Press.

Saunders, C.C. 1978. *The Annexation of the Transkeian Territories*. Pretoria: The Government Printer.

Tabata, I.B. 1952. The Boycott as Weapon of Struggle. Cape Town: All African Convention Committee.

Tabata, I.B. 1950. *The All African Convention: The Awakening of a People*. Johannesburg: People Press.

Wa Thiong'o, N. 1994. *Decolonising the mind: The politics of language in African literature*. Nairobi: East African Publishers.

SECTION I
DECOLONISING HISTORIOGRAPHY

CHAPTER 2

Of Definitions and Naming: "I am the earth itself. God made me a chief on the very first day of creation."[1]

Nomathamsanqa Tisani[2]

Continuous use of 'pre-colonial' and its associated terms 'colonial' and 'post-colonial' for periodisation and the defining of African pasts, is a misnomer that has to be discarded as part of new research questions and knowledge production that have to be created in African studies. Regarding 'colonialism' Eze asks, "Why should colonialism be accorded the status and role of a singular and dominant prism through which the nature and boundaries of African philosophy ought to be thematised and articulated?" (1997:4). On the other hand, these concepts, especially 'post-colonial', are not exclusively used to denote time in academia. Indeed, post-colonial Studies as an academic field has come to signify research that "intermingles the past with the present, ... [European] imperial appropriation of the world ... to be followed in the 20th century by [the indigenous] people taking power and control back for themselves" (Young 2001:2). Retention or failure to interrogate these concepts which are "discourses that have been coded in advance" (Mudimbe 1994:191) locks those who wish to participate in 'catalytic' engagements in some kind of epistemological bondage.

---

[1] Williams 1983:121.
[2] thami.tisani@gmail.com

Thus, taken at a literal level, the word 'colonial' may be seen as innocent, simply conveying a phase in history. A deeper analysis, however, throws up a multiplicity of meanings. The word is usually used in a historical context of a particular group of people – those whose lives were invaded and had their land and possessions taken by Europeans that had embarked on voyages into the 'New World'. 'Pre-colonial' also exists *in tandem* with colonial and post-colonial phases. 'Pre-colonial' is never used as part of a European time schedule, except in the case of Ireland, which was itself a victim of intrusion, even though the Europeans themselves were the main participants in the colonisation movement.[3] These terms, and even [academic] disciplines have undermined the very possibility of understanding African reality (Mbembe 2001:7) and are part of a whole glossary that was constructed to define and name the people by dividing up their history, or stating the absence thereof (Fanon 1967:21), invading their lands (Mbembe 2001:25), baptising them with new names and re-casting their landscape (Tisani 2000:6) and making all these fit into pre-conceived patterns to create "new reality through erasures and re-inscriptions" (Ashcroft 2001:131).

The duration of the colonial experience for indigenous people of the world ranged from a period of five hundred years ago, taking off from Columbus's 1492 adventure in the colonially-named Americas, and the Portuguese presence in what became Mozambique to just a hundred years ago in countries like Zimbabwe. In South Africa the time span of European colonialism stretches from the 17th century in the western region to the 19th century in the eastern regions. In relation to the long life of African people beginning from the evolution of *Homo Sapiens* (Ramose 2005:30), the period of the invading European adventurers represents a mere fraction of their past. Thus, collapsing the pre-European contact as one phase, effectively erases African history and its epochs which include, for example, domestication of animals, adoption of crops from neighbouring regions and continents, evolution of political systems like the rise of African kingdoms, as well as the spread and adoption of religions like Christianity and Islam as discussed by Diop quoted in Mamdani (2012:53-56). Moreover, when academia succumbs to truncating narratives about autochthons before the encounter with Europeans, they are in cahoots with pervading stigmatisation and "negative interpretation" (Mbembe 2001:1) which continues to describe Africa. Periodisation framed around coloniality amounts to a continuation of the brutalising experience by which unquantifiable losses were suffered and also through which "disease, slavery and violence" (Young 2001:1) were experienced

---

[3] See for example works published by authors such as Lloyd (1993).

by the indigenous people. So new research frameworks on the African past should entail "inserting into the discourse arena totally different meanings and registers" (Hoppers ndg:15).

Without underestimating the pervading and overwhelming presence of settler culture among indigenous communities of the world as the autochthon continues to speak and write through the language of the coloniser, pursues his/her philosophy and knowledge system (Fanon 1967:xv), there still is a need, in view of the catastrophic effects of colonialism, to unwrap the shroud that continues to cling around the African body. In many ways this includes construction of knowledge that has been made sacrosanct and given as truth even in colonial academia and interpreted as "epistemological violence " (Mudimbe 2013:5). Such thinking is propelled by an awareness about the relativity of the once proclaimed universal Eurocentric epistemology. Put in other words, De Sousa Santos calls for "a learned ignorant [which] is to know that the epistemological diversity of the [people of] the world is potentially infinite" (2014:111).

In pursuit of such diversity and infinity the discussion in this chapter explores aspects of African social systems on healing, making whole and re-generation as applied in academia. In the African world a situation of disease, imbalance and disturbance of wholeness (Mostert 1992:958) of an individual, family and people as a whole can manifest itself in the form of a calamity which is addressed in various activities that seek to bring about redress to the imbalance. Among the Taita of Kenya, the process of reconciliation, *kutasa*, is followed in search of "peace, health and general well-being" (Magesa 1997:235]. The initiative of the Truth and Reconciliation Commission (TRC) in a post-apartheid South Africa was undertaken along similar lines. Through searching for truth on apartheid brutalities, the intention was to elicit confessions by perpetrators and, hopefully, bring about healing to both the apartheid agents and the victims including individuals, families and people generally. In a Latin American context, De Sousa Santos writes about a need for a "Manifesto for good living – *buen vivir*" (2014:ix).

Related to academic work a call is made by Amilcar Cabral, quoted by Kunnie (2000:163), that there should be a "return to the source of indigenous cultural resistance in examining the question of educational transformation." As a response to Cabral a suggestion is made in this chapter that as part of the process of seeking and promoting healing and wholeness in academia, a search for new research methods and knowledges is undertaken. One of these should include the process of *Ukuhlambulula* – cleansing – inside and outside, touching the seen and unseen, screening the conscious and unconscious. This includes healing of the body and making whole the inner person, because in African thinking "there is an interconnectedness of all things" (Thabede 2008:238).

Mqhayi[4] explains in the book, *Ityala Lamawele*,[5] that in the Xhosa polity it was, and still is, the duty of *itola ukuhlamba umzi ekungcoleni* – the national doctor/diviner – to cleanse and strengthen the nation from all harm (1981:62). In the same book he demonstrates how *imvisiswano* – social cohesion/wholeness – among amaXhosa was desirable and could be attained even through a national effort, as it happened between the twin characters in the book, to the point that there was an agreement among the peace-makers that social cohesion was even more desirable than the rigid law.

Thus, erasing the concepts – pre-colonial, colonial and post-colonial – for the periodisation of African pasts, as well as re-defining African reality generally, could provide an example of a curriculum on African Studies that foregrounds African values and beliefs within African cosmology. Academics as *amatola* – national doctors and diviners – have to pick up the social cohesion, healing and cleansing agenda through the process of *Ukuhlambulula*. Theirs is not the use of emetics, incense or animal sacrifice, but an identification of methods and frameworks of bringing change. The long process of training in academic divination calls on them to lead *Ukuhlambulula*. Failure to do so will mean that those who seek change will remain hooded by a cowl that will keep them on the beaten track of foregrounding European invasions and thefts, masquerading as civilisation, and thus in the end attain partial academic breakthroughs.

Ukuhlambulula in higher education as a process cannot be an overnight exercise. Considering that it is an initiative that has to undo such a powerful force, as to be likened by Ngugi wa Thiong'o to be a "cultural bomb ... [meant to] annihilate indigenous people's languages, environment, heritages" (1986:3), there is a massive task ahead which should be provided with human resources, adequate funding and time. The human resource aspect should be what Ngugi refers to as the collective effort instead of individual genius (1986:x). In addition, Ngugi acknowledges the time, from 1971-1977, as having been seminal in his growth as he interacted

---

[4] S.E.K. Mqhayi (1875-1975) was a historian, *imbongi*/poet and dramatist who greatly influenced the writing and standardisation of isiXhosa during his life time.
[5] First published in 1914 by Lovedale Press.

with colleagues and students (1996:xi). Debates, contestations, conferencing and consultations which took place in the 1960s in East African universities as part of the reform movement of universities are recalled by Mamdani in his 2017 lecture at the University of Cape Town entitled, "Decolonising the Post-colonial University" (Omoyele 2017) and should be central to a process of *Ukuhlambulula*.

The post-1994 settlement in South Africa ushered a period of hope for a birth of a new dawn in all facets of South African life, including higher education. The 1997 *White Paper* on the transformation of higher education carried seeds of the long-awaited cleansing and re-birth. Crucial principles like redress, equity and structural re-construction of higher education institutions were to facilitate the re-generation of a new higher education. Unfortunately, enthusiasm among higher education practitioners for these long awaited changes seems to have evaporated in the morning mist. Equally, the structural changes proposed and effected through the merger of higher education institutions became a damp squib as practitioners spent energy and resources on technical changes and the coining of new names. The essence of a new curriculum devoid of Eurocentrism remained a challenge. *Ukuhlambulula* has to be re-built on these lost hopes and opportunities, not on the pervading Eurocentric thinking that continues to inform South African higher education.

The decolonisation of curriculum movement in 2015 and 2016 was largely incubated and hatched by students with a few academics in tow (Heleta 2016). The South African society to a large extent recoiled from a movement that seemed to have a Janus face and was led by young people. Atabile Nonxuba, a student, responding to the question about decolonised education, bemoans the fact that, "Our own thinking as Africans has been undermined … [and] we cannot be decolonised by the white people who colonised us" (2016). Nkondo takes the debate further when in his argument moves from the de-colonisation debate to a call for a "polyepistemic" approach (2016:19). The process of *Ukuhlambulula* is a means whereby South Africa does not drop the ball again on curriculum development and academic renewal. *Ukuhlambulula* is thus one of the many ways through which polyepistemicism within the overarching multiversalism can be realised.

The above argument is based on the premise that imperial epistemology is a construct and therefore can be and ought to be dismantled. Firstly, the creation of colonial discourse is and was founded on deep mythical and religious beliefs of Europeans, thus giving it a religious aura to observers. The triune phasing of the colonial period into pre-colonial, colonial and post-colonial is no innocent timeframe. It is deeply embedded in Western thinking that evolved over centuries from writings. Mudimbe (1994), through a number of early European writings and paintings, traces how Europeans informed and misinformed each other about the people and the lands they had ventured into. This was the genesis of the "construction of vague recourses to knowledge gained from books and travelogues " (p.9).

In accordance with colonial discourse, Europeans came upon the indigenous people and saw a people of unmitigated darkness and chaos described in childhood images. Mamdani quotes two leading European intellectuals' description of Africans as children. A South African and a leading world statesman, Jan Smuts, as late as the early 20th century referred to Africans as "child-type and child like humans", while Hegel, a renowned 18th century German philosopher, described Africa as a "land of childhood" (1996:4). Actually, European perception and understanding of the world of the indigenous people as being a period of darkness and chaos before contact with them are aligned to the Biblical story of creation. It opens, "In the beginning of creation, when God made heaven and earth, the earth was without form and void, with darkness over the face of the abyss … " (*The New English Bible* 1961:1).

In my doctoral dissertation I trace how knowledge about indigenous people in southern Africa was constructed. Half-truths, mixed up with medieval fables were written up and used as authentic sources for subsequent writings. As intimated above, it all began with "an erasure and at times a distortion of old names which the indigenous people had used to describe themselves" (Tisani 2000:8-9). Then followed the classification and categorisation of the autochthons using physical classification similar to the one used for classifying animals and plants. Another classification tool was informed by the binary view central to European thinking. Hence "Christian and pagan" and "savage and civilised" came to dominate the writings of the times. Examples that fitted within these categories would even be given. For example, the Tutsi and the Hutu were "tribes" that fitted within the binary thesis (Mamdani 2012:54). Respect for the written word has perpetuated myths about indigenous people.

On getting to what was a new world to the Europeans, the invaders would then systematically break down existing political, economic and social systems (Young 2001:288). New names and groupings would emerge. On these break-ups, Mamdani refers to the 'colonial' state being "bifurcated … Janus-faced" (1996:18). New ethnic names like the *Fingo* in South Africa and the *Yoruba* and *Igbo* in Nigeria are 'colonial' names that the indigenous people had no clue of. Therefore "I argue they were part of the attempt of the invaders to create a new history and identities of the indigenous people" (Tisani 2000:88). In due course some of the new names found their way into the vocabulary of the indigenous people themselves. They were "appropriated" (De Kock 1996:6). Later on divisions were mainly in accordance with relations to the colonisers constructed around the strategy of dividing and ruling them. For example, even though the word '*Fingo/Mfengu*' penetrated into the indigenous languages, the word continued to be a foreign construct. It was never integrated into the definitions and naming that the autochthons used to call themselves. No one, no family, has ever adopted a clan praise[6] like *isiduko/isithakazelo/seboko* which is '*Fingo*' or '*Mfengu*'. Thus the European right to define and name after grabbing was an assumed God-given task through papal bulls like the Treaty of Tordesillas of 1494 which divided the world between Spain and Portugal (De Sousa Santos 2014:121), and other pronouncements. The defining and naming of the world of indigenous people was total – including mountains, gorges and valleys. Such places were usually sacrosanct as they would be used as burial places and spaces for religious ceremonies. Rivers and pools received similar baptism. Plants, trees, animals with which the autochthons had had a sacred relationship, would be re-named and then immediately denuded and hunted, sometimes to extinction. Similar changes would be experienced by individuals and families as they were baptised and given 'Christian' names. The hero of the SS Mendi tragedy of 1917[7] who had been a member of the missionary team that went to Central Africa in 1875, went about with two names.[8] His church and school name was Isaac Williams Wauchope. His family name was Citashe Dyoba (Mqhayi 2009:470-484).

It was under the aegis of the African worldview that the African people led their lives, related to other humans, and engaged with nature, processes which Makang in Eze refers to as "ontology of participation" (1997:325), which are not necessarily fossilised frames of thinking. Further, Africans established systems that guided and governed their lives. It was that worldview around which they rallied as they

---

[6] Clan praises known in isiNguni as *iziduko/izibongo/izithakazelo* are oral texts that mark out one group from the other and into which an individual is born. These praises are also carriers of knowledge on family history. They are also parachutes that take an individual into the world of ancestors.

[7] The ship that sank off the British Channel carrying the 'South African Native Labour Corps'.

[8] The idea of an individual going about with two names is confusing. It however captures the dilemma indigenous people found themselves in as they moved into the European world through formal schooling and baptism. Yet, what Europeans did not fully understand was the fact that Africans did not drop or relinquish their original names, and thus, their identities. Citashe Dyoba could also have used the name in some of his writings as a pseudonym which was a practice some contributors to *Isigidimi* and other newspapers had adopted.

faced colonial onslaught through military setbacks, new definitions and names, displacements, spiritual and physical death.

In discussing African and Western worldviews one is mindful of the fact that these concepts do not refer to homogenous entities. Both worldviews are associated with the wide continents of Africa, Europe and the Americas. Within these multiplicities that include languages, religions and other different cultural practices, there are, however, uniting factors that create a tangible consciousness among people. Mbiti's seminal work on *The Concepts of God in Africa* (1970) has revealed commonality that runs through indigenous people of Africa about their knowledge and belief in a deity. Knowledge of the deity comes through different names, but with shared attributes among the various African societies spread especially in sub-Saharan Africa. In addition, for those who fall under the African worldview the common geographic ancestry and physical features are the most obvious characteristics, as Mazisi Kunene proclaimed in an interview by Azuonye (1996). A final argument that Eze makes as he discusses African philosophy, is the claim that the brutal encounter Africa had with Europe over a period of five hundred years in the form of slavery and colonialism has created a historical consciousness that binds the African people together even after the official end of 'colonialism' (1997:4).

Then there is also a Western worldview. Of even greater importance in tracing the genesis of 'pre-colonial' ideas and theses is the significance of unravelling the cosmological views that underpinned conscious and unconscious thinking of Europeans about autochthons (Magubane 2007). The European worldview, which has since the 20th century become known as the Western worldview, has key elements that inform and guide those who have been nurtured in it and therefore subscribe to it.

Three elements will be covered in this chapter. Firstly, a binary view dominates Western thinking. Reality exists in opposing dichotomies; what Mudimbe refers to as "facile dichotomy" (1997:15). The two opposing ends cannot be reconciled, like day against night, black and white, civilised and barbaric are all examples of opposites that dominate this split in the Western mind. Europeans would thus have perceived the people they had no knowledge of as their opposites. In addition, the dominant European religion, Christianity, also became a determinant in the division between "us and them" as there were Christians versus pagans or barbarians (De Kock 1996:10). Trouble came when the indigenous people accepted Christianity and then expected to be treated as equals and the same with Europeans. Indigenous Christian and European Christian created an anomaly for the 'colonial' period.

The second element in the European worldview is their notion of time. Europeans have tamed time through their application of mathematical knowledge, as well as the use of chronometers. In addition, the big moment in the cosmology of Europeans is framed around the historical person of Jesus. Their notion of time is calculated around the era before the coming, as well as the Year of our Lord, *Anno Domini* (Ramose 2005:26). Perhaps it is because there has been the final coming, through the birth of Jesus Christ, that the European worldview is rigidly linear, forever going forward. Notions of a second coming or of doomsday for that matter are vague and have since been eroded by rationalist thinking of the enlightenment.

A third element in the Western worldview is exclusivity, feeding on the "notion of absolute Otherness" (Mbembe 2001:2). On this point De Sous Santos attributes the exclusionary character to an outlook that does not tolerate co-present. "The other side of the line becomes non-existent" (2014:119). There is a tendency to resist and shut off what is perceived as different and coming from outside. However, at times there is selective exclusion when, for example, it comes to technological knowledge which Europeans will readily adopt as they did with Chinese gunpowder and paper. European exclusivity is predictably bolstered by their religion which claims to be the one and only beholden to "a jealous God" (Mbembe 2001:213). Consequently, a sense of being special and chosen was an attitude they carried around as they dealt with people who were different from them. They acted in ways propelled by superior beliefs about themselves and fortified by the church (Magubane 2007:60). Further, for example, a papal bull like the *Romanus Pontifex* of 1454 proclaimed that the land of those who did not belong to the Christian religions was a *terra nullius*, a no man's land that could be appropriated (Mudimbe 1994:30).

In the end what happened in the places and among the people that Europeans invaded, was an imposition of European cosmological outlook through their cultural practices – mainly their languages, religion, political and economic systems. There was very little attempt to adopt any of the aspects of the cultural world of the indigenous communities they encountered into their colonial systems. An extension of this reluctance to come over to the world of the indigenous people propels Mamdani to ask, "When does a settler become a native [if ever]?" (Mamdani 1996). Displacement through loss of land was nothing compared to loss of knowledge of one's mother tongue which Senghor compares to being uprooted from one's background. (Senghor in Langley 1979:376). In the case of Africans indigenously based in the Southwest, covering mainly the present day Western Cape Province, there was a near extinction of indigenous languages as happened in the case of *iiNgqwayi-ngqwayi*/Khoikhoi/Men of Men (Tisani 2000:9). Instead new Dutch place names like Sneeuberg, Langkloof, Swartkops and others were created as the indigenous ones were erased. That signalled new ownership of the land.

In the current era of catalytic engagements there needs to be a serious shift in thinking about how indigenous people lived in their regions for thousands of years. New research questions have to be formulated and knowledges constructed around a multiplicity of themes. To be probed are questions on how indigenous people built systems on how to relate to one another as individuals, families and socio-politico-economic groupings through languages and religious ceremonious rituals. Knowledge should be excavated on how they wrestled with and tamed nature with all its mysteries. They had survived and were rational beings when Europeans ventured into their shores.

The experiences of the autochthons during the era of contact with Europeans were almost similar the world over. The indigenous people, having lived for thousands of years according to their own socio-economic-political systems, had had no contact with Europeans. The latter were informed by their Graeco-Roman civilisation undergirded by the Christian religion. During the 17th and 18th centuries when the European globetrotters ventured into the southern tip of Africa and West African, the indigenous people did not fully comprehend what was coming. Later they informed Thunberg, a traveller, quoted in Tisani (2000:12), that they had been surprised that the Dutch had been making "every year fresh encroachments [on their land] and forcing them continually further up into the country". Another 18th century traveller, Gordon, quoted Koerikei, an indigenous spokesman, who specifically asked one of the Trekboers what he was doing, occupying all places where land and game were (Tisani 2000:12). Nonetheless Europeans embarked on schemes they had perfected over some time as they hugged the African coastland southwards and then northwards from the mid-15th century. The European agenda was purportedly in search of spices from the East, but in reality it included gathering wealth in the form of minerals, then collecting human cargo as slaves and eventually taking the land (De Sousa Santos 2014:123). Later, during the 19th century, Europeans pushed the 'civilising mission' as a reason for colonial conquests.

It remains important to note that at the time of contact with Europeans, southern Africans were informed by their own worldview, as well as some influences from eastern cosmology. The East African coastline had had contact with people from across the Indian Ocean since the dawn of the Christian era (De Vere Allen 1993). The writings of Al-Mas'udi in Levtzion and Hopkins (1981:30) throw further light on the world of the African coastal people and their trans-Indian Ocean contacts. He was a world traveller who had visited India, Ceylon, China and East Africa at the beginning of the 10th century. He actually visited East Africa from 916-917 (Levtzion & Hopkins 1981:30). That demonstrates links that East Africa enjoyed with the then known world. Traders and travellers would have engaged in trade relations with African communities and would have had a cultural impact on each other in one way or another. Africans in the east had had some contact with people from another world or from another cosmology. But they also had their own distinct African worldview.

The African worldview has key elements that help in keeping it coherent, but also flexible. Mazisi Kunene, quoted by Udefi (2012) argues that there are two cosmic laws that regulate such elements – continuous growth versus cosmic boundaries. One of these elements relates to time. For the African worldview time is both linear and cyclical. The two are appositional rather than oppositional. As is the case in human experience, there is a linear experience of time, as each day follows another day, as seasons succeed other seasons. But there is also the cyclical aspect.

The cyclical aspect in the African world is lived through a belief in the notion of regeneration. A day, after going in a circle, is succeeded by another day, summer succeeded by another summer when the time has gone round. This important notion of time permeates all thinking and understanding of life. The significant factor is that what *is*, is not complete in isolation. In due course what *is* will come again and thus attain its fullness. There is a pregnancy, a potential to regenerate. Pixley Seme (in Langley 1979:261) uses the word "regenerate" when he refers to the re-growth of Africa after colonial onslaught. Significantly, this complex cyclicity also touches on the state of being of individuals. A person is an individual, but *is* also her/his family or clan and forebears, living, as well as the living dead. This is part of the meaning of ancestors for which there is a great fascination among students of African philosophy and religion.

Mbembe observes that the non-linearity of time in African cosmology is the most difficult and misunderstood by Western linear thinking. It is simply attributed to chaos associated with the African world (Mbembe 2001:17). Mbembe argues that "every age is a combination of several temporalities" (2001:15) [that] can be aligned to the notion of cyclicity as discussed above. Mbiti's view that African sense of time "lays greater emphasis on the past and present, making future virtually non-existent beyond a few months or years" (1970:12) does indirectly accommodate the idea of repeated retreats to the past and the sense of belonging to the past. But to argue about a virtually non-existent future is contrary to African experience of human lifespan. There is an expectation of the morrow, of the next season and of generations not yet born that can extend to several decades and up to a century, sometimes.

From the cyclical element there is space and opportunity for new beginnings. When a phenomenon occurs, there is an understanding that it will come again in a cycle in the same way that the winter season re-emerges the following year. That may not necessarily be at the same point of convergence. Again, this may be Mbembe's "interlocking of presents, pasts and futures" (2001:16). When that happens it marks a new beginning at the same time, a new cycle notched at a different level. Smith is mistaken when she claims that, "Traditional African worldview sees time as the perpetual unquestioned present" (2003:247). Certainly there is no notion of doomsday as the Westerners believe, but African cosmology does accommodate a tomorrow within a cycle, but it is the reverting back that cuts into the duration of the future. Mbiti quotes an isolated case of a myth among the Sonjo of Tanzania that foretells of human history moving to the end (1970:246).

On first contact with the Europeans amaXhosa in southern Africa, regarded the visitors as *abantu basemzini*, "People of another House" (Crais 1992:30). After contact and due examination, they recognised them as sharing common humanity with them even though they also acknowledged differences which included skin colour and hair that looked like the spirogyra. The recognition of the humanity of Europeans was mainly within the inclusivity element in the African worldview. That was and is the main difference between the two worldviews under discussion. The advent of Europeans would have also been interpreted as a new beginning in the never ending cycles in the African universe. Thus, European presence and activities would be accommodated in the inclusivity which Kalu describes as "elasticity in African worldview and capacity to make room within its inherited body of traditions for new realities" (Kalu, Hofmeyr & Maritz 2005:3). That did not mean an end to the African worldview. Indeed, it has survived in the face of the actual experience of encounters, as well as in the light of the teachings of Europeans about Africans. This also includes Christian teachings about Africans being the descendants of the cursed Ham, Noah's son. An observation by a renowned philosopher, Hegel, quoted by

Ramose, "Africa can have neither a history nor be itself the subject of history" (2005:20), sums up European thinking about Africa among philosophers of Hegel's time.

In his book *Post-Colonial Transformation* Ashcroft makes a strong argument about the resilience of the indigenous people in the face of prolonged and overwhelming European hegemony. He states, "post-colonial cultures resisted the power of colonial domination in ways so subtle that they transformed both the coloniser and colonised" (2001:3). Resistance was/is both overt and covert. Military resistance has been the key indigenous response around which theorists have constructed narratives about contact. Yet, much more subtle ways of resisting and surviving form the greater part of the indigenous – settler interaction. Resistance was not always oppositional. Even collaboration, absorption and swimming along with the invader could create a challenge of the 'other' being too close to the invader. This was certainly the case when indigenous people converted to Christianity or when they progressed in formal learning.

Resistance and resilience of African maps of the universe should form part of the research questions and initiatives aiming at *Ukuhlambulula* studies about knowledge of the indigenous people of the world. This should result in the "reconstruction of concepts and theories governing the construction of [new] social reality" (Hoppers in Higgs 2000:4). Further, it is argued in this chapter, that resistance and resilience are posited within the cosmological outlooks of the autochthons.

The discussion below seeks to demonstrate the resilience of African maps of reality which continued to exist within the world imposed by the settlers. IsiXhosa-speaking Africans, operating from their worldview, continued to define their world and name themselves despite the new European created world generally known as colonialism. This was part of their resistance and survival. In a few isolated cases in written documents, the African voice is heard loud and clear. The colonial definitions and names at times appear to dominate, but the autochthons, confident of the return of the cycle and the pregnant moment of regeneration would not give in. The argument presented below is built on two examples that demonstrate African thinking at play in mid-19th and end of 20th century contexts at the heart of European presence and dominance.

Below, is the quote that this chapter started with:
> "I am the *earth* (his) itself. God made me a chief on the very first day of creation ... " (Williams 1983:121).

The quotation comes from Reverend Tiyo Soga's *Journal*. These words were spoken by one Mhlehle. He was described by Soga, an African missionary, as a 'Fingo'. Soga himself was not just the first ordained isiXhosa-speaking minister, he was also a Xhosa aristocrat as opposed to a 'Fingo'. Thus, it is likely that he was unsympathetic towards Mhlehle. There was a European constructed tension between Soga, an amXhosa, and Mhlehle, a 'Fingo'. Soga described Mhlehle as a "curious old fellow" (1983:121). Later Soga noted that Mhlehle might have suffered "some rude indignities at the hands of [Boers]" (1983:121). It is how Mhlehle defines and names himself that is important in this discussion.

Mhlehle's definition of himself as the *earth* (his emphasis) has to be understood as coming from someone who needed to defend and assert his identity. The use of the metaphor *earth* was pregnant with meaning when used by someone who had lost all claims to the land under settler pressure and had also lost recognition of his indigenous status as *inkosi* – chief. He called himself with what the contention was all about – earth – *umhlaba,* land. He bolstered his argument by going back to the authority of God and creation time, referring to the Biblical creation. Thus he was using the colonial frame of reference. To emphasise his point, however, he came up with his own defining apparatus, "very first day of creation" (Williams 1983:121). It is usually during momentous times that African maps of the universe surface more distinctly. Through the claims Mhlehle made, he was marking or declaring a new beginning in the cycle of his universe. His African listeners did not challenge what would have appeared to be an absurd claim to a non-African. Instead, Christian Soga went on to appreciate the fact that Mhlehle had explained to them his aristocratic background.

The significance of Mhlehle's statement under discussion is the fact that here was an indigenous person living at the height of invasion, loss of land, loss of identity and being exposed into new cosmological outlooks about God and yet continuing to define himself. In essence in his self-definition he stands against Christian teachings bringing forward his own understanding of God's intervention in his life. Mhlehle's time-span is outside the Western notion of time. It is within the African time sense that Mhlehle seeks to highlight one cosmological reality that is forever regenerating. Mhlehle claims that he was made by God to be chief and that can be interpreted as a response to the aggressive policies that the invaders were pursuing during the early 1860s when they displaced *iinkosi* with magistrates.

Mhlehle's statement therefore is a prime example of multiversality – African and European cosmologies – of reality – that characterises contexts of indigenous-

European contact. There is a complex entanglement that is a key feature that characterises these societies. A focus that foregrounds one cosmological outlook and marginalises or buries the other creates a false view of that society.

The second example of Africanist thinking is one expressed through a speech by Thabo Mbeki, the second president of a democratic South Africa. In her article Smith (2003) discusses Mandela and Mbeki leadership styles and argues that they were both influenced by African values and beliefs. Indeed, Mandela is cited as making repeated reference to his upbringing in the context of *Komkhulu* – The Great Place. Then Smith discusses Mbeki's famous speech "I am an African" (2003:259).

The context of the speech, "I am an African" is important and needs some analysis. It was delivered on the occasion of the adoption by the Constitutional Assembly of the Republic of South Africa Constitution Bill 1996. Even though the statement is said to have been given on behalf of the African National Congress (ANC) it may not be far off the point to say it was also Thabo Mbeki's victory song. Mbeki had left home, South Africa, at the age of 19 years. He only returned when he was in his late forties. During his time of exile, he studied. But the greater part of his life was devoted to the work of the ANC. Describing Mbeki, Gevisser, his biographer, discusses his "parentless childhood" (2007:xxxi). This had to do with Mbeki's huge sacrifices as he travelled the world far from his family and living the "vagabondage of exile" (2007:xxix). An argument can be made therefore that the passing of the Constitution Bill marked a moment that all South Africans especially those who had suffered while working for the liberation of South Africa that Mbeki had dreamt of.

Mbeki introduced his speech, "On an occasion such as this we should perhaps start from the beginning" (Mbeki 1996). What beginning? He never said. Once again, like in the case of Mhlehle, there is reference to time, a beginning. Gevisser narrates that on his return Mbeki had an opportunity to visit his ancestral home where he had been introduced to his family history. This experience, Gevisser argues, made Mbeki, the "Englishman" begin to ask in earnest questions about his identity (Gevisser 2007:16). From that moment, the "Englishman" is said to have started asking questions about his identity.

The question of Mbeki's identity is a salient issue in this discussion. He had left home as a young adult and thereafter lived both in African and European worlds. This was during the time he was a student at British universities. Then later his work involved working with international leaders as he was posted in the office of the ANC leader, Oliver Tambo. But it is in the engagement he had with the International Union of

Students, and particularly with African groups like the Pan-African Youth Movement and All African Students' Union, that he was exposed to young people mainly from the African continent, as his fellow countryman, Nhlapo, testifies (Ndhlovu & Strydom 2016:273). Another African sojourner, Ami Mpungwe, a Tanzanian diplomat, observes that he had known Mbeki to be "a strong committed pan-Africanist" (p.447). John Stremlau, an American academic teaching at Witwatersrand University during the late 1990s adds his voice to the discussion. He experienced and redesigned his curriculum around Mbeki's policies and outreach into Africa through the African Renaissance and the New Partnership for African Development initiatives (p.498). Mbeki had returned home with his African cosmological outlook.

The speech "I am an African" demarcated a clear beginning for Mbeki, marking a "rediscovery of ourselves ... a voyage of discovery into our own antecedents, our own past as Africans" (Mbeki 1996). One would not say Mbeki had no awareness of an African worldview, but the ancestral visit rekindled a fire that had been dormant in the long years of wandering in Europe that burnt brightly as he found his way home. And so through the speech, Mbeki was celebrating a new moment, a Ghana Moment in his African life. Moreover, the speech is a profound example that demonstrates inclusivity. There is a genuine appreciation of all the people who have contributed in the making of his past. Included are "those who were transported from India and China" (1996). Also added are "the immigrants who left Europe to find a new home on our native land. Whatever their own actions, they remain still part of me" (1996). Nor are animals and the rumbling thunder forgotten. Again, Mbeki is operating within an African cosmology that celebrates a close affinity between humans and nature. Through *iziduko/ izithakazelo/ diboko*, clan praises are formed around animals like elephants, crocodiles and hares. Birds are sometimes included like *inkwali*. As Africans identify themselves with particular animals, indeed, they *are* those animals.

In this speech Mbeki defines, describes and names himself:
> I am the grandchild of warrior men and women that Hintsa and Sekhukhune led ...
> My mind and my knowledge of myself is formed by the victories that are jewels in our African crown ...
> I am born of a people who would not tolerate oppression ...
> I come of those who were transported from India and China ...
> I am born of the people of Africa ... (Mbeki 1996).

The two texts provide interesting examples where Africans define and name themselves. This they do outside the colonial textual framing. With new beginnings within the African worldview African voices can be heard cutting across the so called pre-colonial, colonial and even post-colonial phases. This is a major shift even from those arguments that understand the African voice to have been successfully silenced.

In conclusion an argument is made in this chapter that the historical division of three phases framed around colonisation should be debunked. Continued use of such historical maps tethers future research to retaining colonialism as one of the final defining moments in African life and history. Researchers should embark on *Ukuhlambulula* – cleansing and healing the body of African studies from colonial malady. *Ukuhlambulula* as a process will be a consciousness that should imbue all those in search of new epistemologies and pedagogies in birthing a multiversal academic reality. This should mark the end of Eurocentric universalism especially in institutions of higher learning and the curriculum offered there. A new awareness by academics on a path of *Ukuhlambulula* will ask innovative research questions which should include indigenous frameworks in their research work. The two texts of Soga and Mbeki, demonstrate an African time consciousness, different from the Western view and calculation of time, as well as an African social reality. A conscious break from the over-used concept 'colonialism' will challenge researchers to re-imagine and create new frames for self-definition and naming.

References

Ashcroft, B. 2001. *Post-Colonial Transformation.* London: Routledge.

Azuonye, C. 1996. *The Big Canvass: An Interview with Mazisi Kunene.* https://scholarworks.umb.edu/cgi/viewcontent.cgi?article=1001&context=africana_faculty_pubs. [Retieved on 17 April, 2018].

Crais, C.C. 1992. *The Making of the Colonial Order: White Supremacy and Black Resistance in the Eastern Cape 1770-1865.* Johannesburg: Witwatersrand University Press.

De Kock, L. 1996. *Civilising Barbarians Missionary Narratives and African Textual Response in Nineteenth Century South Africa.* Johannesburg: Witwatersrand University Press.

De Sousa Santos, B. 2014. *Epistemologies of the South: Justice Against Epistemicide.* London: Paradigm Publishers.

De Vere Allen, J. 1993. *Swahili Origins: Swahili Culture and the Shungwaya Phenomenon.* London: James Currey.

Eze, E.C. (ed.). 1977. *Post-colonial African Philosophy: A Critical Reader.* Massachusetts: Blackwell Publishers.

Fanon, F. 1967. *Black skin white masks.* Translated by C. Markman. England: Pluto Press.

Gevisser, M. 2007. *Thabo Mbeki: The Dream Deferred.* Johannesburg: Jonathan Ball Publishers.

Heleta, S. 2016. *Decolonisation of higher education: Dismantling epistemic violence and Eurocentrism in South Africa.* www.thejournal.org.za [Retrieved on 23 October 2017]. https://doi.org/10.4102/the.v1i1.9

Higgs, P. 2000. *African voices in education.* Cape Town: Juta and Company Ltd.

Kalu, O.U. 2005. Introduction: The Shape and Flow of African Church Historiography. In: O.U. Kalu, J.W. Hofmeyr & P.J. Maritz (eds.). *African Christianity: An African Story.* Department of Church History, University of Pretoria, Pretoria.

Kunnie, J. 2000. Indigenous African Philosophies and Socioeducational Transformation in 'Post-Apartheid' Azania. In: P. Higgs, N.C.G. Vakalisa, T.V. Mda & N.T. Assie-Lumumba (eds.). *African Voices in Education.* Lansdowne: Juta.

Levtzion, N. & Hopkins, J.F.P. (eds.). 1981. *Corpus of Early Arabic Sources for West African History.* Cambridge: Cambridge University Press.

Lloyd, D. 1993. *Anomalous states: Irish writing and the post-colonial moment.* Durhan: Duke University Press.

Magesa, L. 1997. *African Religion: The Moral Traditions of Abundant Life.* New York: Orbis Books.

Magubane, B.M. 2007. *Race and the Construction of the Dispensable Other.* Pretoria: University of South Africa Press.

Makang, J.M. 1997. Of the Good Use of Tradition: Keeping the Critical Perspective in African Philosophy. In: E.C. Eze (ed.). *Post-colonial African Philosophy: A Critical Reader.* Massachusetts: Blackwell Publishers.

Mamdani, M. 2012. *Define and Rule: Natives as Political Identity.* Johannesburg: Witwatersrand University Press. https://doi.org/10.4159/harvard.9780674067356

Mamdani, M. 1996. *Citizen and Subject: Contemporary Africa and Legacy of Late Colonialism.* Princeton: Princeton University Press.

Mbeki, T. 1998. *Africa: The Time Has Come.* Johannesburg: Mafube Press.

Mbeki, T. 1996. I Am an African- Speech at the Adoption of the Republic of South Africa Constitution Bill.

Mbembe, A. 2001. *On the Postcolony.* Berkeley: University of California.

Mbiti, J.S. 1970. *Concepts of God in Africa.* London: S.P.C.K.

Mostert, N. 1992. *FRONTIERS: The Epic of South Africa's Creation and the Tragedy of the Xhosa People.* New York: Alfred A Knopf.

Mqhayi, S.E.K. 2009. *Abantu Besizwe: Historical and Biographical Writings, 1902-1944.* Trans. O. Opland (ed.). Johannesburg: Wits University Press.

Mqhayi, S.E.K. 1981. *Ityala Lamawele.* Alice: Lovedale Press.

Mudimbe, V.Y. 2013. *On African Faultlines: meditations on Alterity Politics.* Scottsville: University of KwaZulu-Natal Press.

Mudimbe, V.Y. 1994. *The Idea of Africa.* London: James Currey.

Ngugi wa Thiong'o. 1986. *Decolonising the Mind: The Politics of Language in African Literature.* London: James Currey.

Ndlovu, S.M.& Strydom, M. (eds.). 2016.*The Thabo Mbeki I know.* Johannesburg: Picador Africa.

Nkondo, M. 2016. Eurocentric thinking holds us back. In: *The Sunday Independent*, 25 September.

Nonxuba, A. 2016. *What is decolonised education?* www.news24.com [Retrieved 23 October 2017].

Hoppers, C.A.O. ndg. Renegotiating Agency in Knowledge Production, Innovation and Africa's Development in the Context of the Triage Society delivered at an International Symposium on Knowledge and Transformation: Social and Human Sciences in Africa.

Omoyele, I. 2017. Past traps post-colonial varsities. *Mail & Guardian.* 8-14 September, 31.

Ramose, M.B. 2005. *African Philosophy Through Ubuntu.* Harare: Mond Books Publishers.

Seme, P.I. 1979. The Regeneration of Africa. In: J.A. Langley. *Ideologies of Liberation in Black Africa 1856-1970.* London: Rex Collings.

Senghor, L. S. 1979. The Problems of African Language – or Bilingualism as a Solution. In: J.A. Langley. *Ideologies of Liberation in Black Africa 1856-1970.* London: Rex Collings.

Smith, B. 2003. Worldview and Culture: Leadership in Sub-Sahara. In: *New England Journal of Public Policy,* 19(1).

Thabede, D. 2008. The African Worldview as the Basis of Practice in the Helping Professions. *Social Work/ Maatskaplike Werk,* 44(3).

The British and Foreign Bible Society. 1961. *The New English Bible.* Oxford: Oxford University Press.

Tisani, N.C. 2000. Continuity and Change in Xhosa Historiography during the Nineteenth Century: An Exploration through Textual Analysis. Unpublished Doctoral dissertation. Grahamstown: Rhodes University.

Udefi, A. 2012. Philosophy, Mythology and an African Cosmological System. *Global Journal of Human Social Science: Geography and Environmental GeoSciences,* 12(10): 1.0.

Williams, D. 1983. *The Journal and Selected Writings of the Reverend Tiyo Soga.* Cape Town: A.A. Balkema.

Young, R.J.C. 2001. *Post-colonialism: An Historical Introduction.* Oxford: Blackwell Publishers.

CHAPTER 3

Language as Source of Revitalisation and Reclamation of Indigenous Epistemologies

Contesting Assumptions and Re-imagining Women Identities in (African) Xhosa Society

Pamela Maseko[1]

Introduction

While history, art and archaeology, for example, have been used to present evidence of socio-cultural and other practices of pre-colonial Africa, the contribution of language as a source from which one can make presuppositions and conjectures about its speakers' past has not been sufficiently explored.

In a context where African knowledge has been undermined and misinterpreted by scholars whose inclination is to scrutinise African experience from a prejudiced cultural standpoint, the study of the meanings embedded in the lexicon of African languages cannot be overlooked when lifting the veil from Africa's past. Although meanings of words in a language may shift because of contact with other linguistic societies, or because of new domains of language use, one is able to study the etymology of words to elicit original meanings and their evolution in form and meaning, and also make correspondence of such meanings to the thoughts of society as early as present memory can recall.

---

[1] p.maseko@gmail.com

As with all languages, languages of Africa encode thoughts of the people who speak them. The encoded thoughts are expressed in the words that constitute the language. It can be argued, therefore, that language is one of the reliable sources in understanding the thoughts and experiences of the societies which speak it, particularly in relation to their past and the present. The dynamics of the African past have, more than ever, occupied the academy as calls for the African-centred curriculum gained increasing momentum in the #FeesMustFall (#FMF) 2015 and 2016 South African student protests. The calls are motivated by practices in the academy that put worth in European knowledge, and marginalise knowledge rooted in the African experience.

Oyewumi (1997), one of the leading African feminist scholars challenging the imposition of Western-conceived gender identity constructs onto Yoruba culture, argues that the cultural hegemony of the North, primarily Europe and North America, in the production of knowledge in the academy, makes Africa dependent on Western cultural experience to make sense of African experience. This hegemony and power of Western knowledge makes the rest of world depend on it to explain their own experience.

In studying isiXhosa in all facets of language study, this chapter seeks to reconstruct the experiences of a pre-colonial isiXhosa-speaking Nguni society to understand the society's ways of knowing in relation to social roles. I examine, through linguistic evidence, the manner in which social roles are constructed amongst the amaXhosa society. Specifically, I look at whether 'gender' is a key factor in organising relationships and roles in Xhosa society.

Further, in response to the question of the transformation and Africanisation of the curriculum raised during the #FMF student protests, this chapter presents language as a possible source of reliable evidence not only in the reconstruction of the social roles in pre-colonial isiXhosa-speaking Nguni society, but also in the efforts of centring African experiences in knowledge production and dissemination in the academy. If we have to develop knowledge about African society, it makes sense that we listen to what African languages are saying about their society.

Some scholars on African Nguni languages and literature, notably Kuse (1978), Qangule (1979) and Kunene (1981) draw connections between language and knowledge to make presuppositions about Nguni society's sociocultural practices based on literary or pragmatic analysis. Literary analysis generally involves examining the structure or form of literary work and draws conclusions about the character or intentions of the author. Pragmatics is the study of the use of language by its speakers in its social context. Generally, pragmatics deals with how contexts contribute to meaning in conversations, and is typically concerned with questions around what characterises the behaviour of language users in those contexts. Both these literary techniques do not look into meanings embedded in words to link them to cultural practices of the linguistic community from whom the words originate. Kuse and Qangule, in their study of S.E.K. Mqhayi's poetry, explore the poetry in terms of its morphological, syntactical and phonetic configurations, its structural and stylistic function and its thematic content. Further, they study literary devices such as symbolism, euphemism and metaphors to draw conclusions on the humanistic traits in Mqhayi's characters and the society from which these words emerge. In other words, formal properties of isiXhosa, the language medium used by Mqhayi, are not analysed to give an account of meanings of words and the information that these meanings may in turn suggest about the society that speaks that language. Kunene's epic poem, *Anthem of the Decades: A Zulu epic dedicated to the women of Africa* differs from the works above, but it is closer in its ideology to my study. In his introduction he states that this text functions as a corrective to views that "have projected African thought systems as no more than a simple folk-thought meriting no serious classification in the hierarchy of knowledge" (1981:xiii). In his corrective undertaking, he proposes an analysis of meanings of names because names have a close relationship to meanings associated with functions of their bearers (1981:xxxv-xxxix), but also uses literary devices such as repetition to give suggestive meanings linked to repeated sounds. His conclusion from his study is that in studying meanings associated with Zulu gods and goddesses, one can determine the African philosophy of life and its connectedness with cosmology.

This study differs from works by Qangule and Kuse, and maybe to a lesser extent by Kunene. It is a lexico-semantic study that engages Semantics (linguistic study of meaning) and Sociolinguistics (study of language in relation to social factors) techniques to investigate, through historical texts, possible links between knowledge and sociocultural practices of a society and the insights this can provide about the historical knowledge of that society. It studies meanings embedded in lexical units of selected isiXhosa words that refer to social relations and makes a correlation between the meaning and sociocultural beliefs and values of amaXhosa, specifically gender identity, in a historical context.

I start the chapter by locating myself within the research and present a narrative on the value of knowledge in language as presented by elders I grew up with in my village. I argue that these experiences were critical in spurring on my sociolinguistic studies, specifically on the relationship between language and dominance. This is followed by a discussion on language, knowledge and power. These are sociolinguistic concepts which I use in analysing and advancing an argument on how language and the knowledge embedded therein, are used to maintain dominance, and by implication, power of the society which speaks it. This section is followed by the history of literacy in isiXhosa, a history that is predated by a longer history of oracy. I then discuss the concept of gender as a form of social organisation as presented in Gender Studies and, using words, some of which are extracted from texts written at the earliest point of acquisition of the writing skills, I give examples of terms used for naming social relations in an isiXhosa-speaking society. The purpose is to give insight, through words used to name concepts, into how isiXhosa-speaking society conceptualised their social reality and, specifically, provide illustrations of social stratification within the society.

I make propositions throughout. The first proposition is that, while it is not possible to argue against social stratification in African or isiXhosa-speaking society, in the case of this chapter, such stratification is not based on the type of body a member of society has, but rather on other factors. For example, the words that name members of society are linked to responsibility, seniority, rank and status of that member, and not the physiology of the person bearing that name. The second proposition is that the present understanding and articulation of social roles and responsibilities in an isiXhosa-speaking society could possibly be traced back to colonial power, which sought through the naming and engineering of indigenous languages to dominate and erase the experience and knowledge of the native population. In the conclusion I emphasise the importance of language as a valuable and reliable source of evidence that should be considered in understanding social practices of the isiXhosa-speaking Nguni society before contact with the West, and expose the invalidity of some of the widely-held assumption about isiXhosa society. One such assumption is that the suffixal morpheme *–kazi* marks a feminine form for nouns that refer to woman, and as an augmentative form in other contexts. A conclusion is then drawn that this marking of gender in language reflects a gendered society. While this form of the suffix occurs in nouns that refer to a woman, however its semantic function goes beyond the structural form of the marked noun. The purpose of this study is to examine the semantic function of this form, and its significance in making sense of whether a being's sex played a role in the assignment of social roles in isiXhosa-speaking pre-colonial society.

Locating my experience within the research

One of the puzzles of my education, particularly higher education, is the extent to which what I was taught and learnt about myself, both as a member of the isiXhosa-speaking Nguni society and as *umntu wesifazane*[2] – a person who is a great mortal (female) in that society – was too removed from what I know and have experienced. It becomes important that, before I develop the argument further on re-imagining women identities in isiXhosa- speaking society, I position myself by relating two experiences.

I grew up in the land of Chief Ngubengcuka in a village called uMgwali in the Eastern Cape. The village is named uMgwali after a river that runs through it. Tatomkhulu Matiwane, one of the elders of the village, told how the village was named. The river itself was named uMgwali from the musical sound that came through the lush grass that grew alongside it. *Umgwali* is a person who plays music on *ugwali*, a wooden harp. The village, therefore, acquired its name from the name of the river. The concept of "making of song" was transferred to its name, a concept reflecting the manner in which the society as a whole made sense of the natural phenomenon in their midst. This, Matiwane said at the social gathering which he addressed, was a knowledge passed orally, from generation to generation (Matiwane, personal communication, 2010). Matiwane died in 2012. He was 91 years old.

When Chief Ngcubengcuka provided land as a place of refuge to the Wesleyan missionaries who came to this area in the late 1820s, they built a mission station in 1831 and promptly gave my village a new name, Clarkebury, after a certain Mr Adam Clarke, who never set foot in Mgwali, but was the Wesleyan Secretary of mission in England during this period.

In comparing these two experiences, it is fascinating in both contexts that the social experiences of the amaXhosa and the English are reflected. On the one hand, uMgwali reflects the manner in which the words that name thoughts reflect in that society's engagement with their natural and social environment. On the other hand, Clarkebury reflects a society's acknowledgement of an individual. From the first experience above, one can deduce that in isiXhosa-speaking Cape Nguni society names and, by implication, knowledge, were derived from the society's perception about a phenomena, whether in terms of characteristics or behaviour. Knowledge

---

[2] Throughout this article I will give literal translation of the terms given. Alongside this I will give, in brackets, what is presented as an English equivalent. This is to show contrast in the literal meaning and the English equivalence.

production, therefore, was communally negotiated by members of the society. The West, on the other hand, focussed on an individual, and celebrated achievement and conquest of a society through an individual.

The second context relates to *umakhulu wam,* my senior mother (grandmother). *uMakhulu* possessed authority in our homestead. She possessed power; power that she shared with *utatomkhulu wam,* my senior father (grandfather). When *oomakazi,* my great mothers (maternal aunts) got married, she gave orders, through my senior father how *lobola* negotiations were to be handled, for example. I grew up in a social context where there was a general understanding that there were members who had profound knowledge and understanding of issues relating to society, regardless of whether they were men or women. *Amaxhegokazi* – the senior womenfolk – of my village lived these traits, and through the tales they told us as young people I got a sense that those traits are common in *abafazi* in isiXhosa-speaking society.

I am often perplexed by scholars on feminism, both from within and outside of the continent, who cannot make sense of this power of women in the African continent. Is it because it presents itself differently from Western epistemologies? For African scholars, is it because we do not know, or is it because we lack an understanding, or an ability to make sense of what we know?

As I undertake this study, I am conscious of the dynamics of scholarship in which I was oriented, a scholarship that does not identify and appreciate African-centred ontology and epistemology (Atanga *et al.* 2013, Buthelezi 2003, Kropf 1899/1915). In reconstructing and making sense of the past from the present, I need the courage to dig down to the roots of my experience and how these are presented in the lexicon of isiXhosa, the language I speak as my primary language to understand what I know and to draw conclusions from it about indigenous ways of life. Part of this requires unlearning the privilege of education, it requires that I remember and relearn my teaching from my senior mother and senior folk in the village and from my contemporary experience. This process of challenging the notion of gender through the reconstruction of social practices in pre-colonial society, using linguistic evidence is the beginning of that process. An understanding of how language constructs the world and how this in turn constructs power around a certain society's knowledge (Gqoba 1887, Foucault 1989) is important in this study.

Language, power and knowledge

The chapter takes, as a point of departure, the important relationship between language, knowledge and power

Language, whether written or spoken, is the medium through which *abantu* – the beings with a soul/people – share their values, thoughts and opinions about their physical, social and spiritual environment. It is the lens through which they construct their ideas, beliefs and thoughts about the world around them. It constitutes the words that *abantu* in a society use to name things and phenomena around them. The words themselves are not random, but are craftily selected to reflect the manner in which the social beings make sense of their surroundings. In other words, the manner in which things are given names reflects society's thoughts about those things.

Language, the words used to communicate, is the source of knowledge for any society speaking that language. Words that make up a language spring from the struggles to name the thoughts we have about different phenomena in our social surroundings. Words are the dress that cover the ideas of a society. This is a universal linguistic phenomenon (Wa Thiong'o 2013). For example, words like *umfazi*, a great mortal, *umfo*, a mortal (a man), *umfana*, a young mortal (young man) and *umfazana*, a newly married great young mortal (a newly married woman) are all derived from the verb *–fa*, 'to die'. The English equivalents of the terms do not begin to convey the concept of 'mortality' that is in the root of all the terms, nor do they transfer the meaning 'greatness' and 'youth' in the morphenes *–(k)azi* and *–ana* respectively. In English the focus is on the 'male-ness' or 'female-ness' in the concept named.

However, while language as a means of communication is important, it is not as important as knowledge, ideas and wisdom embedded in the language itself (Mafeje 1994:64-67). Mafeje argues that any language can be appropriated by different users for authentic representation of knowledge in their own cultural worlds. Knowledge itself is generated from the manner in which a society makes sense of, struggles with, and interacts with its social and natural environment. Knowledge constitutes skills, both abstract and concrete, that *abantu* gain through their lived experiences or education, skills that help them understand the present and predict the future (Gqoba 2015). This understanding of language and knowledge suggests that all beings have a common phenomenon – to use language to express past experiences and to react to the present to make sense of the future.

---

3   Gqoba wrote extensively in 1887 in *Isigidimi SamaXosa*.

The third concept of power in the analytical framework of this study is expressed in William Wellington Gqoba's writing (1887) wherein he postulates that power is constructed when one determines, controls and wields authority on what is to be valued in society. This, he argues, can be constructed through writing. He contends that writing is used as a reservoir of ideas, values, thoughts and knowledge of a society. He makes a point that once knowledge is constructed as powerful in this manner, it 'lives' not only within the confines of where it emerged, but rather because of its power it spreads, gets shared, imposed on others, and others seek to consume it. This can be understood as a state of hegemony. Driven by desire for the history and knowledge of the Cape Nguni to be preserved in the language of the people, and the power of sharing and preserving such knowledge in writing, he writes in *Isigidimi* newspaper, that:

> Imbali yakowethu asikuko nokuba ndinga ingaziwa kakuhle ishicilelwe kuba zonke izizwe ezinembali ziba zihleli azifile noko sukuba sezicitakele. Sifundiswa ngembali zezizwe zaseGreece, Rome, Egypt, nezamaNgesi njalo-njalo, into ezazizo kwanento eziyiyo namhla. Ke ngoko ziphilile, kuba nathi singazange sizibone sazi nto ngazo, namhla ngenxa yeencwadi zembali zazo, siyazibona, siyathetha nazo, siyazekela nentetho nemikhwa ethile kuzo kubume banamhla bazo.
>
> *(My fervent desire is that our history should be well known and brought into print because all nations who possess a history continue to live and do not die even if they become broken up. We are taught the chronological stories of the nations of Greece, Rome, Egypt, of the English and so on, who they were and what they are today. Thus they are very much alive, because even we who never shared their experiences or saw them, at least today we know something about them through their historical books; we see them, we discuss them and make an example of some of their sayings and habits as reflected in their present day legacy).*

Gqoba's argument about the relation between power and literacy is plausible. However, the widely held assumption in the academy, that knowledge is only knowledge because it comes through books, is a fallacy in the context of the isiXhosa. Firstly, the history of recording of people's experience and knowledge through writing came only in the early 1800s in isiXhosa-speaking Nguni society. Therefore, the period of literacy and contact with the West is much shorter compared to oracy. Secondly, prior to the introduction of literacy and contact with Europe, Nguni society used oral literary art forms such as myths, legends, songs, praise songs, proverbs, idioms, etc. to preserve and disseminate knowledge (Jordan 1957, Makalima 1981; Tisani 2000). The medium through which this was communicated was language.

Therefore, given the history of the oral literary art forms, it is therefore possible to look at the etymology of the words that constitute the language to draw conclusions about sociocultural practices and beliefs of a society. The examination of the etymology of the words of a language can suggest contexts in which a named concept emerged.

Except for oral literary art forms in societies with a long, just and systematic history of writing which gives a diachronic development of a language, literary sources also become a reliable source of evidence to complement studies on social issues. In the South African context, literacy and literature development was linked to Christianity and Western education, pioneered primarily by the missionaries from the West. It is widely accepted now that this education was not neutral, but came with cultural and linguistic prejudice with the purpose of exerting the power and dominance of the colonial powers over indigenous populations. Consequently, even in instances where the missionaries or their allies observed powerful indigenous knowledge and discourses that were, for example, significant in making sense of social relations and sociocultural practices in indigenous population, there was deliberate effort to erase these from the memory of the indigenous population, replacing them with newly acquired experiences and knowledge from the West. Secondly, Gqoba and his contemporaries (who wrote at the earliest point of the acquisition of writing) were themselves products of missionary education. Therefore, while they write in their native languages, one cannot escape the fact that even as their writings might have been intentionally subversive to the political and Christian agenda at the time, their acquired education was still through the missionaries. There are even assumptions at times that they served to extend the agenda of the missionaries during their times (Mgqwetho 2007). However, the idea of this study is not validation of the ideology or thoughts of the people, but rather the examination of the lexicon of the language during their writings. Their works present the earliest record of writings by the speakers of the languages.

Therefore, while I do not outrightly reject Mafeje's argument above, that any language can be used in the authentic representation of knowledge from a different cultural context, entering one's world through a different medium, especially in the context of South Africa, can be a challenge. As can be deduced from above, prior to contact with the West amaXhosa had an organised language within which knowledge was preserved. However, encounter with literacy in the Cape Nguni region of South Africa came through English and with a political agenda. Kropf is amongst the first missionaries to offer a comprehensive and systematic lexicographic work in isiXhosa in 1899. This work is rife with instances of cultural and religious (Christian) prejudice. In a few instances he records this prejudice, and acknowledges the missionaries as having replaced certain knowledge with that which would serve the missionary agenda, or that which would be palatable to the colonial governance. Such examples is the missionaries' shifting the meaning of *inkosikazi* (chieftainess) to 'wife' and proudly acknowledges that "this was introduced by the missionaries" (Kropf 1899/1915). This is clearly an indication of the erasure of indigenous knowledge, and replacing it with colonial memory. It is this knowledge, embedded in the language, that this work seeks to recover. In the authentication of knowledge, therefore, drawing from the original meaning of words in the pre-colonial society is somehow more dependable in debunking some of the widely-held assumptions about Africa.

Language reflects a manner in which individuals in a society construct their reality and experience. In this experience is embedded knowledge of the people, knowledge that is shared between members of the society for social cohesion. However, as can be seen in the case of contact with Europe, the power relations between the indigenous population and missionaries, for example, resulted in shifts of meanings of some words. Although this shift might have occurred, the subsets of roots of words remained unchanged, and one can study their original meanings and draw inferences from them, for example, about the socio-cultural identity of the people prior to their shift in meaning. These inferences can assist in the reconstruction of identity of *abantu besifazane* before contact with Europe, in the case of this study. Therefore regardless of the purposeful devaluing of the language and knowledge inherent in it, words in a language can still reflect something about the social history of the people who spoke them, or reconceptualisation of the older meaning.

The section below discusses the early contact of the indigenous population with Europe. It also gives some instances of acknowledgement of the epistemology of the indigenous population, but then distortion was as a result of cultural and linguistic prejudice that was couched in Christian evangelism.

Language and contact in South Africa: acknowledgement, and obliteration of knowledge and wisdom of an indigenous society

One of the primary sources used as evidence to provide an account of African society prior to colonialism is the writings of missionaries. In the case of Sociolinguistic studies, these accounts give evidence of the oral prowess of the African society at the earliest point of contact with the West. Writing in 1850, Appleyard, who worked extensively amongst the Cape Nguni in the Grahamstown and Peddie areas, and led the first translation of the Bible in isiXhosa, is in awe of the exceptional structural organisation of the oral language of amaXhosa, which he expresses as:

> In all grammatical variations of form, Kafir (sic) language is eminently distinguished by system and regularity. It is ... correctly spoken by all classes of the community, which is not the case, perhaps, with any of our European tongues. As a very general, if not invariable rule, a Kafir (sic) will never be heard using an ungrammatical expression... (Appleyard 1850:67-8).

He further states:

> The origin of the Kafir[4] (sic) languages is wrapped in mystery. How came (sic) these people or their ancestors, centuries ago, to express them in this way, and to adopt this system of alliteration. No one can tell; but whatever their language is; and whatever may have been its origin, the Kafirs (sic) themselves are not an *intellectually* (original emphasis) childish race... (Appleyard 1850:67)

From the perspective of language and knowledge, the above statements suggest two issues. The first one is that, even before contact with the West, isiXhosa was characterised by a regular and systematic structure with features characteristic of developed languages. As indicated, this regularity was lacking in European languages at the time. The second issue relates to the manner in which Appleyard draws a connection between the regularity of the language and the intellectuality of the speakers. From our understanding that language is the medium through which we express our knowledge and intellectuality, and this knowledge is a manifestation of people's experience, assumptions can be made about such journaling about the language as source of evidence in the reconstruction of pre-colonial social life. In 1899 Meinof concurs and states that "whosoever wants to gain intimate knowledge

---

[4] Although the term 'Kafir' came to be used in South Africa pejoratively and as a racial slur towards the native population, I have selected to keep it here in order to give the historical and political context in which the texts were written. Therefore, in the context of this contribution, 'Kafir', in all its variations is used to refer to the native population of South Africa and, specifically, those living along the eastern territory of the country.

of the native ... will best do it by studying the fruits of his intellect: those productions which serve ... for the education of both the young and the old, wherein his soul expresses itself, unstifled by foreign intrusion." Holden (1899) quoted in Mostert (1992:202) also states that "Kafir (sic) oral tradition in debates demonstrates gift of logic. They have tenacious memory... and nothing escapes their keen observation and when engraved in the tablet of their memory, it is never obliterated."

Except for determination to succeed in their colonial and evangelising agendas, their moral highhandedness and contemptuous attitude, nothing could explain the missionary epistemic ignorance that followed later. James Stewart quoted in Opland (1983:204), a missionary who established Lovedale College, one of the early missionary schools in the regions, commented in 1871 in the *Kaffir Express* newspaper, an English version of *Isigidimi*, that:

> There is very little in old Kaffirdom (sic) worth preserving – and we think it will be the wisdom of the natives as soon as possible to move forward into day – and secure the blessings which the present time brings to them. We make this statement even while we intend if possible to publish from time to time brief notices of Kaffir (sic) Laws and Customs. These possess a value, as enabling us to understand the native people better – and have an interest as belonging to a certain state of society. But this is a very different thing from holding up that state as worthy of imitation or preservation.

Stewart's comment above stands in sharp contrast to the earlier flattering comments about the language and knowledge of the indigenous population. It illustrates determined efforts to obliterate and/or devalue the indigenous knowledge not just to them as missionaries, but to the indigenous population too. As we reimagine the knowledge and experiences of indigenous South African societies from the language, with the purpose of reconstructing women's identities before contact with Europe, it becomes important that we also rethink the evidence and sources we use to develop our arguments. The writings of the missionaries, some of which are discussed above, as well as those of the early isiXhosa-speaking literates, need to be considered. As can be illustrated in the case of Matiwane above, oral sources are also valuable.

Writing in isiXhosa on the language, culture, history, politics and other significant subjects that reflected intellectuality of amaXhosa, flourished in newspapers in the period between 1870 and 1950 despite the disdainful attitude of the missionaries. In his seminal article *Towards an African Literature* published in 1957, AC Jordan writes about the earliest writings by "any Bantu-speaking African in his (sic) own language in southern Africa" (Jordan 1957:113), written in periodicals and newspapers published at the Lovedale Press from the 1830s. According to Jordan, these were the first missionary converts who, after the acquisition of the skill of reading and writing, wrote literary contributions in newspapers. Amongst the fervent contributors that Jordan lists are Soga, Gqoba, Jabavu, Mhala, Mqhayi and Rubusana whose anthology of the chronicles of 50 years of writing by isiXhosa-speaking writers up to that time, was published in 1906.

There are two critical arguments raised by Jordan in this work. Firstly, he states that although Rubusana might have given insight into the isiXhosa works up to the time of their writing, his anthology does not begin to reflect everything that has been written by isiXhosa-speaking- people in newspapers. Secondly, he makes a point that, although the writings took indigenous art forms, those authors "wrote about serious things in life ... [such as] history, ethnology [and] biography" (Jordan 1957:114), in addition to religious works that were characteristic of the life of any literate African at the time. Jordan concludes this article with a plea, that the heritage of the first fifty years of isiXhosa literary activity should be treasured and appraised not only for its literary attributes or the biographical histories of their writers as is often common with such writings. He argues that it is the ideas, thoughts and knowledge of these intellectuals that should be appraised. I wish to add that these ideas, embedded in the language of these early intellectuals can in turn be analysed to make sense of the pre-colonial past practices around social stratification, in this case, and how, or whether gender is present in the conceptualisation of the isiXhosa-speaking society.

Presenting linguistic evidence in the revitalisation and reclamation of social relations of amaXhosa

This study contends that notions of gender when applied to African social relations, and specifically in isiXhosa-speaking Nguni societies, seem to be premised on Eurocentric conceptions of gender. The term 'gender' commonly refers to the biological state of being male or female. Generally, Gender Studies makes an argument that societies assign social roles to individuals based on their classification as biologically male or female. In English, at birth a child is labelled according to their sex, i.e. as either male or female depending on the type of genitalia they bear. The social roles then are said to be given based on this biological distinction. In other words, one's gender identity is linked to the sex one is assigned to at birth. The language is also characterised by this gender markedness. For example, the most common gender markers are the pronouns 'he' and 'she' depicting a male and female body respectively.

Several studies on language and gender in (southern) Africa have followed this trend of thinking about gender, using the English lens in looking at a phenomenon in an African context. The claim is that African languages encrypt and convey gendered norms and values which exhibit social hierarchy (Bagwasi & Sutherland 2007; Rudwick & Shange, 2006). These studies then posit that there is differentiation in the language used to refer to men and women and, consequently, differentiation in the manner men and women are expected to behave in a particular social context. The argument made is that identities around 'body type' are constructed, transmitted and sustained using language. A conclusion is then drawn, that women in the African society are invisibilised and are perpetually subservient to menfolk. The implication of such a conclusion is that African languages' words encode gender-stratified society and, therefore, African society is gendered.

According to sociocultural theory, and as argued above, language is one of the most important transmitters of a society's knowledge, cultural values and norms. In the context of this research, I attempt to show whether words that assign 'sex' to an individual exist in isiXhosa lexicon, and whether social roles are then assigned according to sex. The meanings of the words, should be able to offer an understanding of how the words originated, and how their origin reflects the conceptualisation of the earliest isiXhosa-speaking society around the different roles of *abantu* in society.

As indicated earlier, language is used in Gender Studies to justify gender stratification in society. The remaining section of this contribution presents linguistic data largely drawn from the isiXhosa lexicon and the works of literature by Jordan (1940) and Gqoba (1873-1888/2015). It uses language, specifically grammar and linguistic discourse to support the argument advanced in this chapter. Such evidence will then be used to support an argument on the manner in which social roles were conceptualised in isiXhosa-speaking pre-colonial society. Using language, I will first examine the manner in which identity of a child is given at birth amongst amaXhosa and the function of the isiXhosa nominal marker. I will follow this up with a discussion on the pronouns, the morpheme *-kazi* and the verb *-lingana* to make sense of family formations amongst amaXhosa. This linguistic evidence is used to provide an answer to the question of whether the biological body is an essential category in social organisation amongst amaXhosa, and what assumptions we can make from this evidence about amaXhosa before contact with foreign speech communities.

When a child is born in an isiXhosa-speaking society, the question asked to determine whether a child is a boy or girl is, *Ngumntwana mni?* Literally, *-ni?* is an interrogative morpheme that can be suffixed to some lexical items to convey a question, e.g. *ntoni* (what?), *njani* (how?), *nini* (when?) and *bani* (who?). In *Ngumntwana mni? –ni* is suffixed to *m-* linking it to *umntwana*, a young being (child) the subject noun. The response to the question can be *yintombi (s/he[5] is* a girl) or *yintombazana* (s/he is a young girl) or *yindodana*, or *ngumfana*, or *yinkwenkwe*, meaning 's/he young man', 's/he is a young mortal' and 's/he is a boy' respectively.

In English, the question asked at birth of a child relates to the 'sex' of the child and requires a response that denotes two categories of either male or female to a newborn child, but in isiXhosa this is different. In fact, there does not seem to have been a word for 'sex' relating to the two 'English' categories. In Kropf's *Kafir[6]-English Dictionary* (1899/1915) the terms referring to sex are only in reference to sexual encounter, and not body type. In making reference to a child born of Nobantu, *inkosikazi yasemaMpondomiseni*, Jordan states, in his classical novel *Ingqumbo Yeminyanya*, '...*inkosikazi ibelekile – umntwana oyindoda*' (1940:151). This can be loosely translated as 'the chieftainess has born a young being who is a man'. Summarily, an identity at birth conveys what a child *is* or *will become*, i.e. 'a young being who is a man', or 'a young being who is a young girl.' The term that is presently in the lexicon of the language as an equivalent for 'sex' – *isini* – does not appear in the early literary or lexicographic works of isiXhosa. It would appear that this is a derivation from the concept *-ni* and, though now *isini* carries the meaning of 'sex', the two are not necessarily related etymologically. While this is an illustration of how language expands its lexicon in response to language contact, this also suggests that this term that seeks to identify whether a being is anatomically male or female is as a result of the linguistic influence from the European languages; although the morpheme *-ni* existed, but *isini* as a concept that denotes the binary sex identity of male or female, at least did not exist in isiXhosa (Kropf 1899/1915, Jordan 1940, Gqoba 1873-1888/2014).

In examining further the grammar of isiXhosa, the obvious 'non-genderedness' of the language is the absence of pronominal gender markers that are characteristic of the English language (also see footnote 4). This is another illustration that isiXhosa is not fixated on type of body the carriers of the name possesses, but rather on the being. For example, most nouns that depict a living being, *umntu* (human), are prefixed

---

[5] I use 's/he' to indicate that there is no masculine or feminine pronoun. Using 'she' and 'he' in this context would be translating an English context into an isiXhosa context, yet this gender marking pronoun is not present in isiXhosa.

[6] The spelling shifted in the different historical literacy periods in South Africa (and the world).

with *u-*, whether male or female, and their connectedness with the verb is with the compulsory prefix of the subject noun, not a gendered marker as with the English 'he' or 'she'. Nouns like 'u*Paul*' and 'u*Sarah*' for example, take the same marker '*u-*' with the verb and consequently, one will not distinguish gender when these nouns are used in a sentence. In a verbal phrase like *uyabona*, the prefix '*u-*' represents a living being, which could either be Paul or Sarah, and *–bona* is a verb denoting 'see' (i.e. a living being sees). This is also the case with pronouns. For example, *yena* is neither she nor he, but represents what stands in place of *umntu*.

There are also morphemes in isiXhosa that, when added to the root of a noun or adjective, they change the meaning. For purposes of this contribution, I will explore the morpheme *-kazi* (also *-azi*). When added to a noun as a suffix, this morpheme adds a kind of superlative, a degree of greatness and awesomeness in the noun. *Inkosikazi* (great chief) also given above, is one such example. The prevalence of this morpheme is in words that refer to 'woman', but not exclusively. It is this prevalence that led missionaries, as early grammarians, to describe the morpheme primarily as a suffix distinguishing feminine nouns from masculine nouns (Boyce 1863:13, Bennie 1826, Maclaren 1944). This notion has been carried through in the isiXhosa descriptive grammar. When the terms *indodakazi*, great man (sister-in-law), *ubawokazi*, great father (paternal uncle), *umhlekazi*, awesome/beautiful one (sir) and *umakazi*, great mother (maternal aunt) are translated into English they do not begin to convey the meaning embedded in the root and suffix of the word. In isiXhosa, the responsibility of the carrier of the name and the connection in terms of social relation is, instead, of great worth.

The sister of one's partner in marriage has a significant social role in her brother's homestead, a role that she carries throughout her life. She is *indodakazi*, a 'great partner' to her brother's 'wife', and *udadobawo*, 'sister of the father' to her brother's children. Equally, *ubawokazi* is one's father's elder brother. The term is an extension of *ubawo* (father, isiXhosa etymology cannot be established). The responsibility of *ubawokazi*, the great father, is equal to, if not greater than that of a father. *Umakazi*, one's mother's sister, i.e. aunt in English, denotes her responsibility towards her sister's children. *Umhlekazi* was used to address the chief and chieftainess, as in 'Your Majesty or Your Excellency' in English (Kropf 1899/1915:157). The terms of kinship given here as examples illustrate no social stratification or responsibility in terms of the gender on whom the name is bestowed. Rather, what is evident is that responsibility, seniority and rank are some of the categories used to explain social organising in isiXhosa-speaking Nguni societies; *-kazi* reinforces the intensity of the idea of the root word, not only in size, but in attributes. The fact that most of the words that carry such a suffix are in reference to terms relating to women leads us to make assumptions about the important position of women amongst amaXhosa. These lexical items provide a clue on the sociocultural interactions of pre-colonial amaXhosa, particularly their sociocultural interactions and family formation. This is critical in how we make sense of family formations in the pre-colonial past, and in the reconstruction of this past, and reclaiming these as we positively focus on Africa in the disciplines such as Gender Studies. This language analysis suggests that 'sex' and 'gender' did not correspond in pre-colonial society. The linguistic information also suggests the kind of relational dynamics that existed between members of society in the past, are not in relation to the binary embodied identities.

Literature is generally perceived as a reflection of a society's knowledge and wisdom. Through fictionalised or factual accounts, one gives an account of the social experiences of the society. I am mindful that literacy was pioneered by European missionaries so much that, even when the early isiXhosa-speaking intellectuals wrote about their own experiences in their own languages, it is possible, although not certain, that their writings were influenced by Western knowledge that they were indoctrinated into through Christianity and education. However, in addition to being amongst the earliest writing by the isiXhosa-speaking literates after the acquisition of the pen, these works are the earliest accounts the isiXhosa-speaking people published after contact with European education and Christianity. They are studied here in terms of their etymology, and any shifts and added meaning that emerge are given, as in *isini* above.

In *Ingqumbo Yeminyanya* (1940), Jordan provides, in a story set in the 18th century kingdom of Mpondomise, an intricate account of a traditional system about ascendency to throne following the rule of a regent. The lexicon and discourse drawn from this literary work especially that which points to family formations, gives us possibilities of reimagining the socio-cultural history of the amaXhosa and assists us in making inferences about social relations. The story in *Ingqumbo Yeminyanya* is couched in a historical context of powerlessness experienced by an indigenous population over colonial rule. In the opening scene of the book, there is a heavy delegation of men waiting next to the kraal of Mamiya and Dlangamandla's homestead. The purpose of their visit is to chart a way for Zwelinzima to take his place as the rightful chief of Mpondomise. Mamiya enters her homestead and greets the visitors, and joins them next to the kraal. She is clearly knowledgeable about the circumstances of the visit. When her partner, Dlangamandla, arrives moments later, she remains part of the conversation with her partner and the other men next to the kraal, and she is fully acknowledged. Besides this 'presence', Mamiya sits next to a kraal, a traditional meeting place in a homestead, which in the present feminist discourse symbolises a domain where women are excluded and silenced in terms of decision-making. The presence of women in positions of power throughout this novel is significant. For example, Thembeka, the displaced chief's partner, *umlingane,* at college, is integral in plans that pave his way back to the throne. This lexical evidence *-lingana* (equal) to support the notion of equity in gender roles is also evident in the concepts used in novels to name people in a marriage partnership. Jordan (1940:4-5,23), for example, refers many times to both Mamiya and Dlangamandla as equals, *abalingane,* as well as Zwelinzima and Thembeka, and Mphuthumi and Nomvuyo who are husband and wife in the English conceptualisation of this kind of relationship. *Abalingane* is a term derived from the verb *-lingana,* to be equal. This evidence presented in sociocultural practices as presented in early literature, as well as the lexicon of the language are significant in studying the foundations of isiXhosa society's social relations.

Conclusion

The concepts used to refer to beings in isiXhosa-speaking society are not primarily fixed according to the anatomical categorisation of that being, nor are roles assigned to this anatomical categorisation. Words to name people rather consider seniority, for example *umakhulu* and *utatomkhulu.* In seniority one possesses power in the family, the smallest unit of social organisation and in wider society. Some names bear an implied semantic function of responsibility in terms of lineage e.g. *ubawokazi, indodakazi,* or social status e.g. *umhlekazi* and royal status *inkosikazi,* while other terms relay equality in a social relationship, e.g. *umlingane.* The absence of a gender marking morpheme in the language, and the general marking of living beings with verbal agreement *u-* and the personal pronoun *yena* are other indicators of this absence of anatomical categorisation in isiXhosa-speaking society. The high frequency of the grammatical form *–kazi*[7] mostly refers to 'woman' and its semantic meaning of augmentative-ness and greatness. Again, these should provide an insight into how pre-colonial isiXhosa-speaking Nguni society conceptually engaged with the idea of social relations, and how these manifest in their naming patterns.

---

7   *-kazi* grammatically is also described as an augmentative form and when suffixed to a noun or other parts of speech, it generally reinforces the idea of the meaning of the noun to which it is suffixed, for example, in terms of attributes.

We have seen that language can be used reliably as a source of information about a society's past. In making sense of our pre-colonial past, the etymology of words can be used to trace the original meanings of words, and therefore make inferences about a society's values and norms in relation to its sociocultural practices. This linguistic evidence is provided to make sense of the pre-colonial social relations. Even though there is evidence of the colonialists' agenda purposefully expunging the language of important knowledge derived from the social experiences of the people, traces of society's experiences remain in the language.

IsiXhosa does not have a long literary heritage, but in addition to the lexicon of the language, the literary works written almost two centuries ago by isiXhosa-speaking intellectuals after the acquisition of writing as a form of preservation of memory, are closer to the pre-colonial past and are able to reconstruct aspects of the past social life of the amaXhosa.

The etymological examination of the meanings of words and morphemes relating to social beings transcend the binary labels of English words where an anatomical label corresponds to the gender of the being carrying that label. Without the linguistic evidence, the contemporary dominant discourse on social relations in South Africa, specifically the isiXhosa-speaking Nguni, is dependent on the 'translation' of an African experience into Western experience, and African scholars' dependency on tools borrowed from outside of Africa in making sense of the self. The importance of a language is not just as a means of basic communication, but also includes its ability to convey knowledge embedded in it, knowledge that encodes the values, norms, ideas and thoughts of a society that speaks it. Given the brutal colonial history of South Africa that introduced literacy, and used this as a tool to construct power around Western languages and knowledge, the challenge is that we need to corroborate literary sources with oral sources where these can provide a reliable source of evidence.

Without diminishing the value of this linguistic evidence in providing insight into pre-colonial social relations amongst amaXhosa, I wish to point out that this does not mean that the social stratification in terms of social relations between men and women was less complex, or that imbalance in power relations between men and women did not occur in pre-colonial societies. I rather explore this evidence to show that various forms of evidence used uncritically, as they present themselves in other cultural contexts, can inaccurately reinforce and perpetuate assumptions and stereotypes about African society.

References

Appleyard, J. 1850. *The Kafir Language*. King William's Town: Weslyan Missionary Printing.

Atanga, L.L.; Ellece, S.E.; Litosseliti, L. & Sunderland, J. (eds.). 2013. *Gender and language in sub-Saharan Africa: Tradition, struggle and change* (Vol. 33). Amsterdam, Philadelphia: John Benjamins Publishing. https://doi.org/10.1075/impact.33

Bagwasi, M. & J. Sutherland, R. 2007. Language, Gender and age(ism) in Setswana. In: L. Atanga, S. Ellece, L. Litosseliti & J. Sunderland (2013). *Gender and Language in Sub-Saharan Africa: Tradition, struggle and change*. Amsterdam/Philadelphia: John Benjamins Publishing Company. https://doi.org/10.1075/impact.33.04bag

Bennie, J. 1826. *A systematic vocabulary of the Kaffrarian language*. Alice: Lovedale Press.

Boyce, W.J. 1863. *A Grammar of the Kafir Language*. London: Wesleyan Missionary Society.

Buthelezi, T. 2003. The Invisible Females: Analysing Gender in the OBE-Orientated Language Books for the Intermediate Phase in South African Schools. *Alternation*, 10 (2): 25-42.

Foucault, M. 1989. *The Archaeology of Knowledge*. London & New York: Routledge.

Gqoba, W.W. 2015. *Isizwe esinembali: Xhosa histories and poetry (1873-1888)*. Edited by J. Opland, W. Kuse & P. Maseko. Pietermaritzburg: UKZN Press.

Jordan, A.C. 1957. *Towards African Literature: The Emergence of a Literary Art Form in Xhosa*. Berkeley: University of California Press.

Jordan, A.C. 1940. *Ingqumbo Yeminyanya*. Alice: Lovedale Press.

Kropf, A. 1899/1915. *Kafir-English Dictionary*. Alice: Lovedale Mission Press.

Kunene, M. 1981. *Anthem of the Decades: A Zulu epic dedicated to the women of Africa*. London: Heinemann.

Kuse, W.F. 1978. The Form and Themes of Mqhayi's Poetry and Prose. Unpublished PhD dissertation. Madison: University of Wisconsin.

Maclaren, J. 1906/1944. *A Grammar of the Kaffir Language*. London: Longmans.

Mafeje, A. 1994. Beyond Academic Freedom: The Struggle for Authenticity in African Social Discourse. In M. Diouf & M. Mamdani (eds.). *Academic Freedom in Africa*, Dakar: CODESRIA.

Mafeje. A. 1971. The Ideology of Tribalism. *Journal of Modern African Studies*, 9 (2): 253-261. https://doi.org/10.1017/S0022278X00024927

Makalima, R.G.S. 1981. An Assessment of the Educational Implications of the Development of Xhosa as a Written Medium from 1820 to 1950 – A historical-didactical analysis. Unpublished Master's thesis. Alice: University of Fort Hare.

Matiwane, G. 2005. Personal Communication. Mgwali, Engcobo.

Meinhof, C. 1899. *An introduction to the study of African languages*. London: J.M. Dent & Sons.

Mostert, N. 1992. *Frontiers: The Epic of South Africa's Creation and the Tragedy of the Xhosa*. Cape Town: Longmans.

Mgqwetho, N. 2007. *The Nation's Bounty: The Xhosa Poetry of Nontsizi Mgqwetho*. Edited by J. Opland. Johannesburg: Wits Press.

Opland, J. 1983. *Xhosa Oral Poetry: Aspects of a Black South African Tradition*. Cambridge: Cambridge University Press.

Oyewumi, O. 1997. *The Invention of Women: Making an African sense of Western Gender Discourse*. Minneapolis & London: University of Minnesota Press.

Qangule, Z.S. 1979. A Study of Theme and Technique in the Creative Works of S.E.K.L.N. Mqhayi. Unpublished Master's thesis. Cape Town: University of Cape Town.

Rudwick, S. & Shange, M. 2006. Sociolinguistic oppression or expression of 'Zuluness'? 'IsiHlonipho' among isiZulu-speaking females. *Southern African Linguistics and Applied Language Studies* 2006, 24 (4): 1-10. https://doi.org/10.2989/16073610609486435

Tisani, N. 2000. Continuity and Change in Xhosa Historiography during the Nineteenth Century: An Exploration Through Textual Analysis. Unpublished PhD dissertation. Grahamstown: Rhodes University.

Vilakazi, B.W. 1945. The Oral and Written Literature in Nguni. Unpublished PhD dissertation. Johannesburg: University of the Witwatersrand.

Wa Thiong'o, N. 2013. Tongue and pen: a challenge to philosophers from Africa: A translation of 'Rūrīmī na karamu: ithoga harī athamaki a Abirika. *Journal of African Cultural Studies*, 25 (2): 158-163. https://doi.org/10.1080/13696815.2013.789251

CHAPTER 4

The Missing Idiom of African Historiography

African Historical Writing in Walter Rubusana's Zemk'inkomo Magwalandini

Nomalanga Mkhize[1]

Zemk'inkomo Magwalandini is a compendium of Eastern Cape clan histories, Xhosa idioms and oral traditions, which was compiled and first published by Walter Rubusana in 1906, with a second edition appearing in 1911.[2] It consists of collected writings by various Xhosa African writers, the majority being taken from the pages of the early Black newspapers in the Cape and others from books published in the years of the early Xhosa writers in the late 1800s.[3] Like other texts of the mid to late 19th century which focus on recovering, recording and recounting the history of Africans, *Zemk'inkomo* fits into the tradition of works produced by a network of mission-educated Africans from the late 1800s and the early part of the 20th century. These writers aimed to record, for posterity, the history of Africans in

---

[1] naledi.nomalanga@gmail.com
[2] In this chapter I rely on the 2015 reprinted edition edited by S.C. Satyo: Rubusana, W.B. (2015). *Zemk'inkomo Magwalandini*. New Africa Books. All English translations from the book are mine and may be imprecise as I am not a mother tongue isiXhosa speaker. I tried my best by consulting those who speak the language and take full responsibility for any potential mistranslations arising.
[3] The terms 'African' and 'Black' are used interchangeably in this chapter. While African includes, so-called 'Coloured', it excludes South Africans historically of 'Indian' origin, while 'Black' generally encompasses Indians. The discussion focuses specifically on 'Black Xhosa' writers.

the days prior to European colonisation; to give a sense of the origins of the various clans and nations that Africans identified themselves by.

Writing in the introduction to *Zemk'inkomo Magwalandini*, Walter Rubusana states that:

> Ukufa kwamadoda amakhulu abesazi amabali ethu, loo mabali engazuzwanga kuwo abhalwe, kube yilahleko enkulu kuthi thina maXhosa. Ngoko ke, nakuba siqale sekusemva, sithi masesihlanganisa imvuthuluka eseleyo yaloo mabali, ukuze izizukulwana ezizayo zazi ukuba kwakhe kwakho izizwe ezisithi. (Rubusana 2015:no page number)
>
> *The death of great men who knew our historical accounts, without us having the benefit of being able to write down those historical accounts, has been a great loss to us amaXhosa. As such, even if we are on the backfoot, we put together what fragments are left of those accounts, so that generations hereafter will know of our nations. (Author's translation).*

Even though 19th century African writers such as Rubusana were actively engaged in historiographical production through texts such as *Zemk'inkomo*, within South African mainstream historical scholarship there has been limited and fragmentary scholarly engagement with the historiographical import of African writers. Over thirty years ago Peires (1979:71) noted this historiographical deficit, arguing that: "The special features of written vernacular history as a specific category of African historical documentation still await a general theoretical analysis." Within the mainstream South African academy, there is still no coherent, synthesised and systematised conception of a body of work called 'African historiography' which adequately synthesises the historical writings of the 19th and early 20th century published Black historians. However, African writers such as William Gqoba, Magema Fuze, Richard Tainton Kawa, John Henderson Soga, Thomas Mofolo, SEK Mqhayi, Petros Lamula and others autonomously produced African histories for African audiences (Fuze & Cope 1979; Kawa 1929).[4] It was the tradition of mission educated African writers to actively write histories according to their understanding of passed down oral histories, their own observation of events that had happened within the lifetimes and every other text they read at the time, including the works of missionaries. African writers deliberately set out to write as historians – they engaged, sourced, debated, and haggled with dominant mission interpretations of African history at the time. This was historiographical production in action, and yet, because many of these works, including *Zemk'inkomo*, appear as collections of printed oral traditions it has been the general tendency within South African

---

[4] See also Mqhayi in Opland 2009; Lamula 1930 and Mofolo 1931.

historical studies to approach them as primary sources without situating their very production as being part of sustained historiographical effort by 19th century African writers – even though their white colonial contemporaries have been accorded historiographical status as progenitors of the South African historical studies tradition.

For Rubusana the importance of the *Zemk'inkomo* collection was not only the content, but its preservation of traditional oral history forms, stating that: "*Incwadi le ikholise ngezibongo, kuba iyeyona ntetho bophele kuyo bonke ubuciko besiXhosa, yaye iyeyona ntetho ishwankathela zonke izafobe zokuthetha esiXhoseni.*" (Rubusana 2015:n.d.) (The book holds to praise poetry because this is the form of orality in which Xhosa wisdom is tied, and it is the oral that encompasses the idioms of the Xhosa.)

It is important that Rubusana made the case for the reproduction of the collected knowledge in the form of oral traditions such as praise poems and clan genealogies – *iziduko/izithakazelo* – because these forms not only recorded history, but also the didactic mechanisms for the impartation of historical consciousness itself. Preserving the indigenous literary form was thus a deliberate and conscious historiographical choice made by Rubusana when collecting these works. Praise poetry and poems, *izibongo* and *imibongo*, of royals and commoners, are particularly important because they provide an account and an interpretation of events. While presented in 'praise' form, *izibongo* are not merely flattery, as Mafeje (1967) points out, they convey political analysis, critique and a sense of public mood and sentiment on the political machinations of the day. These oral tradition forms embody literary, philosophical, idiomatic and historiographical expression, as Tisani (2001:246) states, "*Izibongo* [are] a popular medium for expressing lofty thoughts, including historical topics." In bringing together its selection of oral traditions, *Zemk'inkomo* provides an empirical and idiomatic record of African people's history as conveyed by themselves, for themselves.

However, despite their historiographical significance, texts such as *Zemk'inkomo* have been largely ignored in mainstream South African historical studies. In part, this owes to the fact that the texts are in African languages and the content presented in the traditional oral forms which are usually left to the realm of literary and linguistic studies. It is no surprise that much of the analytical work done on the writings of early African writers has precisely been in the realm of literary studies by the likes of Sizwe Satyo, Peter Mtuze and Jeff Opland, where Xhosa writers are specifically concerned (Satyo 1977; Mtuze 1990; Opland 1983, 2004:22-46).[5] To a certain extent, the indifference of academic historians to African writers owes to the Eurocentric idea of 'historiography' as a discursive form of non-fiction prose that conforms to the stylistic conventions of the 19th century university. Texts such as *Zemk'inkomo* which convey traditional oral literary genres have thus not been recognised as works of 'real' historiography.

The result of the omission of African language texts from historiographical analysis by historians is that, by and large, South African historiography refers to white writers writing on South Africa, in Afrikaans and English. Where history teaching in universities refers to schools of historiography categorised as "colonial", "Afrikaner nationalist", "liberal", "radical/ Marxist", "Africanist" and "social history", it refers largely to white historians. "Africanist" largely referred to white historians who wrote about Africans sympathetically through a nationalist lens such as the likes of J.D. Omer Cooper (Omer-Cooper 1966).

Ironically, even the so-called 'radical' turn of the 1970s and 1980s was a particularly narrow debate that circumscribed major questions of South African history to the particularist theoretical interests of white historians. It omitted large bodies of oral tradition from the historical canon, as well as the work of radical Black scholars such as Archie Mafeje and Bernard Magubane who continuously criticised university historians and anthropologists for failing to see African perspectives of their own histories and oppression (Morris 1988; Murray 1989:645-665; Keegan 1989; Bradford 1990:59-88). Commenting on this "radical turn", Mafeje (1981:137) criticised Marxist scholars such as Harold Wolpe and Mike Morris for failing to grasp the concepts necessary for understanding the organisation of social forms amongst Africans, stating that "it is apparent that most South African Marxist theorising about Africans is based on texts which are largely divorced from context". (Wolpe 1972)[6] Magubane (2006:273-274) noted that the so-called radicals failed to understand Black nationalist sentiment and liberation struggles:

> The radical historians created an opening to the left, but their range of awareness was narrow. Hughes says that what seems to have touched the heart in the writings of most of these authors "is merely the abstract pain." The radical historians have produced an enormous body of historical dissertations (many later published as books), articles, and reviews... I must confess that I find the argument and the main postulates of both

---

[5] Satyo is the editor of the edition of the *Zemk'inkomo* that is used in this chapter.
[6] Mafeje was responding to Wolpe's seminal article – Wolpe 1972.

liberal and Neo-Marxist studies to be exercises in irrelevance and they revealed a gross misunderstanding of the African reality and especially the nature of the Africans' struggles.

It is thus no exaggeration to say that the body of work called 'South African historiography' is largely a historiography of white writing in which the analytical perspectives of Africans came to be marginalised. This marginalisation occurred not just through omission. Within the body of white historical writing, the works and perspectives of African writers were used mostly as primary sources or background information upon which some white historians drew. African writing in these instances was approached as a source archive rather than a historiographical body of work in and of itself. Such, for example, was the relationship between Walter Rubusana, as well as others, with the famous Monica Hunter whose *Reaction to Conquest* formed a kind of standard account of the life of amaXhosa in the shadow of colonialism. Hunter knew Rubusana and visited his home often. Bank (2008:567-568) argues that the Rubusanas were of "generous spirit" and facilitated more than mere access for Hunter when she conducted her fieldwork, stating that "Monica Hunter's passing acknowledgement of the 'Rubisanas' *(sic)* in *Reaction to Conquest* does not do full justice to the influence they had on her fieldwork. They did very much more than offer her security and a stamp of approval." Rubusana became a de facto 'native informant' to Hunter whose work became the standard reference on the history of amaXhosa in university scholarship for many decades. Lekgoathi (2009:80) showed that white ethnographers have relied heavily on African researchers to act as interlocutors "in making African societies fathomable to white ethnographers", even though white researchers often missed the depth of idiomatic richness within the information compiled or conveyed by Africans.

Thus many of the unique insights and analytical understandings of the African writers came to be written through white scholars who inhabited the privileged domains of the white South African academe. The institutional exclusion of Black scholars thus led to the exclusion of African historiography, for as Magubane (2010:249) noted, the power of white academics in the academy who "through their control of institutional and foundation resources, passed as filters of African views and attitudes." Given this history, works such as *Zemk'inkomo* do not constitute core historiography in South African universities.

Historiographical implications of missing the African idiom

The filtering of African writers erased their contribution as authors and also led to conceptual depletion in historiographical theorising because the indigenous concepts used by African writers were not well studied in historiographical scrutiny. Thus, conceptual possibilities offered by the idiomatic depth that characterises Xhosa oral poetry forms in *Zemk'inkomo* for example, are largely lost to South African historiography. This is in large part because to engage and theorise, academics would have had to be competent in African languages and the idiomatic analysis applicable to indigenous oral traditions.

Idiomatic engagement in historiographical analysis cannot be underestimated. At one level, idiomatic grasp of vernacular forms such as *izibongo* and *iziduko* address empirical questions – the 'who' and 'what' of history. At another, vernacular idiom addresses questions of how to understand African societies and the development of their modes of social organising. Tisani (2001:144) has argued that "the study of African history stands to be enriched and broadened through the analysis of clan histories as sources" and while historians have done this, clan historiography is quite underdeveloped in South Africa, and this is evident in particular, in the debates on abaMbo clans within South African historiography.

The preoccupation with abaMbo Mfecane clans in South African historiography

Perhaps there has been no greater controversy in South African historical scholarship than the issue of the *difaqane/ Mfecane* and the identities of those called abaMbo. Etherington (2001:23) states that of the coastal clans "the most fascinating is the Mbo; while the other large groupings persist, the Mbo disappear. Who were they?" The South African historiographical preoccupation with the 'abaMbo' owes in large part to debates around the expansion of the Zulu state under Shaka and associated 19th century migrations. Broadly speaking, uMbo is a major Iron Age 'stem' clan of several lineages which migrated from central Africa all the while splintering off into different sub-clans some of which settled in southern Africa. When this happened is not really clear. Since the mid-19th century, beginning with colonial missionaries and settler writers, there has been continuous concern within South African historiography on *abaMbo*, their origins, their relation to other stem clans, but overwhelmingly, the greatest interest turns on their 19th century dispersals in relation to Shaka's Zulu state. The story of amaMfengu, in particular, is a centrepiece of the academic debate on 19th century Eastern Cape abaMbo and their 'identity' within the historiographical contentions over the Mfecane.

In the late 1980s and early 1990s, there was a major revision of the historiography of the wars and conflicts of the early 19th century, known as the Mfecane, which had been hitherto attributed to the aggressive expansionism of Shaka ka Senzangakhona and his Zulu state. Led primarily by Julian Cobbing, the revision of the 'Shakacentric' explanation for the wars and upheavals of the early 19th century brought the long-standing presence of white colonial expansion into the analysis of what appeared to be 'intra-African' Mfecane conflict (Cobbing 1984, 1988, 1998; Wright 1989). The Mfecane revision had far reaching historiographical (and political) implications because it put Shaka's wars in the context of broader European destabilisation of African societies in southern Africa and included the exploits of hitherto under-analysed groupings such as the Griqua. Cobbing (1984/1988) pointed to the convergent forces of European slaving along the eastern seaboard and the labour raiding coming from the Cape Colony as having knock-on effects on the rise of militarisation and state-building amongst Africa societies of the early 1800s. The Mfecane debate, while radical in the sense of its complete attack on white settler-colonial discourses, came under criticism for some of its analytical excesses (Eldredge 1992:1-35). One of the other shortcomings of the debate, which is the point of this discussion, is that this pivotal debate dismissed African oral traditions on the Mfecane epoch as 'tainted' by missionary influence and did not even engage the work of most early African writers such as Rubusana. In effect, the Mfecane debate was a white academic debate.

The missing African idiom in South African historiography of abaMbo and the Mfecane

It is not the intent of this piece to fixate on the Mfecane debate in and of itself. Of significance is to point out that the works of 19th century African writers which provide the most comprehensive clan genealogies of abaMbo have been all but ignored in terms of academic historiography until recently. Tisani (2001) took up a historiographical analysis of William Gqoba's writings on *abaMbo* in *Isigidimi SamaXhosa*, and Maxengana (2012) took up Richard Tainton Kawa's *Ibali lamaMfengu* to write a history about abaMbo who became amaMfengu. Nhanha and Peires (Kawa 2011:xv) have called for works like Kawa's to be given their historiographical due, particularly in the history of *abaMbo*.

There was clearly a longstanding discussion amongst Africans on the abaMbo and Mfengu clans in the Cape Colony. Below I sample three texts which are key to African historiography of *abaMbo*.

These are:

1. *Zemk'inkomo* (first published in 1906) which in Chapter 37 provides a brief account of the origins of Eastern Cape abaMbo-Mfengu, likely written by William Gqoba.
2. Richard T Kawa's *Ibali lamaMfengu* (first published in 1929) which provides genealogical details on certain family segments of Eastern Cape abaMbo houses.
3. John Henderson Soga's English translation of *South-Eastern Bantu* (first published in 1930) which argues Mfengu are not abaMbo but originally amaLala and amaKalanga.

All three of these texts draw on a variety of sources for engagement, including missionary texts, for African writers that formed part of a global world of letters. More importantly, the authors rely on oral traditions to grapple with competing versions on who abaMbo were. African writers debated the question and subjected it to their own scrutiny. In *Zemk'inkomo*, (1911:208) questions are raised on which precise Mfengu clans were abaMbo:

> Into esingayaziyo yile yokuba ngabaphi na abaMbo, ekho amaHlubi, ekho amaZizi, ekho amaBhele. Kambe amaHlubi athi ngawo angabaMbo.
>
> *What we do not know is which of these are abaMbo when there are amaHlubi, there are amaZizi, there are amaBhele. It is amaHlubi who say they are abaMbo.*

Earlier in 1885, William Gqoba had questioned the blanket application of the abaMbo clanship to all amaMfengu in the newspaper *Isigidimi samaXhosa*, quoted in Tisani (2001:251), asking:

> Sicela imbali maxhego akowethu nonke. Sifuna ezaseBunguni zonke. Sifuna ezaseMbo zonke. Sifuna ukwazi ngalamarwintsela akhoyo pantsi kweli gama liti 'abaMbo'. Kanti akutetwa Mamfengu onke, njengoko inxenye ihlala inqwena ukunga kungatshiwo.
>
> *We seek the histories from you our old men. We want those of abeNguni. We want those of abaseMbo. We want to know about [the details] under this name of 'abaMbo'. It is said it does not speak of all the Mfengu, even though a segment does wish it could be said to be so.*

For example, Soga (1930:65) outright rejects Fingo as abaMbo, and thus by extension, the Hlubi, stating emphatically that "Fingos are not abaMbo. The majority of Fingos are of Lala or Kalanga origin. The principal Fingo tribes are Hlubis, Beles, Zizis and

Tolos." Kawa (2011:9) recognised Hlubis as abaMbo, but not amaBele or amaZizi stating that:

> Kusamiwe ezweni laseNtla abaMbo, ayengama Hlubi qwaba!
> *When they still resided in the North, abaMbo were only amaHlubi!*

Here Kawa appears to be speaking back to the missionary writings which merely lumped all Mfengu as abaMbo. For these writers, clan details – *iziduko* – are important to their debate.

While the 19th century Xhosa African writers clearly were having an abaMbo debate within their press and subsequent published writings, decades later, their debates seemed to have not really penetrated the important academic debates on the Mfecane after Cobbing's interventions. For example, Cobbing (1988) would go on to reject the idea that amaMfengu were even Mfecane refugees, arguing that they were in fact amaXhosa who had been captured by colonial labour raids. The argument was influential, and taken up by Alan Webster (1991), who elaborated on the labour-raid thesis, rejecting any claim that amaMfengu were abaMbo refugees from KwaZulu-Natal (KZN) and agreed with Cobbing that they were Gcaleka Xhosa (Cobbing 1988; Webster 1991; Stapleton 1996:233-250).

While this revised 'radical' version scrutinised the effects of colonial activity in the Eastern Cape, it completely dismissed the legitimacy of accounts of the abaMbo clan migration into the land of amaXhosa. Peires (1993:310) correctly contested the Cobbing thesis by drawing on African oral tradition and argued in fact that "neither Cobbing nor his acolytes have bothered to learn an African language or consult an African source." However, Richner (2005:120) who was also influenced by the Cobbing thesis, took for granted that the exclusion of oral tradition was of no historiographical importance by stating that, "Articles on African history published by Africans in the vernacular during this period appeared mainly in African-language newspapers, as well as missionary, church and teachers' periodicals. These articles had no impact on the development of Mfecane historiography, as none of the English-speaking writers read them." In contrast, Maxengana (2012:51) revisits the African writing on the Mfecane debates by drawing on Kawa, and thus challenging some of the "Mfengu fabrication" aspects of the Cobbing thesis, arguing:

> The term 'Mfecane', however, has become questionable. It has been questioned by professional historians ever since Julian Cobbing's controversial article, 'The Mfecane as Alibi', published in 1988. Alan Webster, one of Cobbing's students, extended his argument with specific reference to the amaMfengu. Webster argued that the majority of 'Fingos'

did not originate in KZN, but were people enslaved by the British during the War of 1835. It is not possible to get into details, but it should be sufficient to point out that Webster did not consult even one isiXhosa language source. R.T. Kawa, K.K. Ncwana and others expended much energy identifying the precise nations which later became known as amaMfengu, and everyone of them originated in KZN.

Key to the origins of amaMfengu is that their *iziduko* provided the point of identification, and African writers such as Kawa recorded these. Idiomatically, *iziduko* are key points of identification of variants of Mfecane refugees which came to be assimilated into Eastern Cape Xhosa polities. The conceptual significance of *iziduko* as kin-identification forms ought not have been overlooked by revisionist writers. Put differently, revisionist historians used the master's epistemological tools to dismantle the master's house without sufficient engagement with the vernacular methodologies employed by Xhosa writers preoccupied with the same questions.

Fundamentally, the trouble for revisionist historians who overlooked the idiomatic framing of African genealogical forms was this preoccupation with the notion of 'identity' as a 'social construction' that has been in vogue in humanities academe in the past 30 years. There are deep flaws here if not understood carefully in relation to the problem of using English singularly as a historiographical language. For example, as Mama (2001:63) has argued there is no precise equivalent for the word 'identity' in African languages, observing that: "In English the word 'identity' implies a singular, individual subject with clear ego boundaries. In Africa, if I were to generalise, ask a person who he or she is, a name will quickly follow as a qualifier, a communal term that will indicate ethnic or clan origins." Thus, if the aim is to 'deconstruct' 'Mfengu' 'identity', southern African genealogical tradition ought to prompt one to ask the question of – *isiduko* – which in isiXhosa implies clanship (not ethnicity), an ontological question of origins and family belonging. Clanship as a form of identification in siNtu epistemology is best understood through the concept of '*ubuni*' which asks the one to identify themselves in relation to ontological ancestral claims that are linked to *amasiko*: ritual custom. *Amasiko*: ritual custom (even if dynamic and changing) functions as elements of grafting persons into the social and spiritual realms of related persons. Mafeje (1971:254) argued that the function of a clan name is to answer the question: 'Whose [which Chief's] land do you come from?" African writers understood this and framed their debates on the question of *abaMfengu* through this underlying notion of belonging identification of *ubuni*. Thus, Kawa (2011:47) engages the question of who the Mfengu is with clanship and *ubuni* in mind, stating on Hlubi origins that "*abati besaku buzwa imvela-pi, bengamanina*", the – '*ni*' – which means 'who' being not fully translatable into English, suffice it to say that in idiom it implies clanship and ancestral ontology not easily reducible to the concept of 'identity'.

The shortcomings of the Anglicised notion of 'identity' in understanding the meaning of identification and belonging sometimes create conceptual fuzziness for African historians. For example, in grappling with post-Mfecane muMbo clanship, John Wright speculates (1989; Hamilton & Wright 2017) that Zihlandlo's Mkhize were given exclusive claim to *izithakazelo* zaseMbo by Shaka because no other clan appears to use this *isithakazelo* anymore in KZN.[7] The implication here is that weaker eMbo clans were deprived of the muMbo clanship by Shaka's royal edict; an implication which requires far greater evidence than mere speculation since *izithakazelo* are inherited and closely related to clan customs in the form of *amasiko* (Kuse 1979).[8] As Ndimande (2001:180) argues, rituals and clan names are interconnected:

> Izibongo nezithakazelo ziyisisekelo sempilo yomuntu ongumZulu. Izibongo, nezithakazelo zabantu abangamaZulu zenza imisebenzi emininji. Okokuqala, ziyabahlukanisa abantu kwabanye, okwesibili, zisetshenziswa ukugcina amasiko esiZulu, kungabalwa umhlonyane, umemulo, umgcagco, umsebenzi wokubonga, uma wenza imbeleko njalonjalo. Abantu abangamaZulu bakholelwa kakhulu ebukhoneni babantu abadala/ amadlozi. Uma kwenziwa imicimbi ebalwe ngenhla, kuyaye kushiswe impepho ukuze kuxhunyanwe nabaphansi/amadlozi. Ngesikhathi kushiswa impepho, kuyaye kubizwe okhokho ngamagama abo, okuyizibongo nezithakazelo zethu thina bantu abaphilayo ukuba basondele eduze. Ngenye indlela, umuntu oyaye aphike ukuthi idlozi likhona, usuke eziphika yena uqobo lwakhe ngoba yena usuke ezibiza ngegama likakhokho wakhe. Izibongo nezithakazelo zabantu abangamaZulu zikhombisa isikompilo labantu, inkolo kanye nobudlelwano obukhona kubantu.

---

[7] Wright (1989:316-319) speculated that: "In the Thukela valley, the Mkhize were able to assert an exclusive claim to the isithakazelo 'abaMbo', which reflected the position of local dominance that they were able to achieve by dint of being Shaka's 'favourites'. In the coastlands, by contrast, the Cele, Thuli and other people came to be designated by the insulting appellations of amaLala and inyakeni, which reflected the positions which they occupied at the bottom of the Zulu-dominated social and political order."
My own understanding as a Mkhize is that umuMbo is a deeply held ancestral identity that cannot be made politically exclusive. In talking to my own father about Wright's formulation, he stated of the Mkhize that "They were abaMbo anyway, babengabaMbo vele" (2017, informal discussion)." It seems unlikely that ubuMbo clanship could have been instrumentalised exclusively as a political construct to cement Mkhize-Shaka allegiance".

[8] That clan titles can be bestowed, and the assemblages reformed and assimilated is not in dispute; after all, naming and renaming (ukuqamba/ ukuthiya) is an integral element of *izibongo*. According to historian Jabulani Sithole, Shaka disrespected tradition and regularly went about upsetting and challenging social norms, even going as far as taking others' clan names to himself as part of state-building. The question is to what degree Shaka tampered with *izithakazelo* of tributary clans and to what extent acts of naming or renaming could obliterate well established kin-genealogies from the oral traditions.

> *Clan praises and clan names are the foundation of life for Zulu people. Clan praises, and clan names of Zulu people have several functions. Firstly, they distinguish between different people; secondly, they preserve Zulu traditions, such as umhlonyane, umemulo, umgcagco, umsebenzi wokubonga, and imbeleko and so forth. People in the Zulu culture believe in the existence of ancestral elders. When there are customary activities, incense is burnt so that there can be a connection with the ancestors. When incense is burnt, the names of these ancestors are called (recited), these are the praise names and clan names of those of us who are living so that they come closer to our. In a way, a person who denies the existence of the ancestral guide, denies their very essence because they are named after that ancestor. The poetic praise names and clan names of Zulu people show the culture of the people, their beliefs and relations amongst the people.*

Koopman (2005:73) describes the ontological nature of *iziduko-izithakazelo* as an ancestral naming form:

> Western thinking generally perceives life as starting at birth and ending with death (excluding here adherents to notions of 'eternal afterlife' and re-incarnation). In Zulu thinking one's own life is simply a small chunk in an ongoing process of life that starts as far back as one can remember one's ancestors, and continues almost infinitely in the confident belief that one's sons will beget sons who will continue to beget sons. Ancestors are alive in memory as long as their names are remembered, and with Zulu clan izithakazelo (clan praises) still a feature of Zulu life, ancestors may be remembered in this manner for many generations back. When an Mkhize father teaches his son the Mkhize izithakazelo, "Mkhize! Wena kaKhabazela! Wena kaMavovo! Wena kaZihlandlo kaGcwabe kaSiyingele kaSibiside!" ('Mkhize! You the son of Khabazela! You the son of Mavovo! You the son of Zihlandlo son of Gcwabe son of Siyingele son of Sibiside!') he is referring to chiefs and heroes of the Mkhize past who go back to the time of Shaka and even further back.

Recently, Hamilton and Wright (2017:671) revisit some of their earlier approaches to conceptualising pre-colonial identities, and they ask: "If the groupings formed in the KZN region before the establishment of colonialism were not ethnic in character, then how can we describe them?" In this chapter I have preferred to use the notion of clanship. I would agree with, Peires (1993) who cautioned fellow historians that kin-clanship genealogical form is more rigid than it at first appears. This rigidity I argue lies in the ontological function of *iziduko* and *izithakazelo* in grafting people into lineages of ancestors through *amasiko* and *totemic* identification that has a psycho-social ritual function beyond political ethnic identity. In that sense then, understanding the psycho-social element of *iziduko* provides sharper insights for eMbo and Mfengu historiography than notions of ethnic identity constructionism that cannot be singularly conceptualised.

AbaMbo nezibongo zabo: Chapter 37 of *Zemk'inkomo Magwalandini*

I now want to turn closer attention to what *Zemk'inkomo* offers in relation to the name *abaMbo*. In putting *Zemk'inkomo* together, Rubusana collected as many writings as he could from the early African newspapers *Imvo Zabantsundu* and the paper he edited *Izwi Labantu*. He also obtained writing from other published sources and private collections, and also used the writings of missionaries to guide how the collection was put together.

The writings of the African writers themselves were not pure oral tradition as many writers already had been engaging missionary writing on African history as part of their contemporary public engagements. In fact, part of the key to doing historiographical analysis of African writers' historical work is to come to grips with the relationship of their writing with the missionary writing. Tisani (2001) does extensive excavation of how the history of amaXhosa came to be written by various groups in the Cape Colony over 100 years, beginning with European travelers through to missionaries and colonial writers such as Theal.

In the chapter *abaMbo nezibongo zabo*, several forms of historical data are provided:

i) an account of how and why abaMbo clans arrived at emaXhoseni

ii) an account of the origins and meaning of the name abaMbo and iii) clan praise poems of amaHlubi and some of their kings.

The challenge, however, is that no author is attributed to the chapter, and it can be assumed that the author was Kawa as a shorter version of this oral tradition is reprinted in the later published *Ibali lamaMfengu* (1929). Either way, the account in *Zemk'inkomo* provides some points of exploration of pre-colonial questions other than the *Mfecane*.

The account of the history and clan names of *abaMbo* in *Zemk'inkomo* is as follows:

> Zathi ke ezi ntlanga zakuchithwa nguTshaka zabalekela nganeno kweli lasemaXhoseni. Kwafika kwaGcaleka uGocina, noMvundlela, noGacula, bephethe impondo zendlovu, besithi bavela eMbo ngowe-1819. Banikwa amanxuwa nguHintsa, bahlala bazeka nabafazi kunye naloompi babenayo.

> *When these groups were dispersed by Shaka they escaped towards this direction to the land of amaXhosa. At Gcaleka's arrived Gocina, Mvundla and Gacula, carrying the tusks of an elephant saying they are from eMbo – this was 1819. They were given sites by Hintsa and there they stayed and took wives even as they had conflicts.*

One can speculate that the elephant tusks were brought as a form of tribute, as an act of voluntary submission to Hintsa by the new arrivals. Tisani (2001:248) argues that "under the rule of *iinkosi* subjects were still expected to give tribute in the form of elephant tusks, leopard skins, buffalo breast and skins of *inamba* (python)." The description of this voluntary *vassalship – ukukhonza* in Nguni languages – supports the contention made by these early African writers that amaMfengu were never enslaved by the Gcaleka and were assimilated into the Xhosa polities on friendly, rather than oppressive, terms.[9]

The writer continues with their account, and begins to explain what they believe to be the origins of the term 'Mbo':

> Umbo lo bazibiza ngaye ngezi mini asinkosi, asigama lomhlaba, ligama lelitye. (Rubusana 2015:207).
>
> *This Mbo they call themselves by is not a king, not a land, but the name of a type of rock.*

It continues further:

> Kuthiwa, ngabakudala, aba bantu bathi ukuhla kwabo bavela kuTshaka bahamba besenza iminquba. Bahambe bada baza kufika mayela nelamaSwazi, kufuphi kule mingxuma, iyimiwonyo, kuthiwa ngoku ziZimbambwe (Zimbyebye okanye Zimbabwe Ruins). Bathe bakufika khona bamisa kwa iminquba, bemba kuloo mingxuma ilitye legolide abathe bona ukulibiza 'yimbo'. Baye'le mbo' bebemana beyihlohla ezingcongolweni, baze baye kuyithengisa elwagcibeni kumaPhuthukezi ukuze bazuze iziziba (calico) zokushubela.
>
> *It is said, by the elders (?), upon migrating down these people said they came from Shaka, they travelled making shelters. They travelled until they reached the land of the Swazis, near the diggings and cliffs called Zimbambwe (Zimbyebye or Zimbabwe Ruins). When they got there they put up their shelters, and started digging gold rock there, which they called 'imbo' – something dug up. This 'imbo' they would put in reeds and then would trade it at the river mouth with the Portuguese in exchange for calico (textiles).*

The account continues:

> AmaSwazi athi ngokungabazi ukuba ngabantu bani na, athi ukubabiza 'ngaBembi' kuba babesimba. Baziwe ngelo gama ngabo kwada kwalixesha. Lisuke, emva kwexesha, lonakala elo gama njengokuba enjalo namanye ukonakala ngokuphimisela kokubiza kwabantu. Bathi endaweni yokuthi 'AbeMbi', basuke bathi, 'abaMbo. (Rubusana 2015:207)

---

9   Kawa (2011:47), who identifies Goceni and Mvundlela as amaHlubi, states this emphatically in *Ibali lamaMfengu* that Indawo yokuba amaMfengu enziwa amakoboka; ndiyayipika unompela; yayingeko. (The idea that the Mfengu were enslaved is something I refute; it never happened.)

Because the Swazis did not know these people, they called them 'ngaBembi' 'diggers'- because they dug. That is how they came to be known by that name until today. It was only after some time that the word came to be distorted, as other words get distorted in the glibness of people's speaking. In the place of saying 'AbeMbi' (diggers), they said 'abaMbo'.

The account then explains how the movement of abaMbo and the precious metal culture, that came to be incorporated into the linguistic idiom of amaXhosa:

Bahle nalo ke eli litye labo liyi "mbo" bade baza kufika nalo emaXhoseni, iyinto abahoba ngayo ngenxa yokuba lihle kwalo. Bebuziwe igama lalo bathe 'yiMbo' Ubuhle balo, nokunqaba kwalo, kwaba basemaXhoseni, kuvelise iqhalo elithi, "Ungazilahleli imbo yakho ngoPhoyiyana, kuba uPhoyiyana uyemka ngomso" ...eyona ndawo inamandla kulo bubuhle nokunqaba kwaloo nto sukuba kusithiwa yiMbo. Linjalo ke thina ukulazi kwethu ibali lika 'Mbo'. Into esingayaziyo yile yokuba ngabaphi na abaMbo, ekho amaHlubi, ekho amaZizi, ekho amaBhele. Kambe amaHlubi athi ngawo angabaMbo.

They came down with their rock 'mbo' until they arrived here among amaXhosa and it was the thing they decorated with because of its beauty. When asked what it was called, they said 'yiMbo'. The beauty of it, and its scarcity amongst amaXhosa, resulted in an idiom arising that says "Do not throw away your precious rock on account of some flimsy person because the flimsy person is leaving on the morrow". The most significant matter here is the beauty and scarcity of the thing that is regarded as 'yiMbo'. That is how we came to the knowledge of this story of 'Mbo'. What we do not know is precisely to whom abaMbo refers; there are amaHlubi, there are amaZizi, there are amaBhele. AmaHlubi tells us they are abaMbo.

This explanation of the origins of '-*Mbo*' itself, is somewhat dubious, given the many iterations of the term '*eMbo*' in Nguni nomenclature. The significance of this account is that it links '*abaMbo*' clans with pre-colonial mining in the Great Zimbabwe area, and with trade in metal. Furthermore, we do get a sense of the intrigue brought about by the migrating abaMbo clans in the eyes of amaXhosa perhaps because of new trade goods they brought with them.

It is highly likely that the author, being educated, would have encountered writing and news reports on the Zimbabwe ruins. What we must ask is how abaMbo are linked to it and how, indeed, they would have brought with them their precious *imbo* into the Eastern Cape. The description of the gold mining pits is key as is the association made with the Swazi of the region. How did these abaMbo come to be miners of gold and not merely of iron, as one tends to associate south eastern Nguni groups with iron metal workings, and not with gold? Were they perhaps merely middle-men and not gold miners themselves? How much gold trade happened between Africans and for what aesthetic use was this precious metal rock used, outside of trading it with the Portuguese?

The author does not offer answers, but the historian is left with key questions. Probing these questions may not in and of itself lead us to new sources, but it does force us to ask questions of detail – is it true that *abaMbo* mined for gold near Zimbabwe? If there is some truth to the story, upon migrating with the metal, what forms of exchange developed with amaXhosa to the degree that an idiom relating to the *imbo* precious metal emerged?

Here perhaps we must return to Soga's (1930) contention of Kalanga origins of some of Hlubi elements. Is it possible that the *imbo* story speaks to the migration of gold mining amaKalanga who come to be incorporated into amaHlubi? A historical puzzle emerges, and requires further investigation. For the purposes of this chapter, however, what has been important is to argue for the mainstream incorporation of Xhosa texts into the body of South African historiography. These texts are not epistemically perfect, but they must be engaged on equal terms for the historiographical debates they bring about.

References

Bank, A. 2008. The 'intimate politics' of fieldwork: Monica Hunter and her African assistants, Pondoland and the Eastern Cape, 1931–1932. *Journal of Southern African Studies*, 34 (3): 557-574. https://doi.org/10.1080/03057070802259787

Bradford, H. 1990. Highways, Byways and Cul-de-Sacs: The Transition to Agrarian Capitalism in Revisionist South African History. *Radical History Review*, 46 (7): 59-88. https://doi.org/10.1215/01636545-1990-46-47-59

Cobbing, J. 1984. *The case against the Mfecane*. African studies Seminar Paper. Johannesburg: Wits University.

Cobbing, J. 1988. The Mfecane as alibi: thoughts on Dithakong and Mbolompo. *The Journal of African History*, 29 (3): 487-519. https://doi.org/10.1017/S0021853700030590

Cobbing, J. 1998. *Jettisoning the Mfecane (with Perestroika)*. Johannesburg: University of Witwatersrand, Institute of African Studies, Paper presented at Seminar August 1998, Nr 241.

Etherington, N. 2001. *The Great Treks: the transformation of southern Africa 1815-1854*. London: Routledge.

Fuze, M.M. & Cope, A.T. 1979. *The Black People and whence they came: A Zulu view*. Scotsville: University of Natal Press.

Hamilton, C. & Wright, J. 2017. Moving Beyond Ethnic Framing: Political Differentiation in the Chiefdoms of the KwaZulu-Natal Region before 1830. *Journal of Southern African Studies*, 1-17. https://doi.org/10.1080/03057070.2017.1323539

Kawa, R.T. 2011. *Ibali LamaMfengu*. Alice: Lovedale Press.

Keegan, T. 1989. The Origins of Agrarian Capitalism in South Africa: A Reply. *Journal of Southern African Studies*, 15 (4): 666-684. https://doi.org/10.1080/03057078908708220

Koopman, A. 2005. Benedict Wallet Vilakazi: A Poet in Exile. *Natalia*, 35, 63-74. Available online at http://natalia.org.za/Files/35/Natalia%2035%20pp63-74%20C.pdf

Kuse, W.F. 1979. "Izibongo Zeenkosi" (The Praises of Kings): Aspects of Xhosa Heroic Poetry. *Research in African Literatures*, 10 (2), 208-238.

Lamula, P. 1930. *uZulu ka Malandela: a most practical and concise compendium of African history, combined with genealogy, chronology, geography and biography.* Marianhill Mission Press

Lekgoathi, S.P. 2009. 'Colonial' Experts, Local Interlocutors, Informants and the Making of An Archive on the 'Transvaal Ndebele', 1930–1989. *The Journal of African History*, 50 (1), 61-80. https://doi.org/10.1017/S0021853708003976

Mafeje, A. 1981. On the articulation of modes of production. *Journal of Southern African Studies*, 8 (1), 123-138. https://doi.org/10.1080/03057078108708037

Mafeje, A. 1971. The ideology of 'tribalism'. *The Journal of Modern African Studies*, 9 (2), 253-261. https://doi.org/10.1017/S0022278X00024927

Mafeje, A. 1967. The role of the bard in a contemporary African community. *Journal of African Languages*, 6 (3), 193-223.

Magubane, B. 2010. *Bernard Magubane: My Life and Times.* Scotsville: University of KwaZulu-Natal Press.

Magubane, B. M. 2006. Whose memory–whose history? The illusion of liberal and radical historical debates. In: *History making and present day politics: The meaning of collective memory in South Africa.* Uppsala, Sweden: Nordiska Afrikainstitutet.

Mama, A. 2001. Challenging subjects: Gender and power in African contexts. *African Sociological Review/Revue Africaine de Sociologie*, 5 (2): 63-73. https://doi.org/10.4314/asr.v5i2.23191

Maxengana, N.S. 2012. *Impact of Missionary Activities and the Establishment of Victoria East, 1824-186*. PhD dissertation. Fort Hare: University of Fort Hare.

Mofolo, T. 1981. *Chaka*. Translated by D. P. Kunene. Oxford: Heinemann.

Morris, M. 1988. Social History and the Transition to Capitalism in the South African Countryside. *Review of African Political Economy.* 41: 60-72. https://doi.org/10.1080/03056248808703763

Murray, M. 1989. The Origins of Agrarian Capitalism in South Africa: A Critique of the "Social History Perspective". *Journal of Southern African Studies*, 15 (4): 645-665. https://doi.org/10.1080/03057078908708219

Mtuze, P.T. 1990. *The Image of Woman in the Prose Works of Selected Xhosa Writers (1909-1980).* PhD dissertation. Cape Town: University of Cape Town.

Ndimande, N.P. 2001. *Ukuqhathaniswa Kwezibongo Zabantu Basentshonalanga-Afrika, Empumalanga-Afrika Nezabasenzansi-Afrika Njengenkomba Yesiko Lobuzwe Obubodwa Base-Afrika.* PhD dissertation. Durban: University of Durban-Westville.

Opland, J. 2009. *Abantu Besizwe: Historical and Biographical Writings, 1902–1944, SEK Mqhayi.* Johannesburg: Wits University Press.

Opland, J. 2004. Nineteenth-century Xhosa literature. *Kronos*, 22-46.

Opland, J. 1983. *Xhosa Oral Poetry: Aspects of a Black South African Tradition.* Cambridge: Cambridge University Press.

Omer-Cooper, J.D. 1966. *The Zulu Aftermath: a nineteenth-century revolution in Bantu Africa* (Vol. 1966). London: Longmans.

Peires, J.B. 1993. Paradigm deleted: the materialist interpretation of the Mfecane. *Journal of Southern African Studies*, 19 (2): 295-313. https://doi.org/10.1080/03057079308708361

Peires, J. 1979. The Lovedale Press: literature for the Bantu revisited. *History in Africa*, 6, 155-175. https://doi.org/10.2307/3171744

Richner, J.E. 2005. *The historiographical development of the concept "mfecane" and the writing of early southern African history, from the 1820s to 1920s*. PhD dissertation. Grahamstown: Rhodes University.

Rubusana, W.B. 2015. *Zemk'inkomo magwalandini*. Cape Town: New Africa Books.

Satyo, S.C. 1977. *Traditional concepts and literary conventions in Sinxo's works*. Pretoria: University of South Africa.

Sithole, J. 2017. Oral History Consultation by author.

Soga, J.H. 1930. *The South-Eastern Bantu-Abe-Nguni, Aba-Mbo, Ama-Lala*, [With a Portrait, Genealogical Trees and a Map]. Johannesburg: Witwatersrand University Press.

Stapleton, T.J. 1996. The Expansion of a Pseudo-Ethnicity in the Eastern Cape: Reconsidering the Fingo "Exodus" of 1865. *The International journal of African historical studies*, 29 (2): 233-250. https://doi.org/10.2307/220517

Tisani, N.C. 2001. *Continuity and change of Xhosa historiography during the nineteenth century: An exploration through textual analysis*. PhD dissertation. Grahamstown: Rhodes University.

Webster, A.C. 1991. *Land Expropriation and Labour Extraction Under Cape Colonial Rule: The War of 1835 and the "emancipation" of the Fingo*. Master's thesis. Grahamstown: Rhodes University.

Wolpe, H. (ed.). 1980. *The Articulation of Modes of Production: essays from economy and society*. London: Routledge.

Wolpe, H. 1972. Capitalism and cheap labour-power in South Africa: from segregation to apartheid. *Economy and Society*, 1 (4): 425-456. https://doi.org/10.1080/03085147200000023

Wright, J. 1989. *The dynamics of power and conflict in the Thukela-Mzimkhulu region in the late 18th and early 19th centuries: a critical reconstruction*. PhD dissertation. Johannesburg: Wits University.

Wright, J. 1989. Political Mythology and the Making of Natal's Mfecane. *Canadian Journal of African Studies/La Revue Canadienne des études Africaines*, 23 (2): 272-291. https://doi.org/10.2307/485525

CHAPTER 5

Repositioning *uMakhulu* as an Institution of Knowledge

Beyond 'Biologism' towards uMakhulu as the body of Indigenous Knowledge

Babalwa Magoqwana[1]

Introduction

Central to the sociology of pre-colonial African society was the elderly woman's leadership in the economy and the household (Amadiume 1987, 2015; Oyewumi 1997; Steady 2011). This role was later eroded by colonisation, religion and today increasingly promoted by 'neo-traditionalism' (concealed as 'African culture') which resembles the colonial patriarchal structures in erasing African women's contribution in African societies (Aidoo 1992:325). It is the invisible and unacknowledged histories of these African women that have reduced them into an ugly 'face of poverty' and underdevelopment in the world today (Aidoo 1992). Elderly African women's role in the economy, markets and in sustaining the rural communities has been reduced to a shadow of what it used to be and today sounds mythical to the younger generation as they see everyday violence against women as the 'norm' entrenched in the social fabric of our communities.

To address this misperception, we need to historicise *uMakhulu* (grandmother or elder Mother in isiXhosa) by reclaiming

---

[1] babalwa.magoqwana@mandela.ac.za

and recognising the elderly African women's bodies as institutions of indigenous knowledge, dissemination and storage in the pre-colonial and contemporary society (Wane 2011:283). The term *uMama-Omkhulu* (elder mother-shortened to *uMakhulu*) is used to assert isiXhosa as a source of knowledge. Using this term avoids the inherent epistemological challenges provided by 'grandmother' in re-inserting the notion of 'extended family' as the norm. The notion of *uMakhulu* can also refer to *UMo'Mkhulu* (senior Mother) who is not directly Mother's/Father's Mother, but elder mother's sister (Sisulu 2003:34). As Ntuli (2002:54) has argued, "language represents a specific worldview and ontology" which is why the isiXhosa term *uMakhulu* rather than 'grandmother' is maintained throughout this chapter. The use of the term attempts to contribute to local concepts rather than adopting "imposed categories, theories and paradigms" that tend to be unfit for local conditions (Adesina 2006).

This chapter seeks to challenge some of the narrow conceptions that define *uMakhulu* purely in economic and seniority terms in African households. I argue that we need to position *uMakhulu* as an institution of knowledge that transfers not only 'history' through *iintsomi* (folktales), but also as a body of indigenous knowledge that stores, transfers and disseminates knowledge and values. In seeking to go beyond the narrative of *uMakhulu* as a safety net or a caregiver under harsh socio-economic conditions in the rural households, I make use of Oyeronke Oyewumi's understanding in *The Invention of Women* (1997) of the bio-logic to argue for *uMakhulu* as a productive, but invisible institution.

It is this institution that shapes our spiritual awareness in the African household, building on Kondiwe Khondlo's (2015) notion of *isazela* (conscience) as part of desired public leadership values. In repositioning *uMakhulu* as the institution of knowledge, I argue, we are then provided with an analytical framework that enables us to move beyond the gendered and binary nature of institutions of learning (public versus private spaces of learning). In this new interdisciplinary framework (beyond the frontiers of binaries), we are then able to integrate local languages and values carried over by our grandmothers in dealing with social, political and economic challenges in our societies. This process of epistemic redress will commence a healing process for our communities from the destructive impact of centuries of colonial thought systems and their impact on our social organisation in our African households.

In my argument, I seek to answer a call by Ifi Amadiume in *Male Daughters and Female Husbands: Gender and Sex in an African Society* (2015) in her preface when she challenges African feminists to centre "Africa's matriarchal heritage" in understanding women's relationship to power in post-colonial society. In repositioning *uMakhulu* as a body of indigenous knowledge, I contend, we are then able to dig deeper in our own local languages and re-historicise our sociological concepts in African societies to produce all-rounded African scholars with firm ontological security.

In using *uMakhulu* as the body of the indigenous knowledge systems, I assert that (as suggested earlier) that we need to go beyond the 'binary biologist' understanding of *uMakhulu* to include the 'historical foundations' she builds in the African households through socialisation of children, oral history (through *intsomi*-folktales and *amabali*-stories) and spiritual labour to induce *isazela* (conscience). It is through modernising these techniques of *uMakhulu* into digital spaces that we can also archive the shared and transferred knowledge systems beyond the rural areas.

In re-centring *uMakhulu* as part of Nguni women histories, I argue we can begin to challenge also the "patriarchal bias" (Tisani 2000:99) that has shaped the understanding of women in Xhosa history through '*isihelegu sika Nongawuse*' (the catastrophe of Nongqawuse) (Peires 1989) to explain landlessness and the suffering of amaXhosa in the 19th to 20th century. This patriarchal bias in the history of the Eastern Cape has been constructed without taking into consideration the rich matriarchal histories of pre-colonial Africa and how women used to influence armies, religious institutions, national economies and political leadership (Steady 2011). Tisani (2000) shows that in the Cape, Xhosa chiefs were in constant communication and advised by the elderly women who sometimes acted as regents in the absence of the older chiefs.

The exclusion of women from the writings belied what was happening at the time. During the 1830s four senior houses in the Xhosa polity, (as listed in the genealogies table in *The Christian Watchman*) had Queen Mothers taking charge of affairs while heirs were minors. With the sudden death of Hintsa in 1835, Nomsa had to step in and support her son who was still *ikrwala* (a young man who just returned from initiation school). When Ngqika died in November 1829, Sutu became regent during the minority of the Rharhabe heir, Sandile (Tisani 2000:100).

This rich matriarchal contribution becomes very clear with the Zulu Monarchy in the 18th and 19th centuries. Shamase (2014) details the "power and strong character" of Mkabayi ka Jama (and her twin sister – Mmama) who "headed the military harems (*izigodlo*) and became a regent when Senzangakhona died in 1781". This history and influence of women among Nguni populations is not unique as Steady (2011) details the history and meanings of African women leadership in West Africa. I make use of the Nguni languages and idioms to illustrate, later in my argument, the link between values, knowledge and spirituality carried by this body of *uMakhulu*.

As the pillar of many African households, *uMakhulu* teaches many of us about resilience or what Motsemme (2001) calls "survival wisdom" in the harsh socio-economic conditions experienced by black households in African societies. I hope to show *uMakhulu* as the embodiment of indigenous knowledge rather than the invisible-unproductive body she is currently perceived to be in our societies (Sigasana 2017).

uMakhulu and the 'bodies that matter'

On 1 October 2017, the United Nations celebrated the "International Day of Older Persons" with the theme *Stepping into the Future: Tapping the Talents, Contributions and Participation of Older Persons in Society.*[2] The theme speaks to the centrality of the elderly in our societies as fountains of knowledge towards ensuring sustainable development. Despite their rich survival wisdom, older persons are often neglected and invisibilised in our societies as 'unproductive bodies'.

Being *uMakhulu* is a life stage that most women cannot escape, as it forms part of the adult life of a woman as soon as they reach menopause. Every isiXhosa African woman (like many other women in Africa since pre-colonial times) inherently knows the knowledge responsibilities embodied by this life stage without question. There is no formal training in entering the life stage as 'institution', but age, knowledge and experience prepare women for it. It is the inevitable nature of this role and position that *uMakhulu* occupies which makes her a significant part of the socialisation process for most African households (Siqwana-Ndulu 1998).

However, later in my argument I move beyond this biology-centred definition of *uMakhulu* towards the spiritual nature of *uGogo* (grandmother in isiZulu) to

---

[2] See https://www.un.org/development/desa/ageing/international-day-of-older-persons-homepage/unidop2017.html [Retrieved 13 June 2018].

problematise age and spirituality. The limits of confining power of *uMakhulu* on aged 'unproductive' bodies, becomes very clear when we discuss the spiritual nature of this institution of knowledge as part of the ontological spiritual foundation of *amaThwasa* (African traditional healers).

The fixation with young and 'productive' bodies or what Oyeronke Oyewumi in *The Invention of Women* (1997) terms 'biologism' in understanding our social issues has resulted in my view to many ignoring the role and significance of *uMakhulu* as an institution of knowledge. Oyewumi's (1997) concept of 'bio-logic' is used to understand how *uMakhulu* has been positioned as an unproductive body within the capitalist logic. This concept is a critique of the Western logic in centring biology as the centre of difference and hierarchy in society. "The notion of society that emerges from this conception is that society is constituted by bodies and as bodies – male bodies, female bodies, white bodies, poor bodies, rich bodies, Jewish bodies, Aryan bodies, black bodies" (Oyewumi 1997:3). She speaks to the physicality that dominated Western thought, which makes the body to always be "in view and on view" (Oyewumi 2005:4). This constant "gaze" tends to define differences in society and forms the centre of the epistemological differences between Western thinking and Yoruba society. The latter tends to privilege the "senses" rather than the "view". She traces the separation between the body and mind dualism to this conception of the body as a "trap to which ideas cannot flow from" (Oyewumi 2005:5).

The 'bio-logic' implies that elder African women's bodies are inherently 'unproductive' and therefore must contribute to the reproductive labour system (care work) performed by mostly other (black) women (Glenn 1992). The emphasis on physicality and hierarchy of bodies has put African women as non-thinkers – but also as 'bodies' – at the bottom of the ladder in knowledge production. This bio-logic does not recognise that in many African households "the female power ultimately lies in postmenopausal women" (Ogunyemi 1996:89) who are respected and feared because of their seniority and wisdom rather than the shape or desirability of their bodies.

Following on Oyewumi's assertion of this epistemological trap, I position *uMakhulu* as the 'body' of indigenous knowledge, from which ideas about history, leadership, and survival do indeed flow. *uMakhulu* forms the centre of what we know and how we know in many African households and directly contributes to the epistemic foundations of knowledge with spirituality as part of 'knowing' in her institution.

uMakhulu – the embodiment of the 'unproductive' body

As indicated earlier, because of her age and non-participation in the labour market, *uMakhulu* tends to be seen as part of the 'unproductive bodies' in our societies, based on her biological and labour market incapacity. She tends to be 'postmenopausal' and therefore has biological limitations on bearing children of her own (even though she has many). This biological determinism connects the body with the capitalist production system, which promotes profit and accumulation. Hence, her biological clock defines her as unproductive as she cannot biologically give birth to more 'productive bodies'. Magubane (2004:19) believes that the characterisation of the "unproductive and therefore undesirable body" is built on Adam Smith's notion of "characteristics of the unproductive workers he disapproves of".

Based on the 'bio-logic' of the productive and unproductive bodies, *uMakhulu* is relegated to the latter, as the capitalist labour system recognises the young and able-bodied who can contribute to the capital accumulation through selling their labour power. Most of the time, she is desexualised (without sexual desire) and therefore deemed only important when it comes to her ability to socialise the children and support the mothers. This is also noted by Lorelle Semley in *Mother is Gold, Father is Glass* (2011) in her introduction on motherhood in Ketu, a West African Yoruba town (Benin). She argues that the 'elder-mother' is a position that is respected and sometimes feared because of the "elder mother's secret knowledge" which might sometimes be termed as 'witchcraft'. "In Yoruba, to see the elder women's authority only in relation to biological motherhood obscures the important role of occult power that shrouds postmenopausal women in particular, which evokes fear as much as respect" (Semley 2011:16). This status of being an 'elder-mother' is granted by not only marriage or giving birth to children, it speaks to seniority that one enjoys in the community as an elder. This is why Oyewumi (2015:10) asserts that seniority is 'socially constructed', not dependent on 'chronological age' or the type of body, but on social relations in the households. The suspicion of witchcraft is therefore linked to the elderly, physical, desexualised body and the powers that seem to be embodied by elderly bodies.

Zine Magubane in *Bringing the Empire Home* (2004) has traced the history of language on how the African woman's body was deemed 'beautiful' before the age of 25. This, she argued, was part of the missionary and later social thinking in the Cape Colony and Scotland. The black woman's body was often contrasted with the African male bodies that were deemed "small, firm, graceful and neat" (2004:20) not subject to temporal changes. Magubane (2004:21) quotes Stephen Kay when he described the bodies of the African women in the Cape in the 1800s:

> As in most barbarous nations, the lot of the *abafazi* [women] is hard indeed ... when young, they are in many instances beautiful [laying aside the prejudice of colour] but the hard labour which they commence as soon as they enter the married state, and which may be regarded as a kind of bondage soon destroys the charms which nature may have gifted them, and they become, at an early age even disgustingly ugly (Magubane 2004:21).

Reading these missionary accounts of beauty and productivity, Magubane (2004:18) then suggests that "to be female is to be, literally and figuratively, a physical extension and manifestation of the system of productive relations". It is this inability of the grandmother to sell her labour power that makes her undesirable to the capitalist system, as she cannot bear children (future labourers) or perform the actual labour that can directly contribute to the market relations. Instead, she becomes a 'burden' for the state in expecting social welfare and being taken care of by the young.

Despite being dubbed as 'unproductive bodies', elderly African women in the apartheid Bantustan reserves have always performed the 'reproductive labour' as they provided an "economic base for the labour needed during the migrant labour system" (Ntantala 1958). Related to this assertion, Cock (1989:309) reminds us that "... the extended family in the reserves fulfills the social security function necessary for the reproduction of the migrant labour workforce". This notion of the 'extended' family mainly refers to elder women who looked after the household. This reproductive function of the elderly African women is not limited to the rural homelands in apartheid South Africa, but continues today under the social welfare system where grandmothers tend to subsidise the unemployed youth (Sigasana 2017). Siqwana-Ndulo (1998:413) also acknowledges the position of the "elderly women [who] were charged with caring for their unmarried daughter's and son's offspring, in addition to relatives of different kids" under the migrant labour system in South Africa. Grandmothers were forced to "care" (Glenn:2010), to supplement the cheap labour system that forced the black man to the city for pittance and exploitation. These women in the reserves sustained the African households, caring for the sick, the young, and disabled (Ntantala 1958).

uMakhulu – the narrator of history for the young

This institution of knowledge cuts across the pre-colonial to the present society with its influence of understanding the past of the African households. In *The Destruction of Black Civilization,* Williams (1987:166) argues that:

> Primary education [in pre-colonial Chiefless Africa] included storytelling, mental arithmetic, community songs, and dances, learning the names of various birds and animals, the identification of poisonous snakes, local plants, and trees, and how to run and climb swiftly when pursued by dangerous animals.

Even during colonial Africa, "legends and folk-tales were very popular forms of entertainment in those days" (Kuzwayo 1990). Many African leaders give credit to *uMakhulu* as the major influence in their socialisation and understanding of oral history (Ellen Khuzwayo, Emma Mashinini, Walter and Albertina Sisulu are among many). In effect, Nkosinathi Biko opens the collection of Biko's writings in *I write What I like* by mentioning *uMakhulu* as the source of 'record keeping' for the history and life of Steve Biko. Even the well-known Zulu King, Shaka ka Senzangakhona's reign tends to be traced back to his paternal grandmother, Mthaniya, who died at 95 years of age with two powerful daughters who later influenced Zulu royal family affairs (Gollock (1932 [1969]:24).

Nomathamsanqa Tisani (1998) confirms this role of *uMakhulu* as a "foundation of historical knowledge" as she transfers knowledge through *iintsomi* and *amabali*. It is the sessions around the fire, at the end of each day, that provided an opportunity for learning by the youth from the grandmother that served as a foundation for historical knowledge and igniting the imagination of the young. This is why Magona in *To My Children's Children* (1990) asks, "How will you know who you are if I do not or cannot tell you the story of your past?" *Iintsomi,* as Magona says (1990:6), are an integral part of the child's socialisation among amaXhosa. These stories taught children about good, bad, duty, obedience, responsibility, honor and orderliness. She goes on to say that the best storyteller around the fire was the maternal grandmother.

Growing up with *uMakhulu* in the 1990s, I have experienced this institution through *iinstomi* and *amabali*. In fact, I still remember stories by my grandmother about pride of who we are, about ancestors, about marriage and so on. I remember Gcina Mhlope, who was always narrating *intsomi* on uMhlobo Wenene FM regional isiXhosa radio on Saturday mornings. With my siblings, we used to sit and listen to Gcina's narration of stories and teachings about animal names, morality and ways of being. This programme continues on this radio station even today under a different host as part of the South African Broadcasting Corporation's education programme.

As illustrated through this radio education programme, *uMakhulu* is indeed a pedagogy in her own right and similar knowledge-making spaces can inform how children are taught in the classroom today. This acknowledgement means we can start using the institution of *uMakhulu's* ways of sharing knowledge as the foundation for young children's curriculum and ways of teaching thereby building towards a more accessible and complimentary primary school curriculum that sees the African household as part of learning spaces rather than divorced from knowledge. This means we start acknowledging children's cultural base, language and innate intelligence, thus valuing their language and sense of being from an early age (Hoppers in Hobongwana-Duley 2014:6).

uMakhulu and the performance of spiritual labour

In situating local knowledge in *uMakhulu's* body, we are not only reasserting the importance of seniority, wisdom and spirituality, but we are also re-centring the invisible embodied knowledges that have contributed to how we know what we know. Tisani asserts that *uMakhulu* is our ontological foundation, "she lives in me".[3] She goes further to highlight the importance of the maternal grandmother in the process of *ukuThwasa* – the spiritual calling. Tisani notes that one can only *thwasa* through maternal grandmother's ancestors. This is confirmed by Mkhize (2018:138-139) in her conversation with Gogo Ngoatjakumba (a practising African doctor) when she says:

> I am not sure why someone is called *baba* [father] even if they are a woman, but the only thing I can think of is that because our lineages are patrilineal but spiritually you are led from your grandmother, so your father '*ubaba*' gives you your law but the gift of calling comes from your grandmother.

This process of *ukuThwasa* gives a clear understanding of the spiritual importance of this institution. When *uMakhulu* provides a historical education through *iziduko* and *ukuzithutha* (clan names and genealogies respectively), she becomes a fundamental base for which to understand oral histories. It is her historical knowledge and spiritual forms of education that make her the integral part of the *ukuThwasa* process. Hence she becomes the ontological spiritual foundation when she passes on

---

3   Tisani, N. An Interview conducted on 12 April 2018 in Grahamstown, Eastern Cape, South Africa.

to the non-living world. Tisani (2017) confirms the spiritual nature of the institution by saying:

> African doctors – 'amaThwasa' – have a revelation and are connected with those who have gone before and the present. When one [recites the family genealogies] *ezithutha*, they revisit their elders because the elders are archives, they pass knowledge and help create new knowledge.

As noted earlier, the pre-colonial African education system was linked to teachings on genealogies, which directly speak to the family histories. This training on genealogies of the family becomes useful in the process of *ukuThwasa* to be *uGogo* (a traditional healer). In isiZulu *uGogo* (grandmother) is also used to refer to "the ancestor of those who have gone through *ukuThwasa*" (Nene 2013:4). This female designation to be *uGogo* transcends gender and the nature of the body, as *uGogo* can be given to both male and female initiates (*amaThwasa*) regardless of physiology.

To those who are invested in biologism, the concept of *uGogo* (and *ubaba*) could be very confusing, as the body in this ancestral plane does not conform to gender binaries. Instead both terms "are transferable across all genders depending on the role [one is] playing, not so much the gender of the person. In the practice of *ukuthwasa*, the *Gogo* principle helps you in the spiritual aspects, and your father – *ubaba* – is the one who helps guide you in the physical world" (Mkhize 2018:138). These gender dynamics on the body of *uGogo* help us imagine a different kind of spirituality that separates the body, gender and hierarchy of power in our societies. *Gogo's* body helps us destabilise the bio-logic that defines hierarchy attached to physical bodies and spirituality, as *uGogo* can be senior without being [physically] older in the age sense. This seniority is derived from the ability of *amaThwasa* to access the archive of knowledge through *abadala* [elders] and help in formulating new knowledge (Tisani:2017). This means one can be *uGogo* through the spiritual process of *ukuthwasa* not by age, hence Oyewumi (2015) maintains that seniority is not 'chronological'.

This spiritual and historical position of an elder mother provides a framework for which we can start building a "woman-centred vernacular theory" (Ogunyemi 1996:56). In fact, the former South African Public Protector, Advocate Thulisile Madonsela, sought to interpret the cultural, political and spiritual link of her duties to the South African public as that of the Vha Venda female spiritual leader – *uMakhadzi*. "An aunt [who] is a non-political figure, serves as a buffer between the ruler and the people. [The *Makhadzi*] enhances the voice of the people while serving as the king's eyes, ears and conscience. [He ignores her] at his own peril" (Thuli Madonsela quoted in Gqubule 2017:79). *Makhadzi*, as articulated by Madonsela here, connects the elder mother to a 'conscience' (*isazela*) of the community and therefore provides a perfect start in theorising beyond the "secularised episteme" (Alexander 2005:7). *Isazela* is not just a learned behaviour like the political consciousness derived from the disembodied and secular institutions. Instead, I argue, *isazela* is a direct result of the spiritual labour performed by *uMakhulu* who provides spiritual and survival wisdom under the harsh socio-economic conditions of the African household (Motsemme 2001:87).

uMakhulu hence provides an inclusive and well-rounded approach of knowing, without segmenting and disconnecting it to everyday life. For instance, her teaching on environmental awareness through recycling in African households is indicative of this institution in seeing the environment, society, and spirituality as a connected unit. Recycling of goods (clothes, tins and saving water) has been part of this institution long before we knew about its 'environmental benefits'. This role illustrates *uMakhulu* as an institution of 'survival knowledge' to the benefit of sustaining our environment, spirituality and economy – by organising knowledge in an accessible and restorative manner. This is a form of pedagogy, which practically helps us to deal with enduring challenges that have shaped our 'body of knowledge' by contributing to imagining new forms of knowing.

Repositioning of *uMakhulu* as an institution of knowledge

To conceptualise *uMakhulu* as an institution is not only to analyse her position in the African household using a 'metaphor', but (I suggest) it is also to provide a new model about where knowledge is situated, how it is communicated, to understand and appreciate the values carried in that knowledge, and to recognise the bodies that carry this knowledge. Positioning *uMakhulu* as an institution of knowledge challenges the categories, definitions, and legitimate sources of knowledge, which are limited to the "certified knowers" (Vilakazi 2002).

This then emphasises the place and importance of local knowledge that is not verified through formal education institutions, making it possible to deal with some of the challenges facing public institutions of knowledge today. Firstly, this challenges the deep historical exclusionary cultures that define formal 'institutions of knowledge' and offers an alternative understanding of the knower, which can complement rather than compete with current forms of knowing. Secondly, this conception of *uMakhulu* as an institution of knowledge automatically deals with the unnecessary separation between the 'informal and formal' institution, which is built on the history of separation between public (productive), and private (reproductive) spaces (Federici 2012). Thirdly, *uMakhulu* offers an alternative understanding of leadership (ethics and consciousness) beyond the current gendered and sometimes racialised public leadership models. The elder mother provides a critique of the "great, masculine, hierarchical, single" leader as representing the old forms of leadership style, which does not take into consideration African matriarchal heritage in leadership (Miller 2016; Amadiume 2015). This is why Steady (2011) and Oyewumi (2015) argue for the "maternal ideology" and "matripotency ethos" embedded in women's leadership in Africa. *uMakhulu* possesses the principles "beyond reproductive and nurturing roles in households, but reflects the normative values and humanistic ideologies that embrace notions of preservation of past, present and future generations" (Steady 2011:22). Finally, to include *uGogo/uMakhulu* as a source of knowledge, we are forced to acknowledge spirituality as part of knowledge making between the living and non-living. Thus through this acknowledgement, we destabilise the "disembodied and binary knowledge system based on secular knowledge" (Motsemme 2001:76). This is why, Oyewumi (2004:1) emphasises "if we are to create relevant scholarship in African knowledge systems, we have no choice but to be cognisant of the metaphysical in the constitution of power, and pay attention to ways in which spirituality undergirds interpretation of the material world".

Conclusion

In my argument, I have sought to answer a call by Ifi Amadiume (2015) in centring Africa's matriarchal heritage in the embodiment of knowledge and its institutions that shape what and how we know. In repositioning *uMakhulu* as an institution of knowledge, we acknowledge the unnecessary divisions between the public and private sphere, the household and state, and knowledge and spirituality. In taking the so-called 'informal' institution as part of learning into the curriculum of our universities and schools, we are then forced to acknowledge the inseparability of the household and learning, the embodiment of knowledge and the inherent ancient African values carried by this boundary-less knowledge stretching back into the pre-colonial era.

Critically engaging with the 'bio-logic' from Oyewumi (1997), I have attempted to reposition *uMakhulu* outside the 'unproductive' biologism that tends to restrictively define her existence in relation to knowledge. Oyewumi's notion of 'senses' as an approach to knowledge speaks to the holistic approach that *uMakhulu* provides in terms of the integration of mind, body and spirit. By moving out of the biological understandings of elderly African women as mere recipients of social welfare and as caregivers, we visibilise and acknowledge them as oral sources of historical knowledge and sources of ontological foundations. Through this paradigm shift, we restore the centrality of spirituality in the African household and indigenous knowledge production process. Through the modernised versions of oral storytelling – digital storytelling – we might be able to have *uMakhulu* influencing not only the rural but also the urban black households. Through these digitised versions of this institution, she might also help many generations in developing survival techniques in the increasing harsh socio-economic realities on the continent.

To conclude, this chapter is explorative in nature, drawing on my own *uMakhulu*-based knowledge experience, designed to spark interest around the contribution of the Nguni (especially isiXhosa) language and elder African women's bodies as institutions of knowledge that can help us improve *how* we teach and *what* we teach today.

References

Adesina, J. 2006. Sociology Beyond Despair: Recovery of Nerve, Endogeneity, and Epistemic Intervention. *South African Review of Sociology*, 37 (2): 41-259.
https://doi.org/10.1080/21528586.2006.10419157

Aidoo, A. 1992. The African Woman Today. *Dissent Magazine: Africa Today Crisis and Change*, Summer: 319-325.

Alexander, M.J. 2005. P*edagogies of Crossing: Meditations on Feminism, Sexual Politics, Memory and the Sacred. City*? Durham, NC: Duke University Press.
https://doi.org/10.1215/9780822386988

Amadiume, I. 1987. Foreword. In: *Male daughters, Female Husbands: Gender and Sex in an African Society*. P. Catlan. London: Zed Books.

Cock, J. 1980. *Maids and Madams: A Study in the Politics of Exploitation*. Johannesburg: Ravan Press.

Duflo, E. 2003. Grandmothers and granddaughters: Old-age pensions and intrahousehold allocation in South Africa. *The World Bank Economic Review*, 17 (1): 1-25.
https://doi.org/10.1093/wber/hg013

Federeci, S. 2012. *Revolution at Point Zero: Housework, Reproduction, and Feminist Struggle*. Brooklyn: PM Press.

Glenn, N.E. 2010. *Forced to Care: Coercion and Caregiving in America*. Cambridge, Massachusetts: Harvard University Press.

Gollock, G.A. 1969. *Daughters of Africa: with Portraits, Illustrations and a Map*. New York: Negro University Press.

Gqubule, T. 2017. *No Longer Whispering to Power: The Story of Thuli Madonsela*. Johannesburg and Cape Town: Jonathan Ball Publishers.

Hobongwane-Duley, H.Y. 2014. Exploring Indigenous Knowledge Practices Concerning Health and Wellbeing: A Case Study of isiXhosa-speaking Women in the Rural Eastern Cape. Unpublished PhD dissertation. Cape Town: University of Cape Town.

Khondlo, K. 2015. Meaning and significance of consciousness and consciousness in public leadership in the post-1994 South Africa. *Journal of Public Administration*, 50 (3): 485-495.

Kuzwayo, E. 1990. *Sit Down and Listen*. Cape Town: David Philip – The Women's Press.

Magona, S. 1990. *To my Children's Children*. Cape Town: David Phillip Publishers.

Magubane, Z. 2004. *Bringing the Empire Home: Race, Class, and Gender in Britain and Colonial South Africa*. Chicago: University of Chicago Press.

Miller, D. 2016. Excavating the vernacular: 'Ugly feminists', Generational Blues and Matriarchal Leadership. In: S. Booysen (ed.), *Fees Must Fall Student Revolt, Decolonisation and Governance in South Africa*. Johannesburg: Wits Press.

Mkhize, N. 2018. A Conversation with Gogo Ngoatjakumba. In: J. Thorpe (ed.) *Feminism: South Africans Speak Their Truth*. Cape Town: David Philips Publishers.

Motsemme, N. 2001. Lived and Embodied Suffering and Healing amongst Mothers and Daughters in Chesterville Township, KwaZulu-Natal. Unpublished PhD dissertation. Pretoria: University of South Africa.

Nene, J.O. 2013. IsiZulu traditional healers' perspective of Ukuhlonipha in Context. Unpublished Master's thesis. Pretoria: University of South Africa.

Ntantala, P. 1958. *The Widows of the Reserves*. http://www.sahistory.org.za/sites/default/files/DC/joa19580600.037.031.001/joa19580600.037.031.001.pdf (Retrieved February 2017).

Ntuli, P. 2002. African knowledge systems and African renaissance. In: C.A.O. Hoppers (ed.), *Indigenous Knowledge and Integration of Knowledge Systems: Towards a Philosophy of Articulation*. Claremont: New Africa Education.

Nyerere, J. 1967. Education for self-reliance. Symposium on Understanding Quality Education, Conference on Envisioning Quality Education, 1-12. http://www.swaraj.org/shikshantar/resources_nyerere.html

Ogunyemi, O. 1996. *Africa Wo/Man Palava: The Nigerian Novel by Women*. Chicago. University of Chicago Press.

Oyewumi, O. 2015. *What Gender is Motherhood? Changing Yoruba Ideals of Power, Procreation and Identity in the Age of Modernity*. New York: Palgrave MacMillan.

Oyewumi, O. 2005. Visualizing the body: Western theories and African subjects. In: O. Oyewumi (ed.), *African Gender Studies: A Reader*. New York: Palgrave MacMillan.

Oyewumi, O. 2004. Conceptualising gender: Eurocentric foundations of feminist concepts and the challenge of African epistemologies. In: CODESRIA (eds.), *African Gender Scholarship: Concepts, Methodologies and Paradigms*. Dakar Imprimerie Saint Pau: CODESRIA.

Oyewumi, O. 1997. *The Invention of Women: Making African Senses of Western Gender Discourses*. Minneapolis: University of Minnesota Press.

Peires, J. 1989. *The Dead Will Arise: Nongwaquse and the Great Xhosa Cattle-Killing of 1856-7*. Johannesburg: Raven Press.

Semley, L. 2011. *Mother is Gold, Father is Glass: Gender and Colonialism in a Yoruba Town*. Bloomington and Indianapolis: Indiana University Press.

Shamase, M. 2014. The Royal Women of the Zulu monarchy-through the key role of oral history: Princess Mkabayi kaJama. *Inkanyiso.Jnl Humanities and Soc Sc*, 6 (1): 15-22.

Sigasana, L. 2017. *South Africa's Elderly Invisible, Neglected and Abused*. The Star Newspaper, 2 October.

Sisulu, E. 2003. *Walter And Albertina Sisulu: In Our Lifetime*. Abacus

Steady, F.C. 2011. *Women and Leadership in West Africa: Mothering the Nation and Humanizing the State*. New York: Palgrave MacMillan. https://doi.org/10.1057/9781137010391

Siqwana-Ndulu, N. 1998. Rural African Family Structure in the Eastern Cape Province, South Africa. *Journal of Comparative Family Studies*, 29 (2): 407-417.

Tisani, N. 2017. Re-visiting and celebrating our literary elders to build a multiversal tomorrow. Paper presented at Colloquium on Rethinking South African Canonical Writing: Centring the isiXhosa Writings of the 19th and Early 20th Centuries. Grahamstown: Rhodes University, 21-22 June.

Tisani, N. 2000. Continuity and Change in Xhosa Historiography During the Nineteenth Century: An Exploration through Textual Analysis. Unpublished PhD dissertation. Grahamstown, Rhodes University.

Tisani, N.1998. Grandmothers' sessions as foundations of historical understanding. Unpublished Seminar Paper- History Department. Grahamstown: Rhodes University.

Vilakazi, H. 2002. The problem of African universities. In: M.W. Makgoba (ed.), *African Renaissance: The New Struggle*. Cape Town, Tafelberg: Mafube Publishers.

Wane, N. 2011. The Kenyan Herbalist Ruptures the Status Quo in Health and Healing. In: *Counterpoints: Indigenous Philosophies and Critical Education: A READER*, 379: 280-298.

Williams, C. 1987. *The Destruction of Black Civilization: Great issue of Race From 4500B.C. to 2000 A.D.* Chicago, Third World Press.

CHAPTER 6

The long southern African past

Enfolded time and the challenges of archive

Carolyn Hamilton[1]

Introduction

In this chapter I delineate some of the terminological problems, temporal complications, and methodological challenges of enquiry into the southern African past before European colonialism. My discussion focuses on the KwaZulu-Natal (KZN) region where these particular complications, problems and challenges have received sustained attention. For this reason, the KZN material is relatively easy to use illustratively in order to explain knotty methodological problems that are shared across southern Africa. I nonetheless also refer to the wider region. Of course, contemporary borders had no meaning in the remote past, but they are relevant to how the past before European colonialism has been treated in subsequent times.

Marked appetite and meagre offerings

Assessments of this field of enquiry are timely, taking place as they do in the context of a surge of interest in the long southern African past. A recent series of developments in the academy is but one signal of this surge. They include the Five Hundred Year Initiative begun in 2006 by a loose grouping of scholars

---

[1] carolyn.hamilton@uct.ac.za

self-consciously working in cross-disciplinary collaborations. This resulted in a conference publication in 2008 (Swanepoel, Esterhuysen & Bonner), a workshop on "History and Archaeology in Conversation – South Africa meets East Africa" held at Wits in July 2009,[2] and a special journal edition in 2012 (Delius & Marks). For the most part the Five Hundred Year Initiative marshalled the energies of established, mostly, though not exclusively, white, scholars, and mostly archaeologists and historians. In 2012, under the auspices of the Minister of Higher Education, dedicated government funding through the National Institute for the Humanities and Social Sciences (NIHSS) was, for the first time, allocated to this area with the express purpose of "catalyzing" and "opening up" new avenues of scholarship.[3] It resulted in two national conferences directly on the subject. The first was a relatively small and low-key gathering in March 2014 featuring mostly, but not exclusively, established archaeologists, historians and linguists. A second larger and more wide-ranging one was held in 2017, a hallmark of which was the animated contributions by a cohort of black scholars, many of whom were based in disciplines hitherto not active in this field, actively posing provocative new research questions.[4] Other recent, conscious attempts to set a new research agenda for the long southern African past include the small colloquium on "*IziThunguthu*: Southern African Pasts Before the Colonial Era, their Archives and their Ongoing Present/Presence," held at the University of Cape Town (UCT) in 2015, as well as a number of projects focused on the Indian Ocean world, with research agendas reaching back to the 11th century.[5]

In the last three years the research developments have intersected with animated debate raging in South African universities, and elsewhere, about the conduct of decolonised forms of research and the possibilities of decolonised university curricula. Indeed, in 2015, a lead article in the UCT student publication, *Varsity*,

---

[2] The workshop papers' content was re-worked as a result of the input at the conference and the papers were published in African Studies, 69 (2). 2010.
[3] See http://www.nihss.ac.za/content/catalytic-projects – sthash.L44 (Retrieved 23 August 2017).
[4] Since the late 2000s scholars working in this area have been able to apply for research funding from South Africa's National Research Foundation's African Origins Platform (AOP). However, the focus there is weighted towards projects with a deep time depth, notably palaeontological and archaeological projects. The NIHSS was established in 2013. It provides funding and support for a series of catalytic projects including the 'Pre-Colonial Catalytic Project'. See http://www.nihss.ac.za/content/catalytic-projects#sthash.L44ZJUvB.dpuf (Retrieved 31 August 2017).
The first conference of the Pre-Colonial Catalytic Project held in 2014 resulted in a volume of conference proceedings (Ntsebeza & Saunders 2014). The second conference was held in March 2017, at Nelson Mandela University, and the second volume of papers is this current publication.
[5] See, for example, the project, Re-Centring Afro-Asia: Musical and Human Migrations in the Pre-Colonial Period 700–1500 AD (http://www.sociology.uct.ac.za/news/re-centring-afroasia-musical-and-human-migrations-pre-colonial-period-700-1500ad, (Retrieved 31 August 2017); and the conference 'Concepts from the Global South', Centre for Indian Studies, University of the Witwatersrand, October 2016.

reported on student demands for "more pre-colonial history" in the university curriculum (Karim 2015). The call for "more pre-colonial history" is not confined to the academy. The extent of the public appetite is so wide-ranging that this essay can only offer a sense of it.

One area in which interest is marked is that of the long histories of the various component groupings subsumed in apartheid times under large ethnic categories like Zulu, Pedi and so on. A dramatic indication of this is provided by the historically significant Ndwandwe identity. The Nongoma area, today in the centre of the royal Zulu heartland, once lay within the large and powerful, but later little known, Ndwandwe kingdom. Ndwandwe was defeated by the Zulu king, Shaka, and its people were either scattered far afield or were incorporated under Zulu rule in a manner that marginalised their Ndwandwe identity and history. Since the late 1990s they have been actively reclaiming their pre-Zulu history and identity (Buthelezi 2012). Also in KZN, the Mkhize clan mobilises pre-Shakan history on multiple fronts (McNulty 2014). In 2007, local historian Siyabonga Mkhize published in isiZulu, and then, presumably under political pressure, withdrew from public circulation, his history of the Mkhize, *Uhlanga Iwas'embo* (Mkhize 2007).

Efforts in historical recovery are not confined to family groupings. The 2008 KZN Heritage Bill set the scene for a provincial government initiative in these kinds of clan or family histories, the ambitious KZN Family Tree project. As the premier at the time, S'bu Ndebele, put it, "This programme sees families, and even whole clans like the Embo, coming together to reconstruct their histories, in an effort to enhance their individual and collective identity and create cohesion among themselves".[6]

Such developments, private and governmental, happen across the country. In 2005 the Mpumalanga Provincial government initiated a heritage project aimed at rediscovering the province's past, including, importantly, the past before the advent of the first Europeans[7] while in the Cape the broad-based Khoisan revivalist movement continuously highlights its attachment to an historical identity traced back to the period prior to the arrival of the Dutch.

Online manifestations offer another line of sight on the extent of public interest in the past before European colonialism. The Mkhize book has been used as a basis for entries on Mbo history in Ulwazi, a project run by the Ethekwini Municipality to

---

[6] See www.info.gov.za/speeches/2008/08112810451001.html (Retrieved 14 July 2011).
[7] See http://www.mpumalanga.gov.za/mpumalangabook/history.html (Retrieved 31 August 2017).

create a collaborative, online indigenous knowledge resource.[8] At the time of writing, entries also existed on Ulwazi for aspects of Duma, Khuzwayo, Ndlela, Qadi, Shange and Shezi clan histories, with more expected. In 2010 the activist Archival Platform[9] established an online initiative on ancestral stories that attracted astonishing public interest. Facebook pages for a variety of kinship-groupings have proliferated and are sites of animated discussion of the past.[10]

A Google search of websites concerned with *izithakazelo* (a form of clan address names and linked praises with extensive historical reach) confirms popular interest in the subject especially where more substantial historical narratives about the distant past are lost or unavailable. The *izithakazelo* address the lineage ancestors, offer poetic tributes to them, and make deep historical allusions. The forms in which they are embraced on the internet suggest that they have a great capacity to be mobilised to tend the psychic wounds left by the policies of the colonial and apartheid states, which effectively denied black South Africans a recognised archive pertinent to the remote past.

The remote past is also the object of attention from heritage practitioners working within the framework of government policies that acknowledge these wounds and the extensive gaps in the recognised record and prioritise addressing them within a policy framework for the promotion of indigenous knowledge.[11] And, in yet another manifestation, contemporary artists, writers and intellectuals wrestle with the challenge of how to recover this past outside the notions of primitive tribalism and immutable ethnicity in which it has been entrapped for the last 150 years (Ntombela 2016).

In addition, there are many ways in which the legacies of the past before European colonialism are invoked in contemporary contestations over resources and authority. In KZN some 11 traditional leaders used the opportunity of the national Commission on Traditional Leadership and Claims hearing held in mid-2007 to stake claims, rooted in the region's history before the reign of King Shaka (c.1816-1828), to the rights, privileges and resources of royalty. The media carried reports that the claims were seen by some Zulu royal councillors as "treason" and had provoked "war talk"

---

[8] See wiki.ulwazi.org (Retrieved 14 July 2011); also see McNulty (2014).
[9] See www.archivalplatform.org
[10] See for example www.facebook.com/AmaHlubi-Amahle-169290819757816
[11] See, for example, South Africa's National Indigenous Knowledge Systems Office, Department of Science and Technology (DST) and the DST-NRF Centre on Indigenous Knowledge (National Research Foundation 2015).

in certain circles, while the head of the Commission described the hostility that the claims had generated as a potential "national danger" (Hlongwane 2007).[12] Though the claims were not ultimately successful, the historical activity undergirding them continued. A year after the Commission's sitting, in a move probably connected to the high-profile Nhlangwini claim on a historically ancient kingship, yet very much about self-discovery, Nomanda Ndola opened a museum in two rooms in her home in the remote southern KZN village of Harding, declaring, "My aim about my research is to keep Nhlangwini material and history for people to see and recognise. That is why I want to open my own museum".[13] This kind of interest was repeated across the country wherever the Commission held its hearings.

For all the demand, there is precious little to feed it in the public domain. School students are little rewarded by what is on offer in the school syllabus or in the extra materials – mostly stories of heroes – now occasionally produced by publishers who sense the gap in the market.[14] In the museums there is next to nothing. And, if the offerings in KZN are slender, the available resources in the rest of the country are more meagre still (Mdanda 2015). What there is, it is mostly presented as consumable heritage like the visitor centre at Mupungubwe, a small number of other stone ruins (mostly poorly presented), and numerous "cultural villages," as well as the occasional statue of a past hero.

Intellectuals, community historians and heritage workers, as well as researchers undertaking work for chiefs and other claimants of various kinds, find their way into libraries and archives to consult published texts and archived documents. In KZN, investigators might end up consulting materials like the James Stuart collection of recorded oral materials (see below), Magema Fuze's book *Abantu Abamnyama Lapa Bavela Ngakona* (1922), and A.T. Bryant's *Olden Times in Zululand and Natal* (1929). These texts are far from straightforward sources open to easy reading for past truths. The researchers will struggle, however, to find much scholarship that they can draw on, beyond a sprinkling of articles, a handful of theses and a few published accounts.

---

12 The newspaper article by Hlongwane listed as the claimants "Mzondeni Alfred Hlongwane of the amaNgwane tribe, S D Mngomezulu (Mngomezulu tribe), Mboneni Absolom Mavuso (amaNgwane tribe), Melizwe Zeluxolo Dlamini (Nhlangwini tribe), Mabhudu Israel Tembe (amaThonga tribe), Mbhekeni Shaclack Ndwandwe (amaNguni tribe), Michael Mfanafuthi Miya (amaZizi tribe), Dumisani Elias Msomi and Vusimuzi Andries Madlala," together with the leaders of the Nhlangwini and Hlubi.
13 www.cavershamcentre.org/newsletters/Hourglass_Jan09.pdf (Retrieved 14 July 2011).
14 See Wylie 2011; saheritagepublishers.co.za (Retrieved 28 October 2017).

There are many more indications that I could cite that show in a compelling way that, in its own right, the history of southern Africa in the many eras before European colonialism is a matter of widespread active public interest and concern that is only weakly served by scholarly research. There can be no doubt about its relevance to people all over southern Africa, and to their sense of place in, and understanding of, the world. There is also a further imperative in paying attention to the region's neglected long history, and what it can contribute to the imagining of new and different futures. Such imaginings are rendered urgent by the extent of present failures on so many fronts: politically, economically, socially and environmentally, locally and globally. Rooted in the nature of the current world order, the failed present is also shaped in powerful ways in this region by the legacies of European colonialism that so forcefully negated the region's deeper history. To make points of this kind about the relevance of the long past in the present and for the future is not to try to go back to atavistic forms of existence, or to haul past institutions and ways of doing things, insofar as we can recover them, into the present and to endorse them as tradition or as models. Rather it is to make them available as resources to fuel creative thinking about the future.

To unlock these resources is to ask and attempt to answer a wide range of questions about the past. What political, cosmological, ontological and epistemological ideas held sway before the establishment of European colonialism? What forms of past consciousness or past ideas of the common good might we find illuminating or inspiring today? What ideas of political contestation, of publicness, of social consensus, of mediating collective life, of accommodating incomers, of the balance between freedom and responsibility, of the relationship between knower and what is known, of what it is to be human, of relationships between humans and animals and the biosphere existed before the arrival of the first Europeans? How did ideas about legitimacy, illegitimacy, sovereignty, power, authority and classes of citizens, and indeed, subjects, play out in social and political life and how did they change across time, eventually to become what the ethnographers of the 1920s and 1930s wrote about, using a host of imported concepts to analyse them? In posing questions of this kind, the English language in which this essay is written inexorably roots concepts in Ancient Greek and Roman times. What versions, or alternatives, with different origins, prevailed in this region and how do the languages of this region attest to alternative intellectual roots? Language as an archive has scarcely been explored.

Such information about the past would resonate with its contemporary residues in the present. It would help to make sense of those residues. It would be likely to appeal to and gain purchase with those who are directly affected by such residues. It would have similar effects in public life more generally where those residues have a presence. Outside a small body of structuralist-orientated archaeology which draws heavily on 20th century ethnography and its key concepts, heavily invested in notions of culture rather than politics (discussed further below), there is almost nothing that speaks to a deep history of ideas, concepts and political discourses, traces of which are yet discernible, and operate with various forms of relevance, in the present. The task is to recover a neglected past and do so with methods, concepts and theories that are not trapped in European colonial legacies. The list of questions to be asked is inexhaustible, the scholarly challenge in responding to them immense.

Some of these issues and linked research questions framed in these terms are beginning to be raised and asked in the latest rounds of conferences and publications.[15] What is clear is that many of the older, more established methods of enquiry rooted in the small set of disciplines and well-worn methods that have long dominated the study of the remote past – archaeology, linguistics, anthropology and history – are often not conducive to questions posed in this way, and may need some rethinking to be able to contribute as fully as possible to the answers.

Periodisation

The readily-used term 'pre-colonial' requires rethinking. Not only is the term imperial in its imposition of a periodisation orientated around a later foreign domination, but it also entrenches a number of unsustainable assumptions. The first of these is that it collapses together the many eras and epochs that preceded European colonialism, thereby suggesting an unchanging past. Without the qualifier 'European', it forecloses on the possibility of other, earlier empires operating within the region. It further proposes the existence of a sharp break associated with the imposition of European colonialism, where in fact, historians know that many aspects of life in the late independent era prevailed, with some adaptations, long after the establishment of formal European overrule. Finally, and this is a point developed more fully below, it resists increasingly demanding conceptual and methodological imperatives to understand how enquiry into the many eras of the remote past is folded into, shaped by and giving shape to, the periods that follow them. Much of the methodological

---

[15] See Buthelezi (2016), as well as the conferences "Concepts from the Global South," Centre for Indian Studies, University of the Witwatersrand, October 2016; and "IziThunguthu: Southern African Pasts Before the Colonial Era, their Archives and their Ongoing Present/Presence," University of Cape Town, July 2015.

complexity that is involved in conducting research into periods before European colonialism follows from how that enfoldedness is understood and negotiated.

The academic discipline of archaeology offers a number of period-marking specialist terms of its own, based on technologies, such as Early and Late Stone Age, and Early and later Iron Age, which break up the uniform 'pre-colonial'. The discipline further makes use of terminology appropriated from linguistics and ethnography, sometimes combined with production descriptors, in order to name past populations, such as Khoi pastoralists and Bantu farmers (also Nguni and Sotho farmers, or increasingly, Bantu-speaking farmers). But these terms, while providing needed descriptive handles, present their own problems. Archaeologists, of course, do not have evidence of the names and terms used in the past; they deal in forms of material culture, and human, animal, and plant remains. The discipline's F practice, based as it is on borrowings from historical linguistics and on a form of analogical reasoning that makes use of 20th century ethnographic studies, assumes continuities in cultural practices and social arrangements across time. At best the naming practice is utilitarian. It is, however, quite obviously mired in the issues that flow from the enfoldedness of time referred to above and elucidated below. In addition, much of the nomenclature involved was given particular shape and meaning under segregation and apartheid in ways that make it unpalatable today, the term "Bantu" being a case in point as a central element in the apartheid government's vocabulary.[16]

Consigned out of history

The history of southern Africa, before the arrival of the first Europeans, was of considerable interest to early European travellers, chroniclers, colonial officials and missionaries, even though it received little substantial academic attention before the 1950s. In part, the lack of academic[17] research was a result of political pressures in the segregation and apartheid eras that played down African occupation of the region before the arrival of the first European settlers in favour of the idea that black farmers arrived south of the Limpopo at roughly the same time as the first white settlers established themselves in the Cape. It also followed from long-held stereotypes about most of the continent having no history worth discussing

---

[16] Nowhere is this more vividly expressed than in contemporary parody. See, for example, McKaiser (2012).

[17] While it is the purpose in this section of the chapter to discuss *academic* research, in a host of other forms in public life – plays, novels, clan-focused ancestral repertoires and much more – the history of the eras before European colonialism has been the object of ongoing attention, largely within counter public spheres of various kinds (see discussion of this in, for example, Peterson 2000; Hamilton, Mbenga & Ross 2010).

(Trevor-Roper 1969:6). At the root of these claims was the belief that there could be no history where there were no documents. If, however, in the time of segregation and apartheid Africans were understood to have no history to speak of, they were credited with customs and cultural traditions. For the most part these were deemed to be the subject of anthropology and ethnology, or ghettoised in Bantu Studies, and were regarded as largely unchanging across time.

We know from situations all around the world and across time that incoming powers put new interpretations of the past into place to justify their rule and to neutralise opposing historical claims. Incoming Europeans initially had little purchase on how local Africans thought about the region's past, though some officials, like Theophilus Shepstone and later James Stuart in Natal, attempted to harness historically-charged local ideas about sovereignty and authority, to their processes of rule (Hamilton 1998). Intimately tied up with ancestors and ancestral matters that the colonised viewed as vitally important arbiters of the present, it was a past that could not be easily forsworn by the indigenous population. Even the forms of Christianity that were imported into the area had to accommodate ancestral matters. So local understandings that proved resilient were either reinterpreted and harnessed in service of what became known as indirect rule, or were dealt with by being displaced out of politics. Pre-existing ideas, processes and practices that were repositioned could continue as a politically neutral custom and culture, rather than potent political history, becoming the domain of the ethnic subject as opposed to that of the political citizen (Mamdani 1996). Paradoxically, the elaborate sequestering out of time of a past that was, and had been for centuries, of consuming interest to the indigenous inhabitants of the region, was a form of recognition of political salience and of the need for it to be effectively bridled.

Large states and 'oral traditions'

The decolonisation of much of Africa in the 1950s and 1960s, however, generated active academic interest in that neglected past and resulted in studies like John Omer-Cooper's *The Zulu Aftermath* (Omer-Cooper 1978), which sought to celebrate the achievement of the early Zulu kingdom. Decolonisation also stimulated academic enquiry into the use of oral sources. Jan Vansina's *Oral Tradition: A Study in Historical Methodology* (first published in French in 1961, and in English in 1965), was the seminal publication in this area, and rapidly became something of a methodological handbook for a new generation of historians of the long African past. It established the existence of 'oral traditions' as potential sources and offered tools for their analysis.

Inspired by these developments and animated by the promising possibilities of the application of materialist analyses and Marxist theory [notably of the French Marxist anthropologists like Claude Meillassoux (1972) and Maurice Godelier (1977)] a generation of southern African scholars did intensive fieldwork recording oral traditions, and used them to write histories of a number of large states that flourished in the late independent era. In the early 1980s a series of monographs appeared, including Jeff Peires on the Xhosa kingdom (1982), Philip Bonner on the Swazi state (1983), and Peter Delius on the Pedi polity (1984). For the most part these studies set up the existence of independent states on the eve of European colonialism, usually in an introductory chapter or two, and then went on to document their loss of sovereignty.

This wave of scholarship mined transcribed, often translated, summaries of the newly recorded oral material for nuggets of fact, using the Vansina toolkit. Southern African historians also began to pay increasing attention to bodies of already recorded oral materials, like the substantial collection of interviews undertaken in the late 19th and early 20th century by the colonial official, James Stuart, and housed in the Killie Campbell African Library in Durban. In later years this kind of raiding of recorded texts for facts began to be challenged by scholars mostly located outside the discipline of history, drawing on ideas and concepts in performance studies and literary analysis (for example Hofmeyr 1993). My own work of the time (Hamilton 1987), itself influenced by literary theory, focussed on contradictions between accounts, seeing them not as the effects of faulty transmission and depredations over time (in the manner suggested by the Vansina approach) but as patterned indications of interventions in, and contestations over, understandings of the past.

In this period archaeologists employing radiocarbon dating decisively pushed the chronology of Iron-Age settlement back to the early centuries of the present era.[18] They began to pay increasing attention to sites occupied by what they described as Iron Age Bantu farmers, focussing in particular on settlement patterns and site layouts, ceramic classification and farming economies. This work made extensive use of analogies drawn from 20th century ethnographies for insight into past social

---

[18] See Norman Etherington's (2010) discussion of the legacy of the discredited short Iron Age, and his argument that the implications of the longer chronology for the rise of large states have yet to be fully explored.

and political relationships and cosmologies (Huffman 1986). Another source of evidence that increasingly caught the attention of academic researchers in the 1970s and early 1980s was that provided by the countless rock paintings and engravings, attributed to 'Bushmen'. The emergent field of rock art studies, positioned as a branch of cognitive archaeology, focused on what was understood to be discrete hunter-gatherer cosmology and initially remained separate from the domain of research into the history of the region. While early work by John Wright (1971) and Patricia Vinnicombe (1976) inaugurated a minority historical approach (Lewis-Williams 1982; Campbell 1986, 1987; Penn 1987), for the most part the often mixed nature of the groupings from whom the painters came and their interactions with settled farmers were neglected topics.

As the 1980s proceeded, the struggle against apartheid in South Africa escalated dramatically and many academic historians who had worked on the history of the loss of independence of the large states turned their attention to historical research with immediate relevance to the prevailing political turmoil and contestation, notably to 20th century labour, social and popular history. In the KZN area, however, the violent political struggle between the United Democratic Front/African National Congress and Inkatha was heavily inflected with claims about the historical existence of a unified Zulu nation. This was accompanied by the aggressive promotion of the figure of its founder, King Shaka, by Inkatha. In the face of the conservative Zulu nationalist organisation's attempts to assert a view of the long past that served their Bantustan-based political interests, historians like myself and John Wright (1989), as well as Mzala (1988) and others, were prompted to provide alternative readings of the history of the early Zulu state, and precursor formations in the region. This was a key reason why in the 1980s interest in what was at the time termed the 'pre-colonial' (and sometimes 'pre colonial' without the hyphen in an early attempt to signal dissatisfaction with the assumptions inherent in the term) was stronger in the KZN area than anywhere else in the country.

Research into the long history of the KZN region was further fuelled by the existence of the James Stuart collection. This collection exceeds in its extent and scope any other corpus of recorded oral materials, pertinent to the late independent periods, other than perhaps, the Bleek and Lloyd archive that focused on the IXam people who were historically resident in the central southern interior of the country. It was also, in part, a consequence of the inordinately high profile – for a multitude of reasons – of the figure of Shaka, both in South Africa and internationally (Hamilton et al. 1998).

Suspect sources, the production of European colonial knowledge and the colonisation of consciousness

In the 1990s scholars of the region began actively to read and make contributions to the growing field of post-colonial studies, paying attention to colonial modes of the drawing of difference, the creation of the inferior, exotic, colonial 'other', the colonisation of the consciousness involved in imperial domination and to the processes behind the establishment of colonial subjects as stable, knowable objects (Pratt 1992; Comaroff & Comaroff 1991; De Kock 1996).

A corollary of this was hesitancy amongst researchers concerning the use of colonial-era sources and suspicions about colonial recordings. In the late 1980s and the 1990s scholarly and public debates proliferated about the extent to which early texts by white writers were 'myths', 'fantasies' and 'tainted' sources. Scholars focussed critical attention on the particular forms of influence that colonial recorders exerted on the texts they recorded (Cobbing 1988; Hamilton 1998; Lalu 2009). For much of the 1990s and early 2000s historical research pertinent to the long past, outside archaeology, was concentrated on these kinds of questions. This resulted in detailed studies of many of the most used and significant sources. The accounts of early travellers, missionaries, reports of colonial officials, and the compilation work and collecting avocations of people like A.T. Bryant and Stuart were the subject of study in their own right (Wright 1989, 1991, 2012; Maclean 1992; Pridmore 1994; Hamilton 1998; Wylie 2000).

Increasingly scholars started to move beyond a relatively simple notion of myth-making and fantasies on the part of the European writers and to grapple with the complexity of the processes of the making of the sources. They began to pay close attention to the people from whom recorders like Stuart solicited information, and to what experiences and inheritances shaped their accounts (Hamilton 1998; Lekgoathi 2009; Wright 2011, 2015; Kriel 2016). They explored the various documented views of the past held, and actively promoted, by a large and diverse range of people of the region. In KZN these views range from those of the Zulu king Cetshwayo kaMpande recorded in 1881 (Webb & Wright 1976), through authors like Petros Lamula, who published *UZulukaMalandela: A Most Practical and Concise Compendium of African History* in 1924 (Lamula 1924; La Hausse 2001) and Magema Magwaza Fuze, who published *Abantu Abamnyama Lapa Bavela Ngakhona* in 1922 (Fuze 1922; Mokoena 2011), to Socwatsha kaPhaphu – in terms of quantity the most significant of James Stuart's interlocutors – recorded at various times between 1897 and 1922, and eventually published in a Reader produced by Stuart (Stuart 1925; Wright 2015). The majority of such men (and there were many of them), and the few women that researchers know about, were involved, in different ways, in the complex politics of their times. The giving of close attention to who they were, what they were doing, and why and how they concerned themselves with historical matters, allows us to grasp something of the intellectual and political manoeuvring, and the conceptual frameworks brought to bear in that manoeuvring, that was going on across KZN in the later 19th and early 20th centuries in response to rapidly changing local and international circumstances. Similar forms of attention are increasingly being paid elsewhere in the region to other political thinkers drawing on history in similar ways and under similar circumstances (Kriel 2016; Schoots 2014).

The making and shaping of the available archive across time

My *Terrific Majesty: the Powers of Shaka Zulu and the Limits of Invention* published in 1998, was one of the first attempts to grapple not only with specific sources, but with the larger forces and factors at work across time that made, shaped and reshaped what came to be the available wider archive, in this particular case, the archive of Shakan times. One aspect of the challenge, as I understood it, was not simply to grasp how a particular source was produced, but how across time some things, mostly documents, came to enjoy the status of archive, and benefit from an expensive apparatus of preservation, while others were repressed, or consigned to other domains such as ethnological records and ethnographic museums.[19]

Increasingly what seemed to me to be the particular archival challenges involved in the study of the remote past started to emerge as problems characteristic of *all* uses of archive, even those relevant to the recent past, but more obvious and more sharply etched in relation to the remote past. The notion of archive that generations of southern African students had been inducted into through the discipline of history became the object of my critical enquiry. In 1998 a group of scholars, radical archivists and artists collaborated in a seminar series and workshop programme that raised a wide variety of critical questions about the notion of archive. This resulted in the production of what is now recognised as something of a seminal text in what is termed "the archival turn", viz., *Refiguring the Archive* (Hamilton *et al.* 2002).

---

[19] A landmark study by Sekibakiba Lekgoathi picked up the issue of ethnological consignation and tackled the making of the vast archive of the government's Ethnological Bureau, brimming as it was with information, textual and photographic, about what were at the time termed 'tribes' and later 'ethnic' groups (Lekgoathi 2006).

The term refiguring had a number of valences. The archive, the book asserted, "– all archive – every archive is figured" (Hamilton et al. 2002:7). The book laid out the challenge involved in getting a grip on that figuring. In South Africa this involved investigation and understanding of how what was established as the available archive was shaped by apartheid, colonialism and even by configurations of power and structures of knowledge that existed before then. The book further suggested that much the same questions needed to be raised wherever the notion of archive was in play. Amongst other things, *Refiguring the Archive* drew attention to the way in which many (but of course, not all) archives are the products of state or institutional machineries, where the record was, and yet is, part of the bureaucratic apparatus, prompting approaches that enable, what anthropologist Ann Stoler already named back then in *Refiguring the Archive*, "reading along the archival grain" (Stoler 2002).

Geared to activities of understanding better and critiquing inherited archives, these kinds of approaches treated archives not simply as collections of *sources* for research, but also as *subjects* of critical enquiry in their own right. As a result, histories and ethnographies of archives began to examine how the inherited archives were made in the past, and how archive-making goes on in the present in countless settings within and outside the official public repositories, as well as what work archives do, and how archives were and are used (Stoler 2002; Ruther 2012; Hamilton 2013; McNulty 2013; Weintroub 2013; Greenwood 2013; Byala 2013; Molins Lliteras 2013; Twidle 2013). Much of this critical work on archive/s is inherently interdisciplinary, with key insights being contributed from outside archive's traditional lair in the discipline of history. While many historians abandoned attempts to write about the periods before colonialism, those who did pay attention to the remote past proceeded by devoting this kind of attention to the available archive.

Structuralist archaeologists initially proved immune to the effects of this interrogation of archive and continued to use early 20th century ethnographies and ideas of stable cultural groups relatively uncritically to interpret their findings concerning much earlier periods. They forged ahead, producing confident typologies, Tom Huffman's 2007 *A Handbook to the Iron Age: The Archaeology of Pre-Colonial Farming Societies in Southern Africa*, being a case in point. In rock art research, however, historically-minded scholars were making extensive use of archival sources, notably the Bleek and Lloyd archive, but also elsewhere, with some of the most novel work paying attention to the interactions between groups of people on the margins of the large states of the late independent period (Blundell 2004; Challis 2012).

In recent years the development of a handful of collaborations between historians and archaeologists across the country has marked a movement away from the resolutely structuralist approach mentioned above (Swanepoel, Esterhuysen & Bonner 2008; Delius & Marks 2012). In some cases this movement still sees the mining of what are regarded as the 'oral traditions' (see, for example, Bonner in Swanepoel *et al.* 2008). It remains the exception rather than the rule that scholars give close attention to the making and reshaping of these materials over time. Many continue to work with translations in English rather than using original vernacular materials where they are available, thereby missing, amongst other things, the immense history of concepts that opens up when language itself is treated as an archive.[20] In particular, the mining approach fails to take advantage of what we might think of as the 'Rosetta stone' archives.

The 'Rosetta stone' analogy points to the capacity of a small number of key archives to enable the interpretation of other texts and sources. It is a capacity derived from the combination in these particular archives of discursive extensiveness, vernacular content, attempts by the respective recorders to capture the words of their interlocutors, variant narratives on a single topic provided by multiple speakers, variant narratives on a single topic given over time by a single speaker, and their contemporary accessibility.

The James Stuart collection is one of these archives.[21] It comprises more than 100 notebooks and numerous loose sheets of papers, on which Stuart recorded his discussions with over 200 different people, mostly Africans, whom he regarded as well informed on the history and affairs of the region that is today KZN and neighbouring Swaziland. The notes were meticulously dated, the circumstances of the conversations were often recorded, his interlocutors were named and numerous details of their ages, statuses and affiliations noted. Large swathes of

---

[20] Where vernacular concepts are deployed this typically involves the use of such concepts as documented and interpreted by 20th century ethnographers. In some cases the extrapolations are illuminating, but methodological reservations remain that can be cleared up through explicit investigation of the history of the concepts. See, for example the work of Gavin Whitelaw (2016).

[21] The already mentioned Bleek and Lloyd archive is another 'Rosetta Stone' archive, comprising some forty-five thousand pages of notes, over 1000 drawings, maps, photographs and genealogies and tens of thousands of dictionary slips elucidating words. Much of the recorded material follows as closely as the recorders could manage, the original words of the speakers. The collection, scattered across a number of institutions, is now available in a digitised form online. The page calculation takes note of the cited figure of ± 13 000 numbered pages (see Skotnes 2007:42) but factors in an estimation of unnumbered facing pages. I am grateful to Pippa Skotnes for her assistance with this. This was first argued in my early work on ideology in the Shakan kingdom (Hamilton 1985), developed further in relation to questions of the nature of rulership and sovereignty in *Terrific Majesty* (1998), then tellingly conceptualised as a form of political theorising in Landau (2012), and built on by Hamilton and Wright (2017).

the notes were recorded in isiZulu, much seemingly verbatim, with peculiarities of expression or dialect often discussed directly with the speakers. Some of the topics covered were obviously introduced by Stuart, others by the speakers. There is now a fairly substantial body of scholarship that deals in detail with the respective extents to which these texts were shaped by Stuart and by his interlocutors. While there is debate on these matters, it is clear that these notes are quite different from Stuart's own writings on many of the same topics, and in numerous respects are characterised by the use of concepts and rhetorical forms that were not Stuart's. Many of these concepts and rhetorical forms depend for elucidation on the wider context in the first instance of the full account given by the speaker, and in the second instance, of the entire corpus. Scholars using this corpus can trace the use of concepts by different speakers across many hundreds of pages, thereby managing to explore their meaning to an unusually extended degree. The editing, annotation and publication with an index of a large part of this corpus, has meant that researchers can do this with relative efficiency. When fully contextualised and interpreted in relation to the wider corpus, a factual nugget extracted from it often fails to bear up as the fact that it purports to be but yields rich returns when treated as an element of discourse. More and more the Stuart collection, handled with increasingly sophisticated methodological care, enables the interpretation or reinterpretation of forms of evidence found in other settings often more firmly tangled up in a European colonial conceptual apparatus.

Acknowledging forms of political discourse and political theorising

One of the spin-offs from working with an extensive corpus like the Stuart collection has been the way in which it has enabled scholars to lift their heads out of the detail of a story of origins, a particular migration or a conquest – three dominant story lines – to discern across those narratives the lineaments of past modes of political discourse and forms of political theorising, the very politics that the categorisation of these materials as custom and culture worked to obfuscate.[22] In particular the research breakthroughs that have happened have been concerned with how understandings of the past were mobilised in relation to political changes in the late independent period, and earlier. The primary challenge here has been how, methodologically, to

---

[22] This was first argued in my early work on ideology in the Shakan kingdom (Hamilton 1985), developed further in relation to questions of the nature of rulership and sovereignty in *Terrific Majesty* (1998), then tellingly conceptualised as a form of political theorising in Landau (2012), and built on by Hamilton and Wright (2017).

recognise aspects of this mobilisation pertinent to political changes at the time of the recorded conversation (at various points between 1897 and 1922) – the *context* of the conversation – as well as what might be relevant to political changes in earlier eras like the Shakan period, which might have been the *subject* of the conversations recorded around 1900 (Hamilton 1998:55-69).

Signs of indigenous political discourses and political theorising are also to be found in the archive that language and names constitute. In this area, the work of Paul Landau on the chiefdoms of the southern Highveld has been insightful in revealing the existence of the kinds of political consciousness and organisation that preceded European colonialism. Giving attention to brotherhoods, rankings and amalgamations, as evidenced very often in language forms, his argument is that in place of the received notion of fixed tribal identities, or discrete ethnicities, we need to see hybridity as lying at the core of a flexible long standing sub-continental political tradition that was geared towards the accommodation of strangers (Landau 2012).

More recently the project on *Tribing and Untribing the Archive* examines closely *how* the idea of tribe came to be imported into Natal in the 19th century (Hamilton & Leibhammer 2016). It looks at how European concepts were mapped onto indigenous ideas in a manner that shaped what was laid down as knowledge of the region's inhabitants, notably as timeless tribal people, in ways that we yet struggle to free ourselves from. Unpacking the legacies of the European colonial conceptual apparatus requires both close historicisation and comparative perspectives from across and beyond the continent (for example, Etherington 2011) that are attentive to the cross-genealogies of the tribal and the modern. This underpins growing critical interrogation of the clutch of inherited concepts like tribe, ethnicity, kinship and tradition that have long been the staples of the study of this time and of the idea that anthropology, linguistics and archaeology are the appropriate specialist disciplines for their study. Increasingly concepts from intellectual history, literary theory, gender studies, cultural studies and other disciplines that are more usually concerned with European metropoles and later periods are being used to ask new questions and gain new perspectives on the remote past, with great purchase.

Tribing and Untribing the Archive took as its central focus the challenges of using evidence in the form of collected material culture, found mostly in ethnographic museums and art galleries. The publication traced how this material came to be marooned in the collecting institutions, often mislabelled, divested of details of provenance and dates of production, in effect doomed to attest to timeless forms of cultural identity. The essays in the publication undertake the kind of research necessary to rehabilitate these materials as historical sources.

There now exists a small, highly specialised subfield concerned with the making and shaping over time of the available sources, carefully situated in changing political and intellectual contexts, and concerned as well with what has been repressed, occluded or consigned elsewhere in the making of that archive. At the same time, the critical work on archive has opened the remote past to new forms of theoretical and conceptual thinking. This, I have argued, allows researchers to go beyond ideas of bias in any collection or archive to recognise how public, political and academic discourses and practices constitute archives, and how in turn archives change those discourses and practices, each shaping and reshaping each other over time in a mutually constituting spiral (Hamilton 2015).

Traces in social practice

Traces of the past that persist over time in social life, subject both to continuity and change in the process, are significantly less theorised as historical sources than colonial records or recorded oral accounts. Such traces are readily described as 'tradition', and are understood to be the doing of things in the present in the ways that they have always, or long, been done. Social practices of all kinds are typically flexible and often what goes as immutable is paradoxically precisely where change takes place, such that some things change, while others hold their ground. The challenge for historians seeking to use traces in a contemporary practice, whether residual or substantial, or as recorded in an ethnography at a particular time, as sources about the distant past is to understand the concept of repertoire at work; the history and conventions of the practice itself, as well as of any form of recording of such a practice; the forces that have changed either the practice or the recording over time; and the factors that might have allowed some elements to continue across time in reasonably intact forms of practice; and finally, what 'reasonably' might mean in a particular case.[23]

---

[23] See, for example, Buthelezi's account of the survival over time of attenuated Ndwandwe historical discourse in Ndwandwe rituals (2012) and my discussion of the custodial imperatives at work in ancestor rituals (Hamilton 2015).

Enfolded time and contiguous space

Developments of these kinds in research using established archives and traces in social practices have prompted me to think in new ways about the contingency of time. Elsewhere I have argued that this involves understanding that past events that are objects of inquiry or reference are perceptible in the present only because of a history across time, and because particular knowledge production processes have brought them into view in a particular way. Materials invoked in contemporary practices that reference the remote past and the documentary sources that researchers might locate in archival folders, are not survivals of past times in the present, but travellers across time that have changed shape and accrued new meanings through time. Such travellers, I argue, were not merely affected by their contexts, but also affected them in turn.[24] The past that is the object of interest is thus not firmly in a place distinct from the present time of enquiry. Rather, both are folded into each other and into what lies in between, and, indeed, into the way in which a hoped for future influences how we handle traces of the past and 'sources' in the present. To engage the materials that attest to the past in order to think about the past is to explore this enfoldedness. It requires an approach that tacks backwards and forwards across time, paying attention to the double-storiedness both of events in the past and of the traces of them in the present. It is a double-storiedness that involves thinking simultaneously about the story of the making of the trace over time, and the making (of the story) of the past to which the trace refers, also often a matter extended across time and itself involving change (Hamilton 2015).

The European notion of archive that took hold in the course of the 19th century resists this sense of enfoldedness by establishing archival items as embalmed material, usually documents, produced at a particular point in time – ideally the time to which they offer archival testimony – and then preserved to arrive in the present in forms as close as possible to their originary ones. It was this notion of archive, as a product of colonial bureaucracy, that was exported to colonies like those in southern Africa. In relation to this notion of archive, so-called traditions, notably oral traditions, but also traditional practices, are regarded as degraded or less satisfactory testatory forms because they are manifestly affected by the periods between their originary moments and the time of their 'capture' through some form of recording. In turn,

---

[24] The idea that archival documents change once they have been placed in a repository is, of course, not an unfamiliar idea to scholars of Europe in Ancient and Medieval times. Indeed, such changes in documents relevant to those periods are the subject of extensive research. The idea of a more unadulterated and stable archive is a legacy of 19th century developments in European government archives, a Rankean approach to history and the export to European colonies of a resultant notion of archives as immutable and reliable records.

this epistemological doubt is all too often countered through assertions of the purity of traditions as unsullied by time.

There are (at least) two problems with ideas that counterpose embalmed archival documents and malleable oral traditions. The first is that under close scrutiny the archival item almost always turns out to have shaped, and been shaped by, the intervening periods, itself then being an item enfolded in time, rather than cutting through it. The second problem is that so-called traditions are often less victims of time than the dominant European epistemological view would have it, being under ongoing pressures across time to preserve their integrity even as they enter time's folds. Pressures understood to be exerted by ancestors are one of the factors that limit the changes that take place. Plausibility is another (Hamilton 1987,2015). Such materials are nonetheless seldom as innocent of time's enfoldings as the champions of purity would have it, often shaping and being shaped by the intervening periods as surely as the archival item. If an Enlightenment notion of time is strictly linear, seeing the present as the product of the past, a sense of time as enfolded understands that the past is equally the product of the present and of all the time between.

Similarly the position of southern Africa in world history requires consideration independent of the dominant axis of European discovery. The out-of-timeness of southern Africa before European colonialism has long been understood to be an effect of its remoteness from Europe. In the 21st century many other former colonies have revised their European designated remoteness through recognising their historical situatedness, and centredness, in other axes of trade, travel and connectedness, such as that of trans-Saharan routes, the Silk Road or exchanges across the Indian Ocean. In relation to these increasingly prominent networks of interaction, southern Africa remains a persistently distant edge. While much is written about trade routes, centres and nexuses, outer margins are seldom theorised as being nonetheless vital, fully relational parts of the larger whole. To be such a margin is not to be insulated and out of the flow of ideas, people, goods and technologies but to be in a particular place with particular dynamics, themselves influenced inevitably by events in other places. The challenge then is to place southern Africa at any point in time firmly in world history and geography, connected to the world if not, or only occasionally, by grand arteries, then by vital capillaries, as well as osmotically by small connections amongst ever contiguous neighbours.

Landscape is able to tell us much about the long past. It has been a kind of source that has been left mostly to archaeologists to explore. But fresh opportunities abound outside archaeology for the exploration of spatial concepts, carefully historicised, as expressed in local languages, and as anchoring narratives, and as fundamental to expressive forms like *izithakazelo*.

All of this makes it clear that we are now surely beyond the limited temporality of European colonial history, the architecture of anthropological time that Johannes Fabian critiqued so powerfully in 1983, and the sweeping arrowed black lines of archaeologically-discerned population movement and European 'discoveries'.

Conclusion

There is today a clear recognition that the long southern African past cannot be only an introductory chapter to European colonialism, nor can it be confined to being the subject of archaeology. The teleological terms 'prehistory' (not much used today) and 'pre-colonial' (fairly persistent), unpalatable archaeological periodisations and linguistic categories, and the lingering effects of disciplinary specialisations for tribal pasts – all of these are ripe for critical engagement. The taking of a long view of history seeks to subvert persistent habits of treating the past before European colonialism as another country, and the advent of that colonialism as the effective starting point of the region's history, with only a passing nod to, or introductory chapter on, what went before. What happens when histories of ideas, modes of thought, institutions and practices, and the changes which they have undergone, are traced across the early state, late independent, early European colonial, apartheid, and even post-apartheid eras, is a pressing question. Even this latter, provisional, periodisation would itself be open to debate and question. The taking of a long view is an opportunity full of possibilities for breaking out of congealed epistemic coloniality.

To my mind the critical work on archive has become a key activity in effecting an epistemic shift in enquiry into the long history of southern Africa. It is fundamental in preparing the ground to meet the challenges of transformation, as articulated in, for example, the demands for curriculum changes and 'more pre-colonial history'. The point is succinctly made by Njabulo Ndebele in recent years: "There can be no transformation of the curriculum, or indeed of knowledge itself, without an interrogation of archive."[25]

---

[25] See http://www.apc.uct.ac.za (Retrieved 31 August 2017).

Acknowledgements

A version of this chapter was first produced in 2014 for the conference "20 Years of South African Democracy: South Africa and the Social Sciences" (hosted by the French Institute and Wiser, University of the Witwatersrand). In the intervening period I have delivered a number of versions of this, most latterly in 2017 to the Second Pre-Colonial Catalytic Conference. In different contexts different aspects of the chapter have given rise to productive discussions. I have benefited from the comments on the chapter made at various times by my associates in the Archive and Public Culture Research Initiative, readers at the conferences and the reviewers. I am grateful to the editors of the two conference volumes for permission to allow the chapter to appear in both publications.

References

Blundell, G. 2004. *Nqabayo's Nomansland: San Rock Art and the Somatic Past*. Uppsala: African and Comparative Archaeology, Dept. of Archaeology and Ancient History. Uppsala University; Johannesburg: Rock Art Research Institute, School of Geography, Archaeology and Environmental Science, University of the Witwatersrand.

Bonner, P. 2008. Swazi Oral Tradition and Northern Nguni Historical Archaeology. In: *Five Hundred Years Rediscovered: Southern African Precedents and Prospects* by N. Swanepoel, A. Esterhuysen & P. Bonner (eds.). 239-255. Johannesburg: Wits University Press.

Bonner, P. 1983. *Kings, commoners, and concessionaries: the evolution and dissolution of the nineteenth-century Swazi state*. Cambridge: Cambridge University Press. https://doi.org/10.1017/CBO9780511563027

Bryant, A.T. 1929. *Olden Times in Natal and Zululand*. London: Longmans.

Buthelezi, M. 2016. Epilogue: We need new names too. In: *Tribing and Untribing the Archive*. Vol. 2 by C. Hamilton & N. Leibhammer, 584-600. Scotsville: University of KwaZulu-Natal Press.

Buthelezi, M. 2012. *Sifuna umlando wethu (We are Searching for Our History): Oral Literature and the Meanings of the Past in Post-apartheid South Africa*. PhD dissertation. New York: Columbia University.

Byala, S. 2013. Museum Africa: Colonial Past, Post-colonial Present. *South African Historical Journal*, 65 (1): 90-104. https://doi.org/10.1080/02582473.2013.768365

Campbell, C. 1987. Contact period Rock Art of the South-eastern Mountains. MSc thesis. Johannesburg: University of the Witwatersrand.

Campbell, C. 1986. Images of War. *World Archaeology*, 18 (2): 255-68. https://doi.org/10.1080/00438243.1986.9980002

Challis, S. 2012. Creolisation on the nineteenth-century frontiers of southern Africa: a case study of the AmaTola 'Bushmen' in the Maloti-Drakensberg. *Journal of Southern African Studies*, 38 (2): 265-280. https://doi.org/10.1080/03057070.2012.666905

Cobbing, J. 1988. A Tainted Well. The Objectives, Historical Fantasies and Working Methods of James Stuart. *Journal of Natal and Zulu History*, 11: 115-154.

Comaroff, J. & Comaroff, J.L. 1991. *Of revelation and revolution: Christianity, colonialism, and consciousness in South Africa. Vol 1.* Chicago: University of Chicago Press. https://doi.org/10.7208/chicago/9780226114477.001.0001

De Kock, L. 1996. *Civilising barbarians: missionary narrative and African textual response in nineteenth-century South Africa.* PhD dissertation. Pretoria: University of South Africa.

Delius, P. 1984. *The land belongs to us: the Pedi polity, the Boers, and the British in the nineteenth-century Transvaal.* Berkeley: University of California Press.

Delius, P. & Marks, S. 2012. Rethinking South Africa's Past: Essays on History and Archaeology. *Journal of Southern African Studies*, 38 (2): 247-255. https://doi.org/10.1080/03057070.2012.683310

Etherington, N. 2011. Barbarians Ancient and Modern. *American Historical Review*, 116 (1): 31-57. https://doi.org/10.1086/ahr.116.1.31

Etherington, N. 2010. Historians, Archaeologists and the Legacy of the Discredited Short Iron-Age Chronology. *African Studies*, 69 (2): 361-375. https://doi.org/10.1080/00020184.2010.499206

Fuze, M.M. 1922. *Abantu abamnyama: lapa bavela ngakona.* Pietermaritzburg: City Printing Works.

Godelier, M. 1977. *Perspectives in Marxist anthropology.* Cambridge: Cambridge University Press.

Greenwood, M. 2013. Watchful Witness: St George's Cathedral and the Crypt Memory and Witness Centre. *South African Historical Journal*, 65 (1): 23-43. https://doi.org/10.1080/02582473.2013.768366

Hamilton, C. 2015. Archives, Ancestors and the Contingencies of Time. In: *Laute, Bilder, Texte* by A. Lüdtke and T. Nanz (eds.), 103-118. Göttingen: V & R Unipress.

Hamilton, C. 2013. Forged and Continually Refashioned in the Crucible of Ongoing Social and Political Life: Archives and Custodial Practices as Subjects of Enquiry. *South African Historical Journal*, 65 (1): 1-22. https://doi.org/10.1080/02582473.2013.763400

Hamilton, C. 1998. *Terrific Majesty: the powers of Shaka Zulu and limits of historical invention.* Cambridge MA: Harvard University Press.

Hamilton, C. 1987. Ideology and Oral Traditions: Listening to the Voices from Below. *History in Africa*, 14: 67-86. https://doi.org/10.2307/3171833

Hamilton, C. 1985. *Ideology, Oral Tradition and the Struggle for Power in the Early Zulu Kingdom.* Master's thesis. University of the Witwatersrand.

Hamilton, C.; Harris, V.; Pickover, M.; Reid, G.; Saleh, R. & Taylor, J. (eds.). 2002. *Refiguring the Archive.* Cape Town: David Philip. https://doi.org/10.1007/978-94-010-0570-8

Hamilton, C. & Leibhammer, N. (eds.). 2016. *Tribing and Untribing the Archive: Identity and the Material Record in Southern KwaZulu-Natal in the Late Independent and Colonial Periods* Vol. 2 Scotsville: University of KwaZulu-Natal.

Hamilton, C. & Wright, J. 2017. Moving Beyond Ethnic Framing: Political Differentiation in the Chiefdoms of the KwaZulu-Natal Region before 1830. *Journal of Southern African Studies*, 43 (4): 663-679. https://doi.org/10.1080/03057070.2017.1323539

Hamilton, C.; Mbenga, B. & Ross, R. (eds.). 2010. *The Cambridge history of South Africa* (Vol. 1). Cambridge: Cambridge University Press.

Hlongwane, A. 2007. *Twelve kings saga sparks KZN war talk.* https://www.iol.co.za/news/politics/twelve-kings-saga-sparks-kzn-war-talk-361027 [Retrieved 14 July 2011].

Hofmeyr, I. 1993. *We Spend Our Years as a Tale that is Told: Oral Historical Narrative in a South African Chiefdom*. Johannesburg: Wits University Press.

Huffman, T. 2007. *A Handbook to the Iron Age. The Archaeology of Pre-Colonial Farming Societies in Southern Africa*. Scotsville: University of KwaZulu-Natal Press.

Huffman, T. 1986. Cognitive studies in the Iron Age in southern Africa. *World Archaeology*, 18. 84-95. https://doi.org/10.1080/00438243.1986.9979990

Karim, A. 2015. Curriculum Transformation. *Varsity*, 12 May. https://issuu.com/varsitynewspaper/docs/2015_edition_6 [Retrieved 31 October 2017].

Kriel, L. 2016. Open-Access Memory? African Interlocutors' Reflective Nostalgia for a Pre-colonial Past as Digitised in the Hoffmann Collection of Cultural Knowledge. In: *Sources and Methods for African History and Culture: Essays in Honour of Adam Jones*. G. Castryck, S. Strickrodt & K. Werthmann (eds.). 275-290. Leipzig: Leipziger Universitätsverlag.

La Hausse de la Louvière, P. 2001. *Restless Identities: Signatures of Nationalism, Zulu Ethnicity and History in the Lives of Petros Lamula (c.1881-1948) and Lymon Maling (1889-c.1936)*. Scotsville: University of KwaZulu-Natal Press.

Lalu, P. 2009. *The Deaths of Hintsa: Postapartheid South Africa and the Shape of Recurring Pasts*. Cape Town: HSRC Press.

Lamula, P. 1924. *UZulukaMalandela: A Most Practical and Concise Compendium of African History*. Durban: Star Printing Works.

Landau, P. 2012. *Popular Politics in the History of South Africa, 1400-1948*. Cambridge: Cambridge University Press.

Lekgoathi, S.P. 2009. 'Colonial' Experts, Local Interlocutors, Informants and the Making of an Archive on the 'Transvaal Ndebele', 1930-1989. *The Journal of African History*, 50 (1): 61-80. https://doi.org/10.1017/S0021853708003976

Lekgoathi, S.P. 2006. *Ethnicity and identity: struggle and contestation in the making of the northern Transvaal Ndebele, ca. 1860-2005*. PhD dissertation. Minneapolis: University of Minnesota.

Lewis-Williams, D. 1982. The economic and social context of southern San rock art. *Current Anthropology*, 23 (4): 429-449. https://doi.org/10.1086/202871

Maclean, C.R. 1992. *The Natal Papers of 'John Ross': Loss of the Brig Mary at Natal with early recollections of that settlement and among the Caffres by S. Grey*. Durban: Killie Campbell Africana Library and Pietermaritzburg: University of Natal Press.

Mamdani, M. 1996. *Citizen and subject: contemporary Africa and the legacy of late colonialism*. Princeton: Princeton University Press.

McKaiser, E. 2012. *A Bantu in my bathroom!: debating race, sexuality and other uncomfortable South African topics*. Johannesburg: Bookstorm.

McNulty, G. 2014. *Custodianship on the Periphery: Archives, Power and Identity Politics in Post-Apartheid Umbumbulu, KwaZulu-Natal*. PhD dissertation. Cape Town: University of Cape Town.

McNulty, G. 2013. Archival Aspirations and Anxieties: Contemporary Preservation and Production of the Past in Umbumbulu, KwaZulu-Natal. *South African Historical Journal*, 65 (1): 44-69. https://doi.org/10.1080/02582473.2012.729602

Mdanda, S. 2015. *Freedom Park film 'Coloniser/Colonised'*. Presentation at the conference Archival Addresses: Photographies, Practices, Positionalities. VIADUCT: University of Johannesburg.

Meillassoux, C. 1972. From reproduction to production. *Economy and Society*, 1 (1): 93-105. https://doi.org/10.1080/03085147200000005

Mkhize, S. 2007. *Uhlanga Lwas'Embo: The History of the Embo People*. Durban: Just Done Productions.

Mokoena, H. 2011. *Magema Fuze: The Making of a Kholwa Intellectual*. Scotsville: University of KwaZulu-Natal Press.

Molins Lliteras, S. 2013. From Toledo to Timbuktu: The Case for a Biography of the Ka'ti archive, and its Sources. *South African Historical Journal*, 65 (1): 105-124. https://doi.org/10.1080/02582473.2013.763402

National Research Foundation. 2015. Indigenous Knowledge Systems KFD Framework Document. *IKS Guide 2015 – National Research Foundation*. www.nrf.ac.za/sites/default/files/documents/IKS%20Guide%202015.pdf [Retrieved 31 August 2017].

Ntombela, N. 2016. Shifting Contexts: Material, Process and contemporary Art. In: *Tribing and Untribing the Archive: Identity and the Material Record in Southern KwaZulu-Natal in the Late Independent and Colonial Periods*, 1. C. Hamilton & N. Leibhammer (eds.), 87-115. Scotsville: University of KwaZulu-Natal Press.

Ntsebeza, L. & Saunders, C. (eds.). 2014. *Papers from the Pre-Colonial Catalytic Project* Vol. 1. Cape Town: Centre for African Studies.

Nxumalo, J. 1988. *Gatsha Buthelezi: chief with a double agenda*. London: Zed Books.

Omer-Cooper, J. 1978. *The Zulu aftermath: a nineteenth-century revolution in Bantu African*. London: Longmans.

Peires, J. 1982. *The house of Phalo: a history of the Xhosa people in the days of their independence*. Berkeley: University of California Press.

Penn, N. 1987. The Frontier in the Western Cape, 1700-1740. In: Papers on the Prehistory of the Western Cape. J. Parkington & M. Hall (eds.). Oxford: *British Archaeological Reports International Series*, 332: 462-503.

Peterson, B. 2000. *Monarchs, Missionaries and African Intellectuals: African Theatre and the Unmaking of Colonial Marginality*. Johannesburg: Witwatersrand University Press.

Pratt, M.L. 1992. *Imperial eyes: travel writing and transculturation*. London: Routledge. https://doi.org/10.4324/9780203163672

Pridmore, J. 1994. The Writings of H.F. Fynn: History, Myth or Fiction? *Alternation*, 1(1):68-78.

Ruther, K. 2012 Through the Eyes of Missionaries and the Archives They Created: The Interwoven Histories of Power and Authority in the Nineteenth-century Transvaal. *Journal of Southern African Studies*, 38(2):369-384. https://doi.org/10.1080/03057070.2012.682840

Schoots, L.J. 2014. *The Sociological Imagination of S.E.K. Mqhayi: Towards an African Sociology*. Minor M.A. thesis. Cape Town: University of Cape Town.

Skotnes, P. 2007. *Claim to the Country: The Archive of Lucy Lloyd and Wilhelm Bleek*. Athens: Ohio University Press.

Stoler, A.L. 2002. Colonial Archives and the Arts of Governance: On the Content in the Form. In: *Refiguring the Archive*, C Hamilton, V. Harris, M. Pickover, G. Reid, R. Saleh & J. Taylor, (eds.) 83–103. Cape Town: David Philip. https://doi.org/10.1007/978-94-010-0570-8_7

Stuart, J. 1925. *UKulumetule*. London: Longmans, Green.

Swanepoel, N.; Esterhuysen, A. & Bonner, P. (eds.). 2008. *Five Hundred Years Rediscovered: Southern African Precedents and Prospects*. Johannesburg: Wits University Press.

Trevor-Roper, H. 1969. The past and the present. History and sociology. *Past & Present,* 42 (1): 3-17. https://doi.org/10.1093/past/42.1.3

Twidle, H. 2013. Writing the Company: From VOC *Daghregister* to Sleigh's *Eilande. South African Historical Journal,* 65 (1): 125-152. https://doi.org/10.1080/02582473.2013.763399

Vansina, J. 1965. *Oral tradition; a study in historical methodology.* London: Routledge.

Vinnicombe, P. 1976. *People of the Eland: Rock Paintings of the Drakensberg Bushmen as a Reflection of their Life and Thought.* Pietermaritzburg: University of Natal Press.

Webb, C.de B. & Wright, J.B. 1976-2014. *The James Stuart archive of recorded oral evidence relating to the history of the Zulu and neighbouring peoples.* Scotsville: University of KwaZulu-Natal Press.

Webb, C.de B. & Wright, J.B. (eds.). 1976. *A Zulu King Speaks: Statements Made by Cetshwayo kaMpande on the History and Customs of his People.* Pietermaritzburg: University of Natal Press; Durban: Killie Campbell Africana Library.

Weintroub, J. 2013. On Biography and Archive: Dorothea Bleek and the Making of the Bleek Collection. *South African Historical Journal,* 65 (1): 70-89. https://doi.org/10.1080/02582473.2013.763401

Whitelaw, G. 2016. *Economy and cosmology in the Iron Age of KwaZulu-Natal.* PhD dissertation. Johannesburg: University of the Witwatersrand.

Wright, J.B. 2015. Socwatsha kaPhaphu, James Stuart, and Their Conversations on the Past, 1897-1922. *Kronos,* 41 (1): 142-165.

Wright, J.B. 2012. A.T. Bryant and the 'Lala'. *Journal of Southern African Studies,* 38: 355-368. https://doi.org/10.1080/03057070.2012.682838

Wright, J.B. 2011. Ndukwana kaMbengwana as an interlocutor on the history of the Zulu kingdom, 1897-1903. *History in Africa,* 38: 343-368. https://doi.org/10.1353/hia.2011.0018

Wright, J.B. 1991. A.T. Bryant and 'the wars of Shaka'. *History in Africa,* 18: 409-425. https://doi.org/10.2307/3172075

Wright, J.B. 1989. Political mythology and the making of Natal's mfecane. *Canadian Journal of African Studies,* 23: 272-291. https://doi.org/10.2307/485525

Wright, J.B. 1971 *Bushman Raiders of the Drakensberg 1840-1870.* Pietermaritzburg: University of Natal Press.

Wylie, D. 2011. *Shaka: A Pocket Biography.* Johannesburg: Jacana.

Wylie, D. 2000. *Savage Delights: White Myths of Shaka.* Pietermaritzburg: University of Natal Press.

SECTION II
THE CHALLENGES OF PRAXIS

CHAPTER 7

The study of earlier African societies before colonial contact in the former Xhalanga magisterial district, Eastern Cape

A case study of three villages in the district

Fani Ncapayi[1] & Mlingani Mayongo[2]

Background and introduction

This case study investigates the lives and living conditions of people in early African societies before colonial contact in the former Xhalanga magisterial district. This is deliberately designed to be a case study from which to gain in-depth knowledge about the living conditions of residents before colonial contact. As Sarantokos (1998:191) puts it, a case study "involves studying individual cases, often in their natural environment...". Case studies "are specific explorations" of a variety of situations, including individuals and communities (Lunenburg & Irby 2008:96). In a case study, "researchers seek out both what is common and what is particular about the case, but the end result regularly presents something unique" (Stake 1994:238). Specifically, the aim is to understand how early African people in three rural communities (Cala Reserve, Mnxe and Tsengiwe)

---

1   f.ncapayi@gmail.com
2   yongos@gmail.com

lived. The chapter does this by tracing the first families in each of the three villages, focusing on origins of the families, the reasons for them coming to the three villages and how the families lived.

The research is conducted under the auspices of the Centre for African Studies (CAS), at the University of Cape Town (UCT), in partnership with the Cala University Students Association (CALUSA).[3] The research is part of a bigger project called "The Pre-Colonial Catalytic Project", which CAS co-ordinates on behalf of other academic institutions such as the "Universities of Cape Town, KwaZulu-Natal, Witwatersrand and Fort Hare, as well as the Director of the South African Democracy Education Trust (SADET), based in Pretoria" (Ntsebeza & Saunders 2014:i).

This chapter is structured as follows: the next section discusses the methodology and research processes. It discusses the research methods employed in the study. The section is followed by a section on data analysis and discussion thereof. The last section constitutes the concluding remarks as well as highlights aspects that need further research.

Methodology and the research process

There are three important points that have to be made about the research and methodology chosen for it. Firstly, the research is undertaken in a context of palpable inter-generational tensions in the communities CALUSA works with, including the three communities. A workshop held in December 2014, where parents sharply expressed their disapproval of the youth's behaviour, highlighted the tensions. It became clear that something had to be done about this state of affairs. The involvement of youth in the research project became CALUSA's strategy of dealing with the tensions. The youth's involvement in the research would lead to closer interaction between them and elderly people. Thus, the involvement of the youth in the research is both a methodological consideration and strategic move to address the identified social problem.

Secondly, CAS and CALUSA decided from the onset to give prominence to oral evidence than to archival records. Since the aim of the study has been to record

---

[3] CALUSA is a non-governmental organisation that is based in Cala with programmes that focus on land access and use; rural governance and youth development. The organisation was established in 1983 by activists, who wanted to contribute in the development of education in the former Xhalanga magisterial district, after their release from prison in 1981. Lungisile Ntsebeza is the only founder member that is active in activities of the organisation.

the history of the communities from the people's point of view, the use of archival sources thus became secondary. The archives constitute records constructed by the colonialists in the context of subjugating the indigenous people. For instance, some records of the colonial administrators depict the indigenous as savages, because these Africans did not follow Christian religion. This indicates that there may have been instances of bias in the construction of some of the archival records. Thus, the use of oral history is chosen as an alternative source of information.

Lastly, the research was approached as a two-way process, where the researchers get information from the respondents and the respondents feed the information back for it to be of use to the communities of the respondents. In other words, the decision was to choose an interactive research approach informed by a desire to ensure that the research provides information to the community. That is why, as will be seen later, CAS and CALUSA chose a participatory research approach. As will be seen below, the workshop involving respondents, where the preliminary research report was presented, constituted a way of feeding the information back and also confirming accuracy of the data and its interpretation.

Photo 1: Young people observing the rock painting in Mnxe

Importantly, the study was conducted in an atmosphere where every member in the research team was regarded as having a contribution to make. The principle informed the adoption of participatory research approaches. As MacDonald (2012:34) states it, "PAR (*participatory action research*) is considered democratic, equitable, liberating, and life-enhancing qualitative inquiry that remains distinct from other qualitative methodologies ... ". One of the reasons participatory research is considered democratic is that it provides those involved in it the space to express themselves. Indeed, space was provided for the young researchers to explore and express themselves in the course of the study. As such, they were required to write reports based on their observations in the field. However, they had to explain themselves during regular reflection meetings held after fieldwork.

Three research teams conducted the in-depth interviews in the three villages between May and August 2015. On the main, the youth in each of the teams led the research with support from the staff members of CALUSA. To ensure accuracy of the information, each research team was required to record the interviews. In turn, each team had to transcribe each interview. Indeed, all the interviews were recorded and transcribed.

The research process proved to be empowering to the research group. For instance, the youth were required to write field reports, which inculcated the culture as well as skill of writing reports. This shows that participatory research processes also empowered those involved. This is an observation Krishnaswamy (2004:1) also confirms by arguing that "(C)apacity building occurs as community members identify research questions, carry out research activities, and in the process develop research skills and techniques. Community members learn to analyze information they have collected and decide how to use this information" (2004:1). Buckner (2004:1) is even more assertive that participatory research methods foster "direct benefits to those involved in the research process ...". As will be seen later, the field reports were presented and discussed not only in the regular action-reflection meetings, but also in the workshop CALUSA organised in August 2015.

In summary, the study used focus group discussions, rock paintings to complement the information obtained during the discussions, in-depth interviews and a workshop, as the strategies of getting information. Below is an account of what happened under each method used.

Focus group discussions

In line with the participatory approach, the three research teams and Professor Ntsebeza met on 7 and 8 March 2015 to discuss and collectively prepare questions for the focus group discussions. The following questions guided the focus group discussions:

- Who the first families in the village were?
- Where did they come from?
- What do the participants know about life before colonial contact?

- The knowledge of the locals about whether Khoisan people ever lived in the area or not?
- If yes, what are the signs of their presence in the area?
- What happened to them?

To complement each other in the recollection of their past, the participants had to be brought together into groups. Freitas, *et al.* (1998:1) argue that, "(D)epending on the research objective, the Focus Group (FG) can be used alone or in conjunction with other methods. The results obtained from the FG application are particularly effective in supplying information about how people think, feel, or act regarding a specific topic" (see also Krueger 2002). In the context of our study, focus group discussions were indeed a useful technique. The focus group discussions allowed the participants to share and support each other in reflecting about their histories.

In setting up the focus group discussions, elderly people of equal gender representation from Cala Reserve and Tsengiwe were invited to be participants in the discussions. The invitees were chosen for their perceived knowledge of the history of their communities. However, no focus group discussions were held in Mnxe due to the long time it took to identify elderly people willing to participate in the discussions. There seemed to be reluctance in some of the elders in Mnxe to participate in the group discussions. Seemingly, the reluctance is associated with sensitivities that exist amongst residents in the community. The sensitivities emanate from struggles of the 1960s which saw fierce clashes including the burning of the houses of others and vice versa. The clashes were due to divisions among the supporters of Chief Daliwonga Matanzima who pushed the introduction of tribal authorities and betterment planning, and people that opposed the processes (see also Ntsebeza 2006). The residents seem not comfortable to talk about those struggles. Thus, the idea was abandoned.

The identification of participants in the focus group discussions was through multiple processes. Firstly, a snowballing approach was employed where key informants were identified and names of other families to be included in the list were solicited from the key informants. Electronic communication between Dr Fani Ncapayi and Professor Ntsebeza set the process in motion, where the names of Messrs Mcebisi Ntamo and Jongilizwe Fani were identified as key informants that should be invited to the focus group discussions in Cala Reserve. The two participants are both leaders in the area and are also elderly people. The 73 year old Mr Mcebisi Ntamo is the chairperson of Siyazakha Land and Development Forum. Mr Jongilizwe Fani has been the headman of Cala Reserve until his retirement in March 2013. He is in his late 70s.

The families identified for further in-depth interviews were amaYirha (Tyandela), amaHlubi (Ntamo and Makhohliso), amaMpondomise (Nophothe), amaGcina (Guata) and amaMpinga (Mabhadi). The informants suggested some of the families to be interviewed.

In Tsengiwe, the key informants were Mr Daliwonga Arosi and Mrs Pumla Yakobi. They are both members of the Committee of 13 in the area.[4] The informants suggested names of local people to be approached for the discussions. Additionally, Mr Daliwonga Arosi has also been helpful in the identification of caves with rock paintings in Tsengiwe on account of his knowledge of Tsengiwe. He even led the researchers to the caves. We will hear more on the rock paintings later.

Based on CALUSA staff members' knowledge of the communities, they also suggested the names of people to be invited. The suggested names were further confirmed with the local people in Cala Reserve and Tsengiwe. In a meeting of the Planning Committee in Cala Reserve the local people added more names of people to be considered.[5] A target of twelve people (six men and six women) was set for each focus group discussion. However, the response of community people was less than the target set. For instance, only five elderly people (three men and two women) turned up for the group discussions in Cala Reserve. Others could not attend for various reasons such as being committed in other activities, including a meeting called by Vulamasango Singene Campaign on the day of the focus group discussions. It was a similar experience in Tsengiwe. Only six people (three men and three women) turned up for the discussions.[6] Some people excused themselves due to prior commitments. Others were not properly informed about the focus group discussions.

---

[4] The Committee of 13 led the struggle to oppose an imposed unelected headman in Tsengiwe from 2007.

[5] The Planning Committee is a local committee of men and women that was formed to work with the headman. It is central in the struggle to democratise governance in Cala Reserve that has ended in the High Court in Bisho.

[6] This is a campaign for the opening of land restitution claims for people affected by the implementation of betterment planning in communal areas of the Eastern Cape; these are claims for rural residents.

Identification of caves with rock paintings and challenges thereof

In trying to put together pieces of the puzzle in the history of families before colonial contact, the research group reasoned that rock paintings would be a useful source of information. The motivation was that some rock paintings reflect the histories of people and their communities. Campbell and Robbins (n.y.) confirm the importance of rock paintings in reflecting the history of people.

In preparation for the field visits to the caves, the youth from each research site was asked to draw maps of their areas. The maps aimed at orientating people to specific features of each village. Consequently, the maps were drawn in such a way that they indicated where the caves were. In other words, the maps reflected the routes, important land marks and the kilometres from the CALUSA offices to the caves. All three groups drew the maps and presented them to a meeting of the research group. The group discussed and endorsed the programme of visiting the caves. Thus, towards the end of March 2015, the research group paid visits to the caves in the three villages. Local people were identified in each area to either lead or guide the research group to the caves. Mr Jongilizwe Tasana acted as a guide who pointed the location of the caves in Cala Reserve. Although he did not physically go to the caves, his directions were spot on. In Tsengiwe, Mr Daliwonga Arosi led the group in the first visit to the caves. He literally led the group up the mountain to the caves. In Mnxe, various elderly people gave directions to the local youth to the caves.

Photo 2: Youth going up the mountain to view caves in Tsengiwe

The first community visited was Tsengiwe. Using the maps, visits were paid to the caves in Tsengiwe to see what the paintings depict. As the picture above shows,

Mr Daliwonga Arosi led the group to the caves. On the first day, the research group could not see paintings in the caves that were visited. The problem was that the caves had collapsed, thus damaging the paintings. In view of this, a different site had to be identified in the area. Indeed, the research team agreed in its reflection meeting after the field trip that another site of rock paintings be identified in Tsengiwe.

In Mnxe, the local youth led the research team members to the caves. As already indicated, the youth got guidance from the local elderly people about the locations of the caves. The caves are about three kilometres, south of Mnxe, about one and half kilometre from the main road running from Cala to Lady Frere.

To the credit of the researchers, the maps proved very helpful as a guide to the caves. Commenting in a reflection meeting on 17 March in 2015, one of the research team members remarked that, "I am grateful to the members who drew the maps. Almost all the maps were able to lead us to the caves".[7] This means the maps were accurate.

In-depth interviews

The participatory approach dictated that the study be qualitative, hence the in-depth interviews. The attempt has been to capture the views and experiences of people in the three villages. Denzil and Lincoln (1994) point out that qualitative research is appropriate in studying things in their natural state and in the interpretation of a phenomenon. This is a point Wisker (2008) also confirms.

As already indicated, respondents for the in-depth interviews were identified during the focus group discussions. According to Boyce & Neale (2006:3), "(I)n-depth interviews are useful when you want detailed information about a person's thoughts and behaviors or want to explore new issues in depth. Interviews are often used to provide context to other data (such as outcome data), offering a more complete picture of what happened in the program and why". Members of the following families were interviewed in Cala Reserve: Messrs Makhohliso, Nophothe, Nobhanda, Mseti, Kula and Tyandela. The respondents confirmed most of the information about the first families in Cala Reserve. In Mnxe, the following families were interviewed: Mr Khubukeli, Msengana and Mr Mgemane for the in-depth interviews. In Tsengiwe, the following families were interviewed: Mr Jam-jam, Mr Arosi and Mrs Makhohliso.

---

[7] Comments of Mlingani Mayongo in the reflection meeting, 17 March 2015.

Workshop as a method of triangulation of the evidence gathered

Following the field reports of the researchers, the research group decided to hold a workshop for all those who participated in the research. Participants in the focus group discussions and the respondents in the in-depth interviews from the three research sites were invited to the workshop. The workshop also involved the youth that are members of Siyazakha, the researchers, CALUSA staff and Professor Ntsebeza. The purpose was to give an opportunity to community members to comment and to critique the research reports. This means the workshop helped in verifying the information the researchers had gathered.

In preparation for the workshop, the young researchers had to write preliminary reports for presentation in the workshop. The reports were to be presented according to an agreed structure that was discussed in the preparatory meeting. The CALUSA staff members were allocated to each research team to assist in writing the reports.

The workshop was held on 28 August 2015. The reports reflected on the whole process, from the focus group discussions to the in-depth interviews of individuals. The expectation of the workshop was that participants would ask questions for clarity, confirm, make additions or challenge what the research teams reported. At the end of the workshop issues needing further investigation were identified. For instance, the issue of cattle and horses that were identified in the rock paintings needed further research as some members felt that the animals were not indigenous. The researchers were asked to investigate whether the animals were indigenous or not.

Nature of data collected and its analysis

Understandably, most of the respondents had no clue of how life was before the colonial period. This was the case during the focus group discussions, during the in-depth interviews as well as during the workshop. Participants could not comprehend lives of the families before colonial contact. Rather than commenting on the period before colonial contact, participants tended to focus on the period they felt most comfortable with, which is the period of the Matanzima regime. This has to do with the ages of the respondents who were mostly born in the 1930s, which is much later in the history of colonial intrusion into African societies. When asked what their parents or grandparents told them about their family histories, one respondent indicated that they never had conversations about the histories of the families with their grandparents or parents. Yet, storytelling was part of knowledge production and transfer. According to Seroto (2011:77):

> The curriculum of indigenous education during the pre-colonial period consisted of traditions, legends and tales and the procedures and knowledge associated with rituals which were handed down orally from generation to generation within each tribe. This process was intimately integrated with the social, cultural, artistic, religious and recreational life of the indigenous peoples.

The comment indicating the collapse of storytelling is interesting given the practice of storytelling in African households. The comment implies that the practice, which served to pass knowledge and information from one generation to the other, has stopped. Explaining why this practice was no longer taking place, one respondent attributed this to the migrant labour system. The respondent argued that migrants did not have time for storytelling to their grandchildren and children because of the limited time they spent with their families.[8] However, the explanation does not address why grandmothers and mothers did not play the role of storytelling in this case. But, what is clear is the collapse of this social activity of passing knowledge from one generation to next.

Indeed, the failure of the storytelling tradition can be seen in the contradictory views expressed by respondents regarding the first families in their villages. The respondents were in agreement on the origins of the early families in Cala Reserve, for instance. They put Makhohliso, amaHlubi, as among the first families in Cala Reserve. Duncan Makhohliso, who was a soldier that participated in one of the wars, became the first headman of the village.[9] The second was the Nophothe family – amaMpondomise who came from Qumbu. The other family was Ntamo, ooDunjane, whose origin is from KwaZulu-Natal. The Dunjane group came and settled in Ngqamakhwe, before coming to Cala Reserve. Mr Mcebisi Ntamo indicated that his father got eight morgen of land in the village as compensation for his participation in the war. However, he was unable to explain which war his father participated in. In addition to the above-mentioned families in Cala Reserve, amaMpinga as represented by the Mabhadi family, and amaGcina represented by Guata are among the early families in the area.[10]

---

[8] Inteview of Zoyisile Tyandela by Mlingani Mayongo and Fani Ncapayi, 28 March 2017.
[9] Recorded views during focus group discussions in Cala Reserve, 7 March 2015.
[10] Recorded views during focus group discussions in Cala Reserve, 7 March 2015.

There were differences of opinions regarding the first headman of Cala Reserve, though. For instance, Mr Zweliphalele Nophothe claimed that Boy Nophothe was the first headman of Cala Reserve. To support his argument, Mr Nophothe even argued that the fact that his family has more arable land in the village which proves that it was his grandfather who was the first headman, and allocated land to other people. Mr Mthuthuzeli Makhohliso challenged this version by pointing out that it was Duncan Makhohliso who was the first headman of the area. He supported his point by stating that it was Duncan Makhohliso who allocated Nophothe the land. Archival records concur with Mr Mthuthuzeli Makhohliso's version that Duncan Makhohliso was the first headman of Cala Reserve.[11]

Another point of disagreement among the participants was with regard to who the first families in Xhalanga were. Mr Jongilizwe Fani, the former headman of Cala Reserve, pointed out that Cala Reserve belonged to amaYirha before the war. According to him, "there is a story to the effect that an old man of the amaYirha clan encouraged his family to flee whilst he remained behind during a certain war. It is not clear what happened to him, but a site of his homestead is still visible".[12] Mr Jongilizwe Fani further mentioned that when the colonialists allocated land after the war, "amaYirha did not get their land back. Instead, it was allocated to other people".[13] Moreover, Mr Jongilizwe Fani reported that during his tenure as the headman of Cala Reserve, the Tyandela family once asked for permission to hold a commemoration on the site, which he granted. Unfortunately, a member of the Tyandela family (Mr Zoyisile Tyandela) could not provide information about this story or his family generally. He indicated that he never had conversations with his father or elderly people in his family about the origins of his family. His argument was that there was never time for that as his parents were workers. He further stated that his father was not an approachable person; something that made communication with him difficult.

Mr Mcebisi Ntamo had a slightly different version though regarding amaYirha. According to him, amaYirha were the first family in the whole of Xhalanga, not only in Cala Reserve. This is based on what his father, who was born in 1887, told him. Me Ntamo's father told him that the Khaliphas were a known family of amaYirha in Xhalanga. There is also agreement among the respondents that some of the amaYirha are still around, e.g. Messrs Tyandela, Ntseke, Khalipha, Nkunkuma, etc.

---

[11] CMT. 3/188
[12] Transcript of the focus group discussions in Cala Reserve on 7 May 2015.
[13] *Op. cit.*

The Tyandela family can also be found in Roma, another village under Cala Reserve. It has not been possible to find out from Mr Jomgilizwe Fani the war he referred to. Even probing him did not yield results. He could be referring to the war in which colonialists pushed Sarhili out of Xhalanga.

Yet, archival records and literature reflect amaTshawe as the first people to settle in Xhalanga. These two sources show that Xhalanga was the land of Sarhili, the chief of amaTshawe who was forced by colonial forces to vacate the land in the 1850s (Ntsebeza 2006).[14]

In Tsengiwe there was agreement among the participants during the focus group discussions on 8 March 2015 regarding the first families. According to Mrs Makhohliso, Richard Tsengiwe was the first headman in Tsengiwe and thus the first family in the area. Richard had a son called Dudu Arthur Tsengiwe who was born in 1926. And, the local teacher training college, Arthur Tsengiwe Teacher Training College, was named after him. The Makhohliso family came from Mzwazwa in 1936. Other community people such as Mr Madikiza and Mr Daliwonga Arosi confirmed that Richard Tsengiwe was among the first families in the village and thus the first headman of Tsengiwe.[15]

As indicated in the methodology section, rock paintings were also considered as another source of information in the study. The caves with rock paintings in Cala Reserve are about five kilometres from the area along the road to the neighbouring village called Roma. In Tsengiwe the caves are on the banks of the Tsomo River between Manzimdaka and Tsengiwe. The paintings are closer to the lower section of Tsengiwe. In Mnxe, the caves with rock paintings are south of the village, on the west of the R410 road, from Cala to Lady Frere.

The paintings in the three villages depict similar animals such as game, wild animals (such as cats, badgers, rabbits, etc.), cattle, horses, and hunters with bows and arrows. The presence of rock paintings in the three areas confirms that there were *abaThwa* and *oNoqhakancu* in the villages.[16] Furthermore, the depiction of *abaThwa* with bows and arrows, game and other wild animals indicates hunting activities by

---

[14] Report and proceedings of the Tembuland Commission with Appendices and Maps. Vol. 1. (G. 66-'83). UCT Library, Government Publications Section.
[15] Transcript of focus group discussions in Tsengiwe, 8 May 2015.
[16] We have avoided using the 'Khoi' and 'San' terms because of the controversies raised about their use in discussions at the Pre-Colonial Catalytic Conference at the Nelson Mandela Metropolitan University held 15-17 March 2017.

The study of earlier African societies before colonial contact • 131

Illustration 1: Paintings in Tsengiwe depicting hunters

Illustration 2: Rock paintings in Mxe depicting badgers

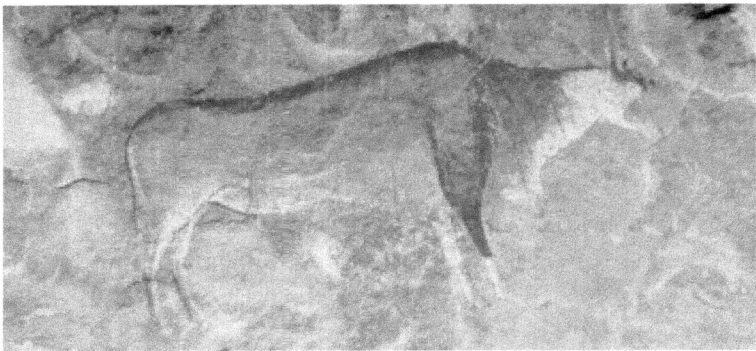

Illustration 3: Rock paintings in Cala Reserve depicting wild animals

abaThwa and other local people for meat. This is in line with Tropp's (2002) claim about hunting activities. In his article entitled *"Dogs, poison and the meaning of colonial intervention in the Transkei",* Tropp describes colonial attempts to curb hunting activities by African people in the Transkei. Moreover, the presence of cattle means the local people consumed meat and milk from the cattle.

However, the presence of cattle and horses in the paintings generated a lot of debate among participants in the workshop of August 2015. At issue was whether cattle and horses are indigenous animals or not. Some participants held a view that the two animals do not originate in present day South Africa. Mr Zikode Khubukeli, for instance, stated that cattle are not indigenous to South Africa. He thus questioned how *abaThwa* could have known about cattle and horses, as the animals would not be around before the arrival of white people.

While the origins of cattle and horses may not be in present day South Africa, some literature locates their origins to different past of Africa, e.g. North Africa, West Africa, East Africa, etc. (Joshi, *et al.* 1957; Felius, M., *et al.* 2011; Warmuth 2011; Venter, n.d.).[17] Warmuth (2011), for instance, confirms that some cattle breeds originate in certain parts of Africa. According to Venter (n.d.:1):

> (T)he Nguni can be classified as a Sanga-type of cattle breed. Nguni people and their livestock migrated from North, Central and East Africa, crossing the Zambezi between 590 and 700 AD. In the process they had to adapt to the environmental extremes of Southern, Central and Eastern Africa. The Nguni cattle breed has over centuries survived seasonal and periodic droughts and therefore has developed into a very hardy breed.

Similarly, some horse breeds originate from North Africa (Jansen, *et al.* 2002; Warmuth 2011). This means both animals have breeds whose origins are in the African continent. The literature also shows that both the cattle and horses came with the African people during their movement southwards.

Furthermore, the depiction of the two animals in the paintings of *abaThwa* means that *abaThwa* must have seen the animals. It can be deduced, therefore, that the animals were drawn after contact between the southern Nguni people and *abaThwa*. As further indication of contact between the southern Nguni people and *abaThwa* is that some clan names show connections with *abaThwa*. For instance, amaMpondomise praise themselves as *amathole omthwakazi* (the offsprings

---

[17] See www.landbou.com/wp-content/.../3bf7de28-c921-4430-991b-209914d0360b.pdf [Retrieved 15 April 2017]. See also Joshi, *et al.*, 1957; Felius, M., *et al.*, 2011; Warmuth, 2011; Venter, undated.

of a female *umThwa*). This also indicates possible inter-marriages between the amaMpondomise and *abaThwa*. In the workshop in August 2015, Mr Jongilizwe Fani confirmed that "there is a story that while hunting people in emaMpondomiseni caught *umThwakazi*, and brought her home". This is a further indication of the inter-marriages between amaMpondomise and *abaThwa*. The clicks in isiXhosa, which are not found in other African languages, is another indication of the contact between the southern Nguni and *abaThwa*.

There is a lot of speculation as to why *abaThwa* left the Xhalanga magisterial district. Lack of evidence makes it impossible to find out. Some participants in the workshop thought that as people who survived on hunting and wild plants, scarcity of wild animals and plants due to the growth in population in the district must have forced *abaThwa* to migrate to other less populated areas. Other participants expressed a view that it was violence the local people meted against *abaThwa* that forced the latter to leave the area. Without evidence it is difficult to dismiss or confirm any of the views.

The presence of cattle, game and other wild animals in the rock paintings indicates that the families were herders and hunters. This signals that meat was one of the sources of food for the families. Indeed, cattle were central in the livelihoods of African families in the Eastern Cape generally (Guy 1987). According to Guy:

> cattle were important as the source of subsistence products: milk in various forms, dung for heating and building, for leather and meat. Moreover cattle are self-reproducing and numbers can increase without absorbing a significant increase in labour time. (1987:19-20).

Moreover, wild plants, roots and fruits were some of the food crops the early families survived on. The respondents confirmed this as they indicated that the early families planted sorghum and also collected wild plants, roots and fruits for food, according to Abongile Cekwana and Solomzi Mntungwa.[18] Literature on the southern Nguni people confirms this claim (Peires 1981; Maylam 1986; Crais 1992). According to Maylam (1986:33), the other food products were "calabashes, watermelons, gourds, beans, pumpkins, potatoes, bananas, sugar, tobacco and dagga". Crais (1992:19) concurs with Maylam on the production of sorghum, beans and melons in African societies in the Cape. The southern Nguni also gathered wild plants such as "berries, mimosa gum, onion-like roots, and the wild spinach which grew in abandoned

---

[18]   See report of the two researchers in the workshop on 29 August 2015.

cattle-enclosures" (Peires 1981:8). Although maize was a foreign crop "from the east coast of Africa, it was also widely planted in the mid-Transkei by the time of colonial contact" (Maylam 1986:33).

Importantly, the caves, interviews and literature show cattle, game, wild plants and roots, fruit and sorghum as sources of livelihoods of the early families. This is in line with the depiction of Ngni families as pastoralists and herders; meaning the families had livestock as they moved around (Oosthuizen 1996).

However, something needs to be done urgently about protection and preservation of the rock paintings, as there is a serious danger of losing them. As shown in the picture below, the rock paintings have either faded or have been defaced. In Mnxe, they have faded due to vandalism by local people. The allegation is that the local youth destroys the rock paintings, especially when herding livestock. There are also signs that some people make fire in the caves as part of traditional rituals, thus smoke affecting the roofs of the caves. The smoke causes the paintings to fade. This has been very evident in paintings in Cala Reserve. There are signs that some people use the caves for traditional rituals. The caves have a big deep and black hole. Seemingly, traditional practitioners enter the hole to perform rituals. Consequently, the roofs of the caves are black from smoke probably from inside the caves. These are indications that people do go inside the caves and make fire. This smoke contributes in defacing the rock paintings. Thus, the condition of the caves highlights an urgent need for plans of protecting them. As in the two areas, the rock paintings in Tsengiwe are fairly clear. However, the fact that they are on the river bank means they are at risk of being destroyed by floods. They are also at risk of being defaced by people.

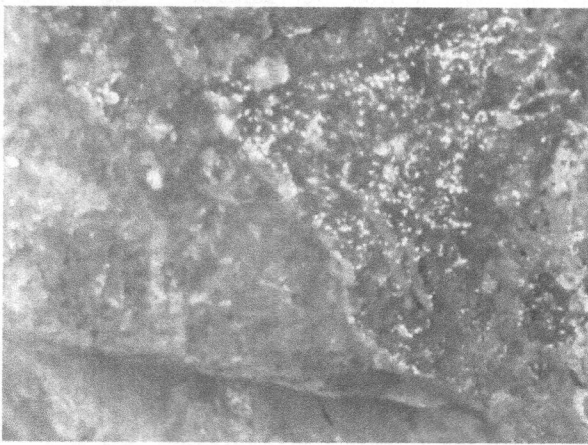

Illustration 4: Picture depicting the damage to the paintings

Clearly, the foregoing discussions show the importance of the caves to various stakeholders ranging from traditional healers, local community members, as well as the municipality. The caves have spiritual significance for traditional leaders and some local residents who conduct rituals in them. For the municipality and local residents, the caves are significant for development of the local economy in communities. For instance, the caves can be promoted for tourism, hence the need for involve of the municipality. Thus, the caves are important not only for purposes of historical record, but also for cultural, spiritual and economic reasons. These considerations highlight a need for discussions by the various stakeholders, including the municipality, regarding the state of the caves. The discussions have to take place in a context where diverse interests in the caves are taken into account.

Additionally, access to the various caves is a huge challenge. The steep slope to the caves and thick bushes make access difficult, especially in the caves in Cala Reserve and Mnxe. Something needs to be done to address the challenges.

Wars contributed to movements and the dispersal of some families across the three communities. Most of the early families who settled in the communities have in one way or the other been forced by war to move until they ended in the villages. The discussions with respondents highlight commonalities in the communities regarding some of the early families who were dispersed by wars, e.g. amaGcina, amaMpondomise, amaMfengu, etc. It would be interesting to establish whether there are connections in the movements of these families to Xhalanga and the villages or not.

Towards a conclusion

The study set out to investigate the lives and living conditions of people in early African societies before colonial contact in three communities in the former Xhalanga magisterial district. Indeed, interviews and the rock paintings provided clues regarding lives and livelihoods of early families in the three communities. The data indicates that early families of Cala Reserve, Mnxe and Tsengiwe led land-based lives relying on cattle and game for meat, wild plants and fruits for food. The study has also highlighted that most of the families came from outside the villages due to dispersal by wars. Other families came for the good grazing lands in the villages.

Although we have an idea of who the first families in the three villages were, there is still a lot that needs to be investigated about the villages and how early families lived.

As intimated earlier, part of the problem is that there is limited knowledge in the communities about the lives of early families. Moreover, a question that kept coming up at various stages of the study, but could not be addressed, was the connection of the local people with religion and the development of the localities. Some residents think the people of Tsengiwe had an association with the Lutheran Church, which in turn contributed to the development of the area. The presence of old church buildings of the Lutheran Church in the area influences this thinking. This is one of the issues that need further investigation.

However, the research initiative was important for the knowledge it impacted on the youth. The research provided information about things the youth never knew of. For instance, some of the youth did not know what the rock paintings signified and their importance to their communities. Thus, the research is in line with CALUSA's idea of promoting education in its broadest sense amongst the youth and residents generally. Additionally, the research also highlights the need to share the knowledge not only with the youth, but also with learners in the local schools.

Moreover, the relationship between CALUSA and CAS could be a model of how social responsiveness of tertiary institutions can be structured. The relationship allows constant interaction between an academic institution and the community. In this instance, CAS's approach helped to bring UCT to the communities. Indeed, the research has not only extracted knowledge from the rural residents, there has also been imparting of knowledge and skills to the communities.

References

Boyce, C. & Neale, P. 2006. *Conducting in-depth interviews: A Guide for Designing and Conducting In-Depth Interviews for Evaluation Input.* Waterton: Pathfinder International.

Buckler, E.S. & Stevens, N.M. 2005. *Maize Origins, Domestication, and Selection.* http://bio-nica.info/Biblioteca/Buckler2005MaizeOrigins.pdf [Retrieved 10 March 2017].

Buckner, S. 2004. *Participatory Action Research in a community development setting – obstacles and opportunities.* University of Central Lancashire. UEL Centre for Narrative Research. www.uel.ac.uk/cnr/documents/CNRWIPJune04Buckner.doc [Retrieved 8 June 2012.]

Campbell, A. & Robbins, L. n.d. Tsodilo Hill, Botswana. http://www.rockartscandinavia.com/images/articles/tsodiloa9.pdf [Retrieved 2 March 2017].

Crais, C. 1992. Representation and the politics of identity in South Africa: An Eastern Cape example. *The International Journal of African Historical Studies,* 25(1): 99-126.

De Wet, J.M.J. 1978. Systematics and Evolution of Sorghum Sect. Sorghum (Gramineae). *American Journal of Botany,* 65, 4: 477-484. https://doi.org/10.1002/j.1537-2197.1978.tb06096.x

Denzin, N.K. & Lincoln, Y.S. 1994. Introduction: Entering the field of qualitative research. In: Denzin & Lincoln (eds.). *Handbook of Qualitative research.* New Delhi: SAGE Publishers, 1-19.

Felius, M.; Koolmees, P.A.; Theunissen, B.; Lenstra, J.A. & European Cattle Generic Diversity Consortium. 2011. *On the Breeds of Cattle—Historic and Current Classifications. Diversity*, 3(4): 660-692. www.mdpi.com/journal/diversity [Retrieved 17 April 2017].

Freitas, H.; Oliveira, M.; Jenkins, M. & Popoy, O. 1998. *The focus group, a qualitative research method: Reviewing the Theory, and Providing Guidelines to Its Planning.* ISRC Working Paper. http://gianti.ea.ufrgs.br/files/artigos/1998/1998_079_ISRC.pdf [Retrieved 7 March 2017].

Guy, J. 1987. Analysing Pre-Capitalist Societies in South Africa. *Journal of South African Studies*, 14(1): 18-37, October 1987.

Gepts, P. 1998. Origin and evolution of common bean: Past events and present trends. University of California. *HortScience*, 33 (7), December 1998.

Haile-Mariam,M.; Malmfors, B & Philipsson, J.2010. *BORAN: Indigenous African cattle with potential.* www.landbou.com/boereblogs/boran-indigenous-african-cattle-with-potential [Retrieved 14 April 2017].

Jansen, T.; Forster, P.; Levine, M.A.; Oelkes, H.; Hurles, M.; Renfrew, C.; Weber, J. & Olek, K. 2002. Mitochondrial DNA and the origins of the domestic chorse., *PNAS*, 99(16), August 2002.

Joshi, N. R.; McLaughlin, E.A. & Philips, F.W. 1957. Types and Breeds of African Cattle. Food and Agriculture Organisation of the nited Nations. *Rome: FAO Agricultural Studies,* 37. http://www.fao.org/docrep/015/an470e/an470e.pdf [Retrieved 10 March 2017].

Krishnaswamy, A. 2004. *Participatory Research: Strategies and Tools.* https://nature.berkeley.edu/ community_forestry/Workshops/powerpoints/tools%20and%20strategies%20of%20PR.pdf [Retrieved 2 March 2017].

Krueger, R.A. 2002. *Designing and Conducting Focus Group Interviews.* http://www.eiu.edu/ihec/ Krueger-FocusGroupInterviews.pdf [Retrieved 7 March 2017].

Lunenburg, F.C. & Irby, B.J. 2008. *Writing a successful Thesis or Dissertation. Tips and strategies in the Social and Behavioural Sciences.* New York: Corwin Press.

MacDonald, C. 2012. Understanding Participatory Action Research: A qualitative Research Methodology Option. *Canadian Journal of Action Research,* 13, 2: 34-50.

Maylam, P. 1986. *A History of the African people of South Africa: From the Early Iron Age to the 1970s.* Cape Town: David Philip.

Ntsebeza, L. 2006. *Democracy compromised. Chiefs and the politics of land in South Africa.* Cape Town: Human Sciences Research Council Press.

Ntsebeza, L. & Saunders, C.C. (eds.). 2014. *Papers from the Pre-Colonial Catalytic Project.* Cape Town: Centre for African Studies, University of Cape Town.

Oosthuizen, M.P. 1996. Uchibidolo: The abundant herds. *A descriptive study of the Sange-Nguni cattle of the Zulu people with special reference to colour-pattern terminology and naming-practice.* PhD dissertation University of Natal, Durban.

Peires, J.B. 1981. *The House of Phalo. A History of the Xhosa People in the days of their independence.* Johannesburg: Jonathan Ball Publishers.

Sarantakos, S. 1998. *Social Research* (Second Edition). Hampshire, London: Macmillan Press.

Seroto, J. 2010. Indigenous education during the pre-colonial period in Southern Africa. *Indilinga – African Journal of Indigenous Knowledge Systems*, 10 (1): 77-88.

Stake, R.E. 1994. Case studies. In: N.K. Denzin & Y.S. Lincoln (eds.). *Handbook of Qualitative Research*. New Delhi: SAGE Publications. 236-247.

Tropp, J. 2002. Dogs, poison and the meaning of colonial intervention in the Transkei, South Africa. *Journal of African History*, 43: 451-72. https://doi.org/10.1017/S0021853702008186

Venter, Y. n.d. *Nguni: The breed from the past for the future*. Bloemfontein: Nguni Catte Breeders Society.

Warmuth, V. 2011. *On the origin and spread of horse domestication*. PhD dissertation. Cambridge: University of Cambridge.

Wisker, G. 2008. *The postgraduate research handbook. Succeed with your MA, MPhil, EdD and PhD. (Second edition)*. New York: Palgrave Macmillan.

CHAPTER 8

The Home of Legends Project

The Potential and Challenges of Using Heritage Sites to Tell the Pre-colonial Stories of the Eastern Cape[1]

Denver A. Webb[2] & Mcebisi Ndletyana[3]

Introduction

The subject of this chapter is a research project – the Home of Legends – undertaken under the auspices of the National Heritage Council (NHC) in terms of a partnership the NHC entered into with the Eastern Cape Office of the Premier. The project is not solely concerned with pre-colonial history of the Eastern Cape, but in its original conception, was intended to span the full spectrum of Eastern Cape narratives from the geological and palaeontological past, the pre-colonial era, the colonial period to the recent past.[4]

The Home of Legends project offers interesting opportunities to provide a broad revisionist overview of the area that now

---

[1] This chapter focuses on the pre-colonial in the Eastern Cape as a *methodological* study to *illustrate* the practical challenges involved in attempts to decolonise heritage studies as integral and related to decolonising historiography. It is not intended as a specific geographical area study in itself nor as a demographic study of Xhosa-speaking South Africans. In a sense, it attempts to provide a working template for any province or region in southern Africa or elsewhere in terms of lessons learnt and for further critical engagement in other contexts.
[2] denver.webb@mandela.ac.za
[3] mcebisin@hotmail.com
[4] See 'Memorandum of Agreement Between the Eastern Cape Office of the Premier and the National Heritage Council, 2015', Annexure.

constitutes the Eastern Cape province, which would be of value to schools, local communities, tourism authorities and heritage agencies in the province. It is an opportunity to insert the pre-colonial into popular narratives of the Eastern Cape and look a little wider than the recent, overwhelmingly political, histories of the area. In the context of this project the term 'Eastern Cape' is used to refer to the post-1994 political and geographical construct as defined in the Constitution (1996:125) and which defines the geographical focus area of the study.

The purpose of this chapter is to share the background and progress on the project to date, and highlight the potential and challenges, especially with regards to pre-colonial history.

Origins and background of the Home of Legends research project

The Home of Legends concept originated as an Eastern Cape branding and marketing exercise that was launched in 2012 at Mqekezweni, near Mthatha. As a branding and marketing campaign it enjoyed somewhat mixed results. It included promoting certain heritage sites; a series of billboards and banners placed at prominent places throughout the province; and a public call inviting citizens to suggest names of individuals whom they believed had achieved legendary status. The concept of a 'legend' was initially very loosely defined by the initiators of the campaign and tended to largely focus on male politicians. The conceptualisation was later redefined to 'include people, places and events that set the Eastern Cape apart from the rest of South Africa'.[5]

There was general consensus in the media[6] (*Daily Dispatch*, 7 August 2013; *Daily Dispatch*, 9 July 2014) that the idea of promoting the Eastern Cape as the Home of Legends held considerable promise, but the manner in which the campaign was being driven suffered from a number of problems.[7] One of the main problems was that the Home of Legends conceptualisation was insufficiently clear on the categories of possible legends and the criteria for what might constitute a 'legend'. Contestation in

---

[5] See National Heritage Council, Concept Note Branding the Eastern Cape: Home of Legends (HoL), 2 June 2015.
[6] 'Home of Legends brand can reshape poor image'; 'Home of Legends campaign can revive brand Eastern Cape' respectively.
[7] See *Daily Dispatch*, 25 October 2014, Legends' campaign a failure.

the media emerged, especially around which political figures ought to be considered as legends and the gender insensitive nature of the selected legends.[8]

The second main problem was that the campaign had not been based on a solid foundation of academic research to provide narrative context and substantiate the choice of legends.[9] There was, however, agreement as expressed in the media that however poorly conceptualised the 'dull' and 'flawed' marketing and branding campaign was, the concept of the Eastern Cape as 'a Home of Legends' was one which could serve as a springboard for retelling stories of the province.[10] Aside from the negative comments in letters to newspapers about who was in the first list and who was out, the general public interest and debate it stimulated was useful in highlighting the potential a reconceptualised Home of Legends research project might have. It was argued that the concept held considerable potential to go beyond the narrow confines of a marketing and branding exercise. The key aspects of public sentiments expressed about the project can be summarised as follows:

- It was an opportunity to have 'a public conversation' about who the people in the Eastern Cape are.
- There was a need to capitalise on the rich Eastern Cape heritage in a similar way to KZN.
- The heritage of the Eastern Cape is unparalleled and constituted a magical unique selling point.
- The educative function should be emphasised and a wider spectrum of figures should be included.
- Possibly look at themes such as pre-colonial Khoisan life; Khoisan-Xhosa co-existence; wars of conquest; missionary life; African intellectuals; literary awakening; journalism; black theology; Pan-Africanism; anti-colonial resistance; gender activism; musical revolution; academic excellence; and working-class protests.
- The process should be lifted above mere marketing to identity formation.

In short, a revitalised Home of Legends project was seen as one way of promoting social cohesion and social justice. The Eastern Cape Office of the Premier and the NHC subsequently entered into an agreement on 15 January 2015[11] to commission

---

[8] See *Daily Dispatch*, 2 August 2013, The forgotten legends. None of the Mbeki family features in provincial branding campaign.
[9] See *Daily Dispatch*, 7 August 2013, Home of Legends brand can reshape poor image.
[10] See *Daily Dispatch*, 2 October 2013, Mistake to underestimate potency of Legends drive.
[11] See 'Memorandum of Agreement Between the Eastern Cape Office of the Premier and the National Heritage Council, 2015'.

research that would provide an academic foundation for a reconceptualised Home of Legends project. One of the key questions posed was how heritage sites in the Eastern Cape could be identified and used to tell the narratives(s) of the province, beginning with the geological and palaeontological past, through the pre-colonial and colonial periods to the recent past. Amongst the underpinning principles was the idea that neglected and marginalised aspects of Eastern Cape history, especially in the pre-colonial period, should be included in the project. As set out in the agreement,[12] the problems the project was reconceptualised to address included:

- The absence of reliable, well-researched, up-to-date accessible reference work on the prehistory and history of the Eastern Cape that can be used for heritage management, tourism marketing and product development.
- An absence of reliable revisionist reference material that can be used in schools and by the general public.
- The lack of a comprehensive database of significant palaeontological, archaeological, historical and cultural sites.

Heritage sites in the context of the Home of Legends, were defined broadly to include any place with geological, palaeontological, historical, cultural, political or similar significance around which a narrative explaining that significance could be contrasted. In embarking on the research, the team was mindful of problems experienced with previous attempts to use heritage sites as drivers of local economic development. Heritage development in the Eastern Cape has since the 1990s largely been driven by twin imperatives of constructing a dominant narrative around the liberation struggle and heritage tourism as a driver of local economic development. The fate of a well-intentioned earlier initiative to use heritage to promote tourism and local economic development illustrated some of the practical pitfalls in heritage tourism projects. In 2006 the Amathole District Municipality (ADM) implemented an innovative project based on the heritage of the area covered by the municipality. The ADM identified and defined a large number of heritage sites, grouping them into 'tourism routes', produced brochures, and promoted them in various ways. Information on the routes was made available in brochures (ADM, n.d., *Amathole Heritage* Routes) and on the ADM website.[13] The lack of coordination between the responsible agencies such as the South African Heritage Resources Agency, its provincial counterpart, the Directorate of Museums and Heritage, the Eastern Cape Parks and Tourism Agency, local municipalities and the ADM in sustaining and

---

[12] *Op. cit.*
[13] See http://www.amathole.gov.za/index.php/tou/heritage-routes [Retrieved 6 June 2018].

adding substance to this project meant that this noteworthy initiative petered out. The central problem is that the important steps in the value chain of identifying sites, getting community buy-in, protecting them, conserving them and interpreting or re-interpreting them were not followed before they were promoted as possible tourist attractions (Mancotywa 2014:91). This is a problem that has repeatedly been identified, as the CEO of the NHC articulated, "[P]ackaging these sites into booklets for tourism needs to be premised on something for the tourist to see and experience. The agencies responsible for the identification, conservation and management of heritage sites must ensure that heritage sites are in a suitable state for visitors and tourists" (Mancotywa 2014:89-90). To this, one could add that communities that are theoretically to benefit from heritage tourism should also be involved from the outset.

The objective was to produce a comprehensive, reliable, well-researched academic reference work on the prehistory and history of the Eastern Cape that could contribute educational material for schools and the general public; that could be used to identify and protect important heritage sites; and which would provide data for the development of tourism products and routes.[14] In seeking to provide a broad, popular, revisionist book, complemented by a database of sites, events and people associated with these events and sites, the book project was inspired by the precedent set by the pioneering work of Peter Delius and his team with the Mpumalanga history and heritage book and its spin-offs (Delius 2007; Delius & Hay 2009), although the approach and methodology were different.

The project deliverables as per the agreement[15] include:

- Conceptual clarity and criteria on what constitutes a legend for the purposes of the Home of Legends.
- History of the Eastern Cape from the dawn of time to the present.
- A database of prominent sites, events and personalities.

The NHC assembled a team of researchers to produce the envisaged book. The core team consisted of the authors of this chapter and Eastern Cape historians Jeff Peires and Thozama April. Mark Mandita and Philani Nongogo were added as specialists in music and sport, respectively. The project is well under way, but some challenges have been experienced, especially around pre-colonial history.

---

[14] See 'Memorandum of Agreement Between the Eastern Cape Office of the Premier and the National Heritage Council, 2015', Annexure A: 3-4.
[15] *Op. cit.* Annexure A: 8.

Pre-colonial history and the Home of Legends

A range of conceptual, methodological and procedural challenges have been experienced in the course of researching and writing up the project.

Firstly, the research team was conscious of the need to avoid hagiographic accounts of provincial history that would err on the side of boosterism. Avoiding the pitfalls of embellishing history for contemporary use was partly addressed through clearly defining what was considered 'legendary'. This included avoiding 'living legends' and ensuring that the definition included events and places, as well as people.[16] It also involved judgement calls around who to include and who not to. Considerable debate, for example, was generated on whether Nongqawuse (1841-1898), notable for her association with the Xhosa cattle killing of 1856-1857, could be considered a 'legendary' figure. The point of departure in this is informed by Edward Said's argument in *Orientalism* that, "[H]uman history is made by human beings. Since the struggle for control over territory is part of that history, so too is the struggle over historical and social meaning. The central task for the critical scholar is not to separate one struggle from another, but to connect them" (Said 1979:331). Whether a balance has been achieved between producing academic research that will withstand rigorous scrutiny and producing something that promotes social justice will be seen once it is completed, but the writing team was conscious of this and from the outset aimed to produce "balanced academic research".[17]

Secondly, the Office of the Premier was initially ambivalent about including the pre-colonial past. After initial enthusiasm, the idea of including chapters on the geological and palaeontological past was dropped at the start of the project. In December 2016, after the first draft of the book was completed, the Office of the Premier decided that the chapters that were initially proposed on the palaeontology and pre-colonial history of the province should be revived. Somewhat belatedly moves were made to include an archaeologist and a geologist/palaeontologist in the research and writing team.[18] This aspect of the project in itself revealed additional challenges in working on an academic project with government officials.

---

[16] See 'National Heritage Council, Concept Note Branding the Eastern Cape: Home of Legends (HoL)', 2 June 2015.
[17] 'Memorandum of Agreement Between the Eastern Cape Office of the Premier and the National Heritage Council, 2015', Annexure A: 2.
[18] See NHC Report, 21 May 2017, Annexure F.

Despite the legally binding contract that set out the parameters of the project and a series of meetings with government officials representing the Office of the Premier, this issue also revealed that a key decision maker in government responsible for releasing funds for the project either did not fully comprehend the nature of the research project or did not study the reports periodically submitted.[19] For a time in 2017, the project teetered on the brink of collapse until various high-level meetings put it back on track.

The project plan included a series of engagements in workshops with local communities to understand which people, sites and events were important to them. These engagements were supposed to have been organised by the Eastern Cape Office of the Premier. Unfortunately, only meetings with the Eastern Cape Intergovernmental Communicators' Forum (on 18 May 2015) and traditional leaders (on 15 October 2015) were organised. The community meetings that were to be arranged by the Office of the Premier through local government structures failed to materialise.[20]

More fundamentally, the pre-colonial section has been conceptualised within the existing epistemologies and paradigms, which still define this lengthy timespan in terms of the colonial period. There has been no significant reflection on the problematic notions of 'pre-colonial' and 'colonial'. Even within this, periodisation like 'Early Stone Age', 'Middle Stone Age', 'Late Stone Age' and 'Early Iron Age' are problematic. Given the scope of the Home of Legends research and the absence of consensus amongst scholars on alternative conceptualisations, we have been forced to work within current orthodoxies knowing that they need reconceptualisation. One of the related challenges is the relative absence of recent research on the pre-colonial period in the Eastern Cape. Coverage of the pre-colonial past in the province is at best patchy. As Peires (2014:35) pointed out at the first Pre-Colonial Catalytic Conference, held at the University of Cape Town in March 2014, very little work has in fact been done on the pre-colonial past in what is now the Eastern Cape and there are a number of possible sites that could potentially yield significant data if properly investigated.

Notwithstanding the relative paucity of information on the pre-colonial period, it is possible to identify a range of sites around which the early history of the

---

19   See *Daily Dispatch*, 19 June 2017, Walkout threat to the Home of Legends; *Daily Dispatch*, 24 June 2017, DG slated for angry outburst; NHC Report, 21 May 2017, Annexure F.
20   *Op. cit.* Annexure F.

Eastern Cape can be narrated. For the 18th and early 19th centuries – what Nomalanga Mkhize referred to in the March 2017 conference session as the 'Late Independence Period' – there is sufficient information in the oral archive (more accurately, published histories that draw on oral traditions) to identify possible sites. The point made that these published works need to be viewed as part of African historiography and recognised as historical accounts in their own right, rather than mere source material, needs to be taken on board. In particular, the works of Soga (1930 and 1931), Bhotomane (1996), Tyabashe (1996), Mqhayi (2001), Citashe (Opland & Nyamende 2008) and Gqoba (Opland, Kuse & Maseko 2015) are especially noteworthy in this regard.

Source material and secondary works on aspects like the pre-colonial relations between the Khoikhoi, San and Xhosa are relatively readily available. For example, two Xhosa traditions highlight divergent perspectives on Khoikhoi-Xhosa relations during the reigns of Rharhabe and Ndlambe, the two most influential leaders in the western parts of Xhosaland in the pre-colonial period. Rharhabe is remembered as a Xhosa chief in conflict with the San and the Khoikhoi. Mqhayi narrated how Rharhabe first fought with the San around Hohita and was then forced to move southwest to the Amatholes where he encountered the Khoikhoi of Queen Hoho. Her followers defended their lands vigorously, forcing Rharhabe to make peace and to purchase the land around the Amathole mountains (Mqhayi 2001:282-285). This is confirmed by Citashe who, recounting a slightly different tradition, described how Rharhabe crossed the Kei River after quarrelling with his brother Gcaleka and was opposed by a large army of Khoikhoi who fought a battle in the bed of the Kei River. After the battle the leaders met to establish peace and permanent friendship as proof of which ten young men and ten young women of either side were to be married (Opland & Nyamende 2008:51). The common issue is that Rharhabe is remembered as a chief who was in conflict with the Khoikhoi and San.

The relationship between Ndlambe and the Khoikhoi and San was remembered in a far more positive light:

> Ama Lawu ayehleli isonwabo ku Ndlambe. Undlambe lo kanjalo ubekwa yincwadi (pass), kuba aba Twa bebisiti bakudibana nom-Xosa bambuze ukuba ulunge kubanina, eko u Ndlambe eko Hahabe (Rarabe). Ubesiti ke umntu ukuze asinde ati ungum-Ndlambe, ukuba uke wati ungum-Rarabe angabinto ikoyo.
>
> *The [Khoikhoi] lived content with Ndlambe. Ndlambe also served as a book (a pass) because when [San] met a Xhosa they would ask who he belonged to, Ndlambe or Hahabe*

(Rharhabe). A person was safe if he said he was a Ndlambe, but he was in trouble if he said he was a Rharhabe (Mqhayi 2001:86-87).

Information on 'late independence' sites such as the Hoho forest, Ntaba kaNdoda, Hohita, Sihota, Hintsa's great place and the Bawa falls that has come to us through such narratives is thus reasonably accessible.

In respect of – for want of better terminology – the 'Middle Stone Age' and 'Late Stone Age' periods the Eastern Cape is blessed with a rich heritage of rock art sites that stretch in a broad swathe from the Baviaanskloof in the west through the Amathole Mountains into the trans-Keian area and north-eastern parts of the province. The challenge here is not the shortage of sites, but the need to work with communities to conserve and interpret them. Local initiatives to involve youth in documenting rock art sites such as the Cala University Students Association (CALUSA) project at Xhalanga, led by Fani Ncapayi and discussed in the previous chapter, are extremely encouraging. The responsible heritage agencies in the province and nationally ought to be investing a lot more in identification, protection, conservation and education programmes for rock art sites. Community initiatives, such as the CALUSA project, should be receiving a lot more support from agencies charged with heritage management.

In terms of other types of pre-colonial sites, particularly those that tell the story of the 'Early Stone Age' and 'Early Iron Age', there are still huge gaps in our knowledge. Except in a few isolated cases, initial pioneering work by Derricourt (1977), Deacon (1970, 1988), Prins and Granger (1993), Feeley and Bell-Cross (2011), Nogwaza (1994) and Binneman (1996) have not been actively taken up. This is, of course, in stark contrast to the amount of work on Eastern Cape colonial history, a selection of which includes Crais (1992, 2002), Keegan (1996), Legassick (2010), Lester (2001), Peires (1981, 1989), Saunders and Derricourt (1974), Stapleton (1994) and Switzer (1993). But even here, all is not lost. Notwithstanding the relative dearth of research on these periods, there are a number of pre-colonial sites around which narratives could potentially be woven. These include Klasies River (Deacon 1988; Wurz 2008), Nahoon Point (Roberts 2008), Amanzi Springs (Webley 2008), Ntsitsana (Prins & Granger 1993), Canasta Place (Nogwaza 1994) and Kulubele (Binneman 1996) – if the appropriate research, interpretative and conservation interventions are made.

The Klasies River site has, if anything, become more significant since the pioneering work at Pinnacle Point at Mossel Bay, which has refocused attention on the emergence of cognitively modern humans (Marean 2010). The trace fossil hominid footprints at Nahoon Point, recently re-dated to 126 000 years before the present, are also something around which an important facet of the story of humanity, in what is now the Eastern Cape, can be told (Roberts 2008:206). Similarly, the Amanzi Springs site at Uitenhage lends itself to some sort of development that would depict *in situ* the story of 'Early Stone Age' life. Following excavations done by amongst others (Deacon 1970), the site has recently been re-dated to about 200 000 years ago. It is unique in several ways, not least as the first 'Early Stone Age' site to be professionally excavated in South Africa. More importantly, the boggy ground around the warm water spring preserved organic remains, "which is extremely rare in sites of this age" (Webley 2008:15).

The recent survey of 'Middle Stone Age' sites in Mpondoland, conducted under the rubric Pondoland Palaeoenvironment, Palaeoclimate, Palaeoecology, and Palaeoanthropology (P5) shows great promise (Fisher 2014). Begun in 2011 as an offshoot of the Pinnacle Point project, the initial research found both 'Early Stone Age' and 'Middle Stone Age' sites along the coast around Mkhambathi, but it is too soon to include any of these sites in the Home of Legends project.

In respect of the 'Early Iron Age' (or early farming settlements) fewer than 20 sites have been discovered to date in what is now the Eastern Cape (Feely & Bell-Cross 2011). Of these only three have been reasonably well investigated. Further research would undoubtedly uncover more such sites. Despite the relative absence of dedicated research into this period of the pre-colonial past in the Eastern Cape, there are at least three sites around which narratives of early farming communities could be constructed.

Ntsitsana near Sipedu village in a deeply rural part of the Ntabankulu area is one of few such sites that have been properly examined. It revealed farming communities living along the middle reaches of the Umzimvubu River in the 7th and 8th centuries. Ceramics, slag, hut floors, grain pits, pottery figurines and stone artefacts suggest an intriguing picture of life along the banks of the Umzimvubu nearly 1 300 years ago. Perhaps even more significantly, as Prins and Granger (1993:169-170) postulate, clay figurines (possibly used for initiation purposes) and the layout of cattle kraals in relation to homesteads, as well as the location of a larger iron smelting site at Ncabela three kilometres away, is suggestive of gender relations and political and economic organisation that would benefit from further research.

Two other early farming sites are located closer to major roads. Kulubele, near the confluence of the Kulubele Stream and the Kei River, is an especially interesting site that provides *in situ* evidence of an early farming settlement with evidence of iron-working living on the west bank of the Kei River in the 8th and 9th centuries (Binneman, Webley & Biggs 1992:108). Canasta Place, near the East London airport and overlooking the Buffalo River, was examined by one of the few African archaeologists to work in the Eastern Cape, Themba Nogwaza. It has been argued that it represents the most south-westerly 'Early Iron Age' site found to date (Nogwaza 1994:103). But the challenges here include access (since the sites are on private land), the absence of interpretative structures, and the lack of formal protection and conservation measures.

This brings us to a final challenge: the need to treat sites associated with indigenous culture and practices in a sensitive and respectful manner when considering promoting them as places around which narratives can be told. The discovery of the well-preserved remains (later identified to be those of a San person) in the Baviaanskloof by Johan Binneman in 1999 provides a case in point. An agreement was reached[21] after a detailed and lengthy engagement between the Eastern Cape Department of Sport, Recreation, Arts and Culture and Khoikhoi and San communities in the Eastern Cape represented by the Council of the Ghonaqua People, the Khoisan Awareness Initiative and the Eastern Cape Council of Khoi Aborigines. The agreement allowed for a non-invasive testing study to be followed by a dignified reburial of the body after two years.[22]

The remains were found to be those of a male, about 30-40 years of age and were dated about 2 000 years before the present. He was buried at the back of a rock overhang, wrapped in medicinal plant leaves, covered with two layers of sticks, leaves and branches. A large, flat stone with San paintings was placed on top. Inter alia, the discovery provided a lot of insight into Late Stone Age burial practices (Steyn, Binneman & Loots 2007:3). There is potentially a considerable amount of information about the site and the human remains that could be used to educate the public, but this has to be balanced with respecting both the sacred nature of the space and the wishes of those identifying with the remains. Sadly, government's

---

21   See 'Minutes of the Consultative Meeting Held in Port Elizabeth at Edufin Building', 22 June 1999.
22   Council of the Ghonaqua Peoples to Permanent Secretary, Department of Sport, Recreation, Arts and Culture, June 1999.

commitment to the reburial of the mummified remains has to date not been honoured and the body continues to languish in the Albany Museum.[23]

Conclusion

In conclusion, the Eastern Cape Home of Legends research project is a work in progress. By attempting to take a long view of the Eastern Cape past, it is endeavouring to insert pre-colonial narratives, however imperfect, back into a general history of the province, geographically constituted according to current provincial boundaries as this may be. The use of heritage sites as pegs on which communities can co-create their stories holds considerable potential, but for this to be realised, a number of fundamentals need to be put in place, including protecting and conserving those sites which illuminate the long past in southern Africa. The project has experienced a number of conceptual, methodological and practical challenges, but it is a first step in producing a more updated, revisionist popular account of a region.

If nothing else, it has highlighted (if emphasis was ever needed) that renewed focus needs to be given to the broad sweep of pre-colonial history in what is now the Eastern Cape.

Acknowledgements

This chapter arose out of the Eastern Cape Home of Legends project, commissioned by the National Heritage Council (NHC). The views and opinions expressed here are those of the authors and not necessarily those of the NHC nor anyone else associated with the project. We would also like to thank Lita Webley for advice on archaeological sites and Margaret Coetzee for her inputs on the "Kouga mummified body" discussed above.

References

ADM (Amathole District Municipality). n.d. *Amathole Heritage Routes brochure*. East London: ADM.
ADM website, http://www.amathole.gov.za/index.php/tou/heritage-routes
    [Retrieved on 6 May 2017].
Bhotomane, N. 1996. Origins of the Xhosa. In H. Scheub, *The Tongue is Fire, South African Storytellers and Apartheid*. Madison: University of Wisconsin Press, 31-47.

---

[23] Personal communication, D.A. Webb with Director of Albany Museum, 23 March 2017.

Binneman, J. 1996. Preliminary Report on the Investigations at Kulubele, an Early Iron Age Farming Settlement in the Great Kei River Valley, Eastern Cape. *South African Field Archaeology*, 5: 28-35.

Binneman, J.; Webley, L. & Biggs, V. 1992. Preliminary Notes on an Early Iron Age Site in the Great Kei River Valley, Eastern Cape. *Southern African Field Archaeology*, 1(2): 108-109.

Constitution of the Republic of South Africa (Act No.108 of 1996) as amended.

Council of the Ghonaqua Peoples to Permanent Secretary, Department of Sport, Recreation, Arts and Culture. 1999. *Recommendations on the Findings of the Khoi-Khoi Mummy*, available on SAHRA website at http://www.sahra.org.za/sahris/sites/default/files/remoteserver/sahrisdepot/scannedfiles/9-2-047-1.pdf [Retrieved 9 March 2017].

Crais, C. 2002. *The Politics of Evil. Magic, State Power and the Political Imagination in South Africa.* Cambridge: Cambridge University Press.

Crais, C. 1992. *The Making of the Colonial Order. White Supremacy and Black Resistance in the Eastern Cape, 1770-1865.* Johannesburg: Witwatersrand University Press.

Daily Dispatch, 24 June 2017, DG slated for angry outburst.

Daily Dispatch, 19 June 2017, Walkout threat to the Home of Legends.

Daily Dispatch, 25 October 2014, Legends campaign a failure.

Daily Dispatch, 9 July 2014, Home of Legends campaign can revive brand Eastern Cape.

Daily Dispatch, 2 October 2013, Mistake to underestimate potency of Legends drive.

Daily Dispatch, 17 September 2013, Legends project flawed.

Daily Dispatch 7 August 2013, Home of Legends brand can reshape poor image.

Daily Dispatch, 2 August 2013, The forgotten legends. None of the Mbeki family features in provincial branding campaign.

Deacon, H.J. 1988. The Stratigraphy and Sedimentology of the Main Site Sequence, Klasies River, South Africa. *South African Archaeological Bulletin*, 43: 5-14. https://doi.org/10.2307/3887608

Deacon, H.J. 1970. The Acheulian Occupation at Amanzi Springs, Uitenhage District, Cape Province. *Annals of the Cape Provincial Museums*, 8: 89-189.

Delius, P. (ed.). 2007. *Mpumalanga: History and Heritage.* Pietermaritzburg: UKZN University Press.

Delius, P. & Hay, M. 2009. *Mpumalanga. An Illustrated History.* Johannesburg: Highveld Press.

Derricourt, R. 1977. *Prehistoric Man in the Ciskei and Transkei.* Cape Town: Struik.

Feely, J.M. & Bell-Cross, S.M. 2011. The Distribution of Early Iron Age Settlement in the Eastern Cape: Some Historical and Ecological Implications. *South African Archaeological Bulletin*, 66(194): 105-112.

Fisher, E.C.; Albert, R.M.; Botha, G.; Cawthra, H.C.; Esteban, I.; Harris J, Jacobs, Z.; Jeradino, A.; Marean, C.; Neumann, F.H.; Pargeter, J.; Poupart, M. & Venter, J. 2014. Archaeological Reconnaissance for Middle Stone Age Sites Along the Pondoland Coast, South Africa. *Paleo Anthropology*, 104-137.

Keegan, T. 1996. *Colonial South Africa and the Origins of the Racial Order.* Charlottesville: University Press of Virginia.

Legassick, M. 2010. *The Struggle for the Eastern Cape 1800-1854: Subjugation and the Roots of South African Democracy.* Johannesburg: KMM.

Lester, A. 2001. *Imperial Networks. Creating Identities in Nineteenth-Century South Africa and Britain.* London: Routledge.

Mancotywa, S. 2014. *Critical Conversations About Heritage: Popularising Contemporary Heritage Issues*. In D.A. Webb (ed.). Pretoria: National Heritage Council.

Marean, C. 2010. Pinnacle Point Cave 13B (Western Cape Province, South Africa) in context: The Cape Floral kingdom, shellfish, and modern human origins., *Journal of Human Evolution*, 5: 425-443. https://doi.org/10.1016/j.jhevol.2010.07.011

Memorandum of Agreement Between the Eastern Cape Office of the Premier and the National Heritage Council on the Repositioning of the Province as the Home of Legends Project, 15 January 2015.

Minutes of the Consultative Meeting Held in Port Elizabeth at Edufin Building on 22 June 1999, available on SAHRA website at http://www.sahra.org.za/sahris/sites/default/files/remoteserver/sahrisdepot/scannedfiles/9-2-047-1.pdf [Retrieved 9 March 2017].

Mqhayi, S.E.K. 2001. *Abantu Besizwe. Historical and Biographical Writings, 1902-1944*. In J. Opland (ed.). Johannesburg: Wits University Press.

National Heritage Council (NHC), Report on the Home of Legends Project, 21 May 2017.

National Heritage Council, Concept Note Branding the Eastern Cape: Home of Legends (HoL), 2 June 2015.

Nogwaza, T. 1994. Early Iron Age Pottery from Canasta Place, East London District. *Southern African Field Archaeology*, 3, 103-106.

Ntsebeza, L. & Saunders, C. (eds.). 2014. *Papers from the Pre-Colonial Catalytic Conference*. Cape Town: UCT Centre for African Studies.

Opland, J. & Nyamende, A. 2008, *Isaac Williams Wauchope. Selected Writings 1874-1916*. Cape Town: Van Riebeeck Society.

Opland, J.; Kuse, W. & Maseko, P. (eds.). 2015. *William Wellington Gqoba. Isizwe esinembali. Xhosa Histories and Poetry*. Pietermaritzburg: UKZN Press.

Peires, J. 2014. Historical Priorities for Eastern Cape Archaeological Research. In: L. Ntsebeza & C. Saunders (eds.), *Papers from the Pre-Colonial Catalytic Conference*, 35-47. Cape Town: UCT Centre for African Studies.

Peires, J. 1989. *The Dead Will Arise. Nongqawuse and the Great Xhosa Cattle-Killing Movement of 1856-7*. Johannesburg: Ravan.

Peires, J. 1981. *The House of Phalo. A History of the Xhosa People in the Days of their Independence*. Johannesburg: Ravan.

Prins, F. & Granger, J.E. 1993. Early farming communities in northern Transkei: The Evidence from Ntsitsana and Adjacent Areas. *Natal Museum Journal of Humanities*, 5: 153-174.

Roberts, D.L. 2008. Last Interglacial Hominid and Associated Vertebrate Fossil Trackways in Coastal Eolianites, South Africa. *Ichnos*, 15(3-4): 190-207. https://doi.org/10.1080/10420940802470482

Said, E. 1979. *Orientalism*. New York: Vintage Books.

Saunders, C. & Derricourt, R. (eds.). 1974. *Beyond the Cape Frontier. Studies in the History of the Transkei and Ciskei*. Cape Town: Longman.

Soga, J.H. 1931. Ama-Xosa: Life and Customs. Lovedale: Lovedale Press.

Soga, J.H. 1930. *The South-Eastern Bantu (Abe-Nguni, Aba-Mbo, Ama-Lala)*. Johannesburg: Witwatersrand University Press.

Stapleton, T.J. 1994. *Maqoma. Xhosa Resistance to Colonial Advance*. Johannesburg: Jonathan Ball.

Steyn, M.; Binneman, J. & Loots, M. 2007. The Kouga Mummified Remains. *South African Archaeological Bulletin*, 62(185): 3-8.

Switzer, L. 1993. *Power and Resistance in an African Society*. Madison: University of Wisconsin Press.

Tyabashe, M. 1996. All the Land of the Mpondomise. In *The Tongue is Fire. South African Storytellers and Apartheid*, 227-274. Madison: University of Wisconsin Press.

Webley, L. 2008. Heritage Impact Assessment for the Farm 294 Amanzi Estate, Portion 4 of the Farm 296 Amanzi Mooi Water, Erf 296 Portion 3 of Rietheuvel and Erf 296 Rietheuvel. In the Nelson Mandela Bay Municipality, Eastern Cape, unpublished. HIA by Public Process Consultants and Archaeology Contracts Office.

Wurz, S. 2008. Modern Behaviour at Klasies River. *Goodwin Series: Current Themes in Middle Stone Age Research*, 10: 150-156.

CHAPTER 9

Considerations towards establishing equitable stakeholder partnerships for transformation in higher education in South Africa

A review of the challenges, constraints and possibilities in working on pre-colonial history[1]

June Bam[2], Bradley Van Sitters[3] & Bongani Ndhlovu[4]

Knowledge production and related praxis on the pre-colonial in South Africa and in the North remain largely untransformed. Much of this phenomenon has been ascribed to the colonial legacy of hegemonic powers of powerful institutions and their relationship with the communities as knowledge bearers of pre-colonial knowledge. There is already a familiar and well established scholarship on this by Africa-centred decolonial theorists (such as the works of Ntuli 2002; Ndlovu-Gatsheni 2013; Kaya & Seleti 2013; Hoppers 2001 & 2002), and those in the Global South (such as Grosfoguel 2013; Spivak 1988).

---

[1] An earlier draft of this chapter was presented by June Bam at the Archive and Public Research Initiative at a Workshop in April 2016 at UCT, followed by the presentation at the Pre-Colonial Catalytic Conference of 15-17 March 2017 in Port Elizabeth.
[2] june.hutchison@gmail.com and june.bam-hutchison@uct.ac.za
[3] bradlox@gmail.com
[4] ndhlovubc@gmail.com

This chapter goes a step further beyond decolonial theory to reflection on decolonial praxis drawing on the triangulated systematic conversations amongst the authors in their self-reflective practice over many years in the diverse Africa-focused heritage field.[5] In terms of knowledge production and praxis, as authors of this chapter, we have individually and collaboratively engaged in partnerships on the pre-colonial with museums, heritage agencies, and various communities over many years. Each of us brings a particular set of knowledges, perspectives and a variety of experiences and interactions on the pre-colonial project.[6]

We have also intermittently worked together in post-apartheid transformation contexts (Bam with Ndhlovu in heritage networks in Johannesburg and Tshwane, and with Van Sitters in the Cape). Much of the triangulation validation of these conversations on the pre-colonial also took place amongst ourselves and with others in intense and much contested discussion forums on knowledge partnerships in our joint work as the members of the new Cape Town Museum Management Committee over the past 2 years. All three of us as authors are researchers in higher education and work directly in the everyday of both scholarship and the pre-colonial.

Of special mention to this 'triangulation' research method (Flick 2004), which is the systematic triangulation of perspectives as a conversation analysis and validation strategy, that we have applied in the three way conversation and collaboration, is the working relationship between Bam (as university-based scholar) and Van Sitters[7] (as the 'keeper of pre-colonial knowledge' and as 'organic intellectual') over the past three years.

This chapter brings together what we have come to consider, through these triangulated conversations, those salient points for strategies in decolonising knowledge production on the pre-colonial, in partnership work with descendent communities in local contexts. These have been woven into five key common shared

---

[5] Here Bam draws also on her experience as Diversity Manager on the creation of the 'London, Sugar and Slavery gallery' 2007-2008 and work with Bongani Serote on Freedom Park etc.

[6] Through the method of triangulation at the Museum of London, this chapter also draws on findings of research done over the past three years by one of the authors, June Bam, on the 'pre-colonial' under the auspices of respective NRF Chairs Carolyn Hamilton (the *Five Hundred Year Archive* project of the Archive and Public Culture Research Initiative) and Lungisile Ntsebeza (the NIHSS Pre-Colonial Catalytic Conference project under 'Democracy and Land Reform'). In terms of conclusions, the chapter reflects on additional research done by Bam on community partnerships and traditional healing in Public Health at UCT; on the Khoi Revivalist Movement and their relationship with the Diaz Museum in Mossel Bay; and a teaching partnership on the pre-colonial at the Cape between Bam and Van Sitters of the Khoi Revivalist Movement for Stanford University over the last three years.

[7] The work of Van Sitters in teaching Khoi language and sharing knowledge passed on is regularly featured on television in South Africa. This is their first writing collaboration, which is also reflective of their work over the past few years in Cape Town.

themes informed by this collaboration. This chapter discusses these key emerging research themes and attempts to identify the possible ways forward for working on the pre-colonial with higher education institutions in the future, and considers what the possible impacts on higher education transformation could look like, should these recommendations be considered.

The five key commonly identified emerging research issues

The five emerging key research issues that we have identified can be grouped in categories of possible research frameworks towards establishing equitable partnerships with higher education institutions on the pre-colonial. These are:

(1) facilitating networks of negotiation and trust;
(2) challenging state political control in 'heritage' for tourism;
(3) developing de-colonising epistemologies;
(4) facilitating multiple and inter-disciplinary skills development strategies; and
(5) addressing equity in partnerships: the land that memory institutions occupy.

Facilitating networks of negotiation and trust

Wounded-ness and Intergenerational Secrecy

We have found that partnerships on the pre-colonial with greater success benefitted from already long established scholarly and community networks. These projects on the 'pre-colonial' have shown that multilingualism and local community connections (through working with ex-students and organic intellectuals[8] in the field) are tremendously helpful in designing a partnership research project. Internal collaboration through such networks within institutions is also paramount to success as these multiple layered networks bring other useful and relevant knowledges, research capacity and networks to projects. These networks are essentially about facilitating networks of trust, negotiation and mitigation in conflict. Community organisations often have to contend with a multitude of pressures and requests from powerful memory institutions 'to do this and that'. For example, in an interview as

---

[8] Using the Gramscian term in this context (as translated from his 'Prison Notebooks', 1971), and referring to activists from NGOs who are loosely affiliated to higher education institutions who benefit from the 'cultural capital' (Bourdieu 2011) they bring to scholarship without acknowledgement in publications or benefit in research funding.

part of a study conducted for the *Five Hundred Year Archive* (FHYA),[9] postdoctoral fellow in the UCT Health Sciences Faculty Anastasia Koch notes that, "like with the FHYA, it took a long time to establish trust in our public health project on tuberculosis (TB) in collaboration with communities, because powerful institutions are known to not 'follow through' and to be fickle ('all of a sudden choosing another organisation')"[10]. The early phases of a community-linked research collaboration can therefore often be difficult, and (as verified by other global examples) it can take a number of years to build trust (Sandell & Nightingale 2013; Barrow, Prescod, Qureshi, Adi, Bressey, Carty, Casely-Hayford, Dadzie, Dalphinis, D'Mello, Fulton 2005; Arokiasamy 2012). Community organisations look for consistency and a genuine commitment, which takes considerable time and effort.[11] Because of its necessary interdisciplinary nature, we found that successful collaborations on the 'pre-colonial' are often informal, flexible and organic and may be initiated from entirely outside the conventional research area – often through networks with organic (public) intellectuals[12] and civic organisations. For example, Koch relates how an artist friend who is a musician took up an offer to make a film about tuberculosis, which then ended in a health workshop and a collaboration with IKhamba Youth [13] facilitated through yet another informal network layer of a fellow doctoral scholar in an entirely different research area in music. These relationships were 'out there', but were never planned and became more consolidated and strategically established over time. "It's got to be an equal, flexible and dynamic relationship; things change and one has to be responsive to change. There needs to be a dialogue and mutual learning. We got the youth to make the films about TB instead of us. They are involved from the filming to production phase."[14] Because of this interactive and community-led research methodology, the project has therefore managed to build up a rich collaborative archive[15] on health and narratives through the films, including the work of traditional healers on tuberculosis.

---

[9] The Five Hundred Year pre-colonial digital archive is located within the Archive and Public Culture Research Initiative, UCT, led by NRF Chair, Carolyn Hamilton. See http://www.apc.uct.ac.za/apc/research/projects/five-hundred-year-archive [Retrieved 13 November 2017].

[10] Interview, July 2016. UCT: Health Sciences.

[11] Koch interview, UCT Health Sciences, July 2016.

[12] Mahmood Mamdani, for instance, emphasised the role of the public intellectual in transforming the university space as an essential part of decolonisation in Africa (T.B. Davies, Memorial Lecture, UCT, 22 August 2017). See also the discussion on the 'committed intellectual', liberatory pedagogical praxis and Freirian conscientisation in contemporary discourse in Fischman & McLaren (2005:425-446).

[13] They offer extra curricula support to youth in Khayelitsha, Nyanga, KwaZulu-Natal, Johannesburg and worldwide to improve learners' marks and access to tertiary education; open for anyone who wants to come.

[14] Interview, July 2016. UCT: Health Sciences.

[15] Whilst the creation of community archives is a growing phenomenon globally, it has been critiqued in the West as threatening standards in scholarship. See for instance, Flinn 2007.

But public health partnerships (a pivotal area relevant to the recognition of pre-colonial knowledge, such as the medicinal value of plants) are not always collaborative. A case in point is traditional medicines[16] and government appropriation of patent and intellectual property processes. In this instance, the Khoi Revivalist Movement cites the case of the appropriation of the *Hoodia* plant as an example of contemporary forms of appropriation that led to the breakdown of trust on working together on pre-colonial cultural capital, linked to economic capital (Bourdieu 2011; Guillory 2013). The knowledge of the *Hoodia* plant which has been used by the San for thousands of years as food and water during hunting expeditions and to treat disease was systematically obliterated along with well documented genocide (Adhikari 2010). It made its appearance in the colonial archive as late as 1796 as part of encounters with the 'Hottentots'[17] and gets documented as 'an edible plant' by the apartheid Council for Scientific Research (CSIR) in 1963. Even though knowledge of these plants existed and continues to be vibrantly alive in descendent communities, the apartheid government embarked on confidential research on the *Hoodia* from around 1986-1995 (Wynberg & Chennells 2009).

Internationally, there were strong campaigns to protect indigenous knowledge in medicine, such as captured in the *Indigenous and tribal peoples: a guide to International Labour Organisastion (ILO) Convention* 1989 (No. 169) (Tomei & Swepston 1996). With the founding of South Africa's first democratic constitution in 1996 the "cultural knowledge" and "rights" of indigenous people were protected and a commission has been established for this purpose. After 1994 patent law and indigenous intellectual property rights became a prominent feature of the new South Africa with appropriation of indigenous knowledge globally being branded 'biopiracy'.[18] This was part of the global movement in the 1990s to protect indigenous knowledge from capitalist appropriation, such as the later creation of the Traditional Knowledge Digital Library in 2001 in India.

These global movements also impacted on awareness of indigenous rights and knowledge in South Africa as it was consolidated in the late 1990s through the first international indigenous people's conference held in Cape Town which discussed some of these rights.

---

[16] There is established early scholarship on this aspect of indigenous knowledge in South Africa. See for example Ngubane 1977.
[17] The derogatory term used in the colonial archive for the Khoi in the Cape.
[18] See 'Struggle over Hoodia patent continues', *Business Day*, Johannesburg, 12 July 2006:6.

However, in recent years there have been increasing concerns regarding the protection of indigenous knowledge as this has not been explicit constitutionally, although chapter 9 of the Constitution outlines protection for institutions of indigenous rights. South Africa also passed the Traditional Health Practitioners Act 22 of 2007.[19] Though the KhoiSan could legally claim profits for their intellectual property in rock paintings in KwaZulu-Natal and through the San Institute for South Africa for plant knowledge, the process has shown to be often difficult and complex (Wynberg, Schroeder & Chennells 2009). Government intent did not often match government support to ensure protection of intellectual property.[20]

It is within these complex constitutional and policy implementation contexts, that the ANC government commenced in negotiations on the *Hoodia* plant with Unilever within the post-apartheid South Africa. The end result of the negotiations was that the patent rights of the plant were sold and today these communities need a permit to access their plants, leading to communities not being able to freely use their thousands of years' pre-colonial knowledge of resources within the natural landscape.

Today, Khoi Revivalists are asking for initiatives on 'secrecy' amongst indigenous communities regarding indigenous knowledge because "who told the world about the plant".[21] Whilst the colonial botanical archive was founded on appropriation of knowledge, indigenous pre-colonial capital and exclusivity, the knowledge within communities continued to exist in a 'secrecy' parallel process, seemingly surviving epistemicide.

Related to the issue of trust between public health institutions and indigenous communities is the deep issue of the not so very distant historical colonial violence on subjugated physical bodies as anatomies for "study" (Legassick & Rassool 2000; Rassool & Hayes 2002; Wits & Rassool 2008). Van Sitters contends that through working with memory and body within contemporary self-identified Khoi communities, there is a direct link between the urge to jealously guard secrecy and the deeply embedded associated fear of the genocide of indigenous people in southern Africa in the past. Because Khoi skeletons were sought for scientific study and as

---

[19] See http://www.chr.up.ac.za/chr_old/indigenous/country_reports/Country_reports_SouthAfrica.pdf [Retrieved 24 June 2018: 8].
[20] See http://www.chr.up.ac.za/chr_old/indigenous/country_reports/Country_reports_SouthAfrica.pdf [Retrieved 24 June 2018: 52].
[21] At the March 2017 conference, the 'secrecy' issue was raised by Khoi Chief Margaret Coetzee, but with a reluctance to spell out in public what that 'secrecy' entails. It was pursued as a debate in the breakaway groups.

collectors' items, Van Sitters explains that there is the general secretive approach to human remains within these psychologically brutalised communities, '*Ons praat nie uit nie*' ('We do not talk out'), referring here to the need in the past (as passed on through oral tradition within the contemporary Khoi Revivalist Movement[22]) to keep secret from such colonial scientists (who monitored communities for impending 'bones') when someone in the Khoi community was close to death due to terminal illness or old age. The gruesome fate of Sarah Baartman is well known and has become household knowledge globally. Furthermore, it was a legal Western practice worldwide during the colonial era for those who were deemed as 'Resurrectionists' to supply scientists with cadavers of the black, poor and indigenous in subjugated communities. Rassool (2015) mentions how South African museums competed with such scientists for access to Bushmen bodies for racial research. One such, being the Austrian anthropologist Rudolf Pöch.[23] This abhorrent practice laid the foundation for the founding of colonial museums in South Africa (Rassool 2015).[24]

This highly sensitive issue of ethics and secrecy (whether about the fear of genocide or of the appropriation of indigenous knowledge) was also raised by Khoi Chief Margaret Coetzee and Chief George Maleiba in conversation with higher education participants at the Pre-colonial conference of March 2017 who cited (amongst other still jealously guarded unnamed reasons) fears around the use of indigenous languages during colonialism at the Cape as it could have 'led to death'.[25] 'Secrecy' within indigenous-descendant communities beyond the knowledge of plants remains a much un-researched aspect and a silence within academia, further complicated by the ongoing fear itself to speak in higher education conferences and seminars (considered still as colonial knowledge practices) about 'secrets'. Because of embedded extractive colonial research practices in universities, academics are often not trusted by communities that are the 'keepers' of 'pre-colonial' knowledge. A case in point, is the Griqua Movement which is renowned for protectively guarding their '*geheime*' – 'secrets',[26] which has typically frustrated white academic researchers on the pre-colonial.[27]

---

[22] This civic movement emerged in recent years in the Cape provinces (Northern, Western and Eastern Cape) to contest heritage spaces through occupation, Khoi language teaching classes and renaming of places and the landscape.
[23] See also Hoffmann 2014.
[24] See also Legassick & Rassool 2000.
[25] Similar to the plight of the indigenous Kurds in present-day Turkey.
[26] Remark made by Eastern Cape historian Jeff Peires at the Pre-Colonial Catalytic Conference of March 2014, African Studies, UCT.
[27] See also a related discussion by Doxtater (2004:618-633).

In light of these strong tensions around exploitation of the body and knowledge forms, we need to consider consultation on a decolonising framework for working with indigenous knowledges and related aspects of 'protocol' and 'secrecy' (discussed earlier). This is not currently covered, for example, in the San Code of Ethics for Research.[28] Patent systems in Africa are equally underutilised, showing this shortcoming in the 'elements of secrecy customs' when digitising knowledge of plants and healing, for instance. Traditional knowledge-holding communities are encouraged to be engaged in policy consultations on plants.[29] For instance, South Africa's Kukula healers from Bushbuckridge in Mpumulanga, want to make sure that their knowledge "is not taken away ... because we have a wealth of knowledge ... traditional knowledge that we have inherited that we want to keep on for new generations ... protocol must be followed even by our researchers".[30]

Challenging state political control in 'heritage' for tourism

From the /Ui!arab (Castle of Good Hope) case study (discussed later), it is becoming apparent that there is constant tension between on the ground decolonial movements for visibility and top down institutional tendencies to respectively visibilise and invisibilise the 'pre-colonial' depending on political agendas that these spaces do get confronted with within post-1994 South Africa. By default, higher education researchers get drawn into such processes of 'curation' as research consultants, which as authors we have observed in a range of projects and exhibitions commemorating various historical anniversaries (such as the bicentenary of the abolition of the transatlantic slave trade at the Museum of London and Iziko Museums in 2007 and the commemoration of 350 years of colonial settlement at the Castle of Good Hope, etc.).

---

[28] See http://trust-project.eu/wp-content/uploads/2017/03/San-Code-of-RESEARCH-Ethics-Booklet-final.pdf
[29] See 'Briefing Note: Managing Benefits from Traditional Knowledge (TK)', published by Open Air, 2014. See also www.youtube.com/user/Afrinnovation
[30] See www.youtube.com/user/Afrinnovation

Illustrations of Visibilisation and Invisibilisation of Pre-colonial History at the Castle of Good Hope

Source: Line engraving from an English edition of Peter Kolbe's 'The Present State of the Cape of Good Hope,' 1731.

Photo 1: A contemporary reconstruction of a pre-colonial Khoi settlement at the Castle of Good Hope, erected in 2016 to commemorate 350 years of the Castle. Source: News 24 (Jenna Etheridge) [Retrieved 18 September 2017]. After the commemoration it was moved outside to a more obscure space on the side at the entrance.

Photo 2: The relocation of the settlement (made much smaller) after the 350 year commemoration to outside the Castle. Source: IOL News [Retrieved 19 September].[31]

Much of what we got to know about the Cape of Good Hope Castle is through the colonial archive and histories (Raven-Hart 1971) that were drummed into the minds of generations of school children during apartheid (1652; Jan Van Riebeeck, etc.). Oppositional historiography exposed much of the colonial history of the Castle through the publications of 1952 to boycott the 300 years apartheid commemoration (Saunders 1986; Rassool & Witz 1993).

Interestingly, the Castle's historiography in praxis has remained much unchanged, hindered by neo-liberal heritage agendas in contemporary South Africa. For instance, as part of the 350 year celebration in 2016, the erected Khoi settlement hut in photo 1 was initially positioned opposite the Torture Chamber at the Castle where indigenous people and the enslaved, amongst others, were notoriously brutally incarcerated from the late 1600s before public executions on the Leerdam Bastion (Shell 1994) or at 'Justice Square' –'Pleets Justisie'[32] as called by the Dutch.

According to the Castle's Annual Report of 2015/6, in line with its 'mandate', it spent over R1 million on its general 'tourism offering' including the construction of a 'Khoi-kraal' (photo 1). The Kraal was opened in the courtyard on 7 February 2016, accompanied with goats, while buchu was burnt and holy water was drunk[33] in the opening ceremonies. In the run up to the celebration in 2015, 'Full moon Khoi

---

[31] Since the land hearings in 2018 the reconstruction has been totally removed from the site of the Castle.
[32] Corner of present day Buitenkant and Darling streets in the city of Cape Town.
[33] http://www.news24.com/SouthAfrica/News/cape-town-castle-commemoration-heralds-new-chapter-of-healing-20160103

ceremonies'[34] and cleansing ceremonies were held at the Castle. A Khoisan Art Exhibition was opened in February 2016 with an ex-Pollsmoor prisoner as 'resident artist' who had a passion for depicting indigenous art as part of his rehabilitation programme.[35]

These initiatives were all largely in response to government political interests for promotion of reconciliation and in part the public pressure that has been exerted by Khoisan activism. Hence, the 2015/6 Castle's Annual Report made a commitment to "missing reinterpretation, reimagining and representation of the full Castle story particularly focusing on indigenous Khoi people" in the new financial year. Youth education programmes on the pre-colonial enjoyed a particular focus as evident in the report, and the Castle reported that it had opened its doors to "organised Khoi and Nguni Cultural Groups".[36] "We are trying to confront the visitor with what they read in history books and we are saying the Castle was not built on open land and unused land. They were people who roamed this land (Hunters and gatherers, the Khoisan people)" (Gilfellan 2015/2016).[37]

In spite of the management's enthusiastic commitment to foreground pre-colonial history at the Castle, at the end of the celebration, the Khoi settlement was removed to be placed outside the Castle (photo 2). It was now out of sight, due to 'security measures' because of the visit by the Minister of Defence, Nosiviwe Mapisa-Nqakula.[38] The goats (a particular attraction for young children) were also removed.[39] The alleged 'security risks' of what a 'pre-colonial hut' could present notwithstanding, the Minister is said to have taken a 'selfie' at the hut and "everyone wanted to take photos of the Khoisan kraal".[40]

---

[34] Much of the pre-colonial rituals are still alive and well amongst descendant communities in places like the Cape Flats. Often such practices, such as the knowledge and consumption of edible plants, are vibrantly and deeply present and not considered new or 'exotic'; therefore perhaps 'invisible'. Even colonial observations record the 'ongoing practices' of rituals and performances in the 1910s such as discussed in Hoernlé 1921:-21.
[35] This was observed during a site visit to the Castle by the authors at the time.
[36] See http://pmg-assets.s3-website-eu-west-1.amazonaws.com/Castle_Control_Board_Annual_Report_2015_2016_FA4.pdf
[37] http://www.leadsa.co.za/articles/12966/castle-of-good-hope-brings-the-history-of-the-khoisan-alive
[38] The Castle is a military site, though part of national heritage. The Castle is managed by the Castle Control Board as a public entity under the Minister of Defence and Military Veterans and mandated by the Castle Management Act (Act 207 of 1993).
[39] Van Sitters was part of the consultation process regarding the goats, and relates that due to animal rights concerns (loud military parade with the noon gun), the goats were given back to their owners. These owners were the same people that used to supply the Castle with horses and carts for tourist 'horse rides' at the Castle (to emulate the colonial experience).
[40] Observation made by Bradley Van Sitters.

The Cape of Good Hope Castle has always been known for its conservative and cautious approach to curation and public programmes in a post-apartheid context since 1994;[41] itself steeped in a deep colonial and brutal history and the much boycotted 300-year Van Riebeeck celebrations in 1952.[42] It has always been a traumatic and much feared site for descendants of the oppressed and indigenous people; many of those generations who lived through apartheid as the oppressed avoid the site because of "what happened there to our people".[43] It is also remarkable, for instance, that it was only recently in 2012 that the Castle management was instructed (amidst public outcry most likely from whites) to remove the old South Africa apartheid flag[44] along with other colonial flags such as the Union Jack, on the Leerdam Bastion, where ironically executions of the incarcerated, enslaved and indigenous people took place in colonial times. There is the problematic assumption in the new South Africa that the pre-colonial people are 'extinct' and that parading violence of early colonial times towards the indigenous people is benign.[45]

Photo 3: The contentious 'Krotoa's bench' at the Castle (unmarked and obscure) unveiled by the Ministry of Defence in Women's Month, August 2016.

Doing the 'pre-colonial' at museums and heritage sites has clearly not been without significant contestations within descendant communities. A case in point is the 'statues of royal prisoners' unveiled on 11 December 2016 by the Minister of Defence of amaHlubi king Langalibalele, Zulu king Cetshwayo, Bapedi king Sekhukhune and

---

[41] Bam served on the Iziko Museums Council in 2002/3 before the Castle was transferred to the Ministry of Defence. Van Sitters has been fully integrated into the everyday public programmes at the Castle for the past few years and Ndhlovu has worked in close partnership with many heritage institutions at the Cape and in South Africa.
[42] See for instance the 1952 protest publications of the Non-European Unity Movement (NEUM).
[43] Van Sitters and Bam in conversation with Khoi activists at the Castle on Heritage Day, 24 September, 2017.
[44] http://www.news24.com/SouthAfrica/News/Shock-as-CTs-Castle-removes-old-SA-flag-20121123
[45] Similarly also the case with the Drostdy Museum with its 'whipping post' in Swellendam. See http://www.iol.co.za/news/politics/welcome-to-the-whipping-post-have-a-seat-1951947

Khoisan freedom fighter Doman[46] who were held captive at the Castle. The ceremony which coincided with "reconciliation month",[47] was attended by IFP[48] leader Mangosuthu Buthelezi 'who saluted as the statue of the Zulu king was unveiled'. As related by Van Sitters, the Khoisan Revivalist Movement expressed their disappointment by the fact that when the four statues were erected at the Castle, they "thought they were building a statue for Krotoa",[49] who was the niece of the Khoi Goringhaicona leader and interpreter, Autshumato ... 'but it was about the four male prisoners that were held there'.

Photo 4: Indigenous male warrior statues prominently erected at the Castle in December 2016 to commemorate 350 years (coinciding with Reconciliation Day).

The Khoisan Revivalist Movement argues that before the colonial prison, there were people; prison was a foreign concept. There was no consultation with the Khoisan Revivalist Movement on the statues. Instead a wooden bench was made for Krotoa without the Khoi Revivalist Movement being consulted. Van Sitters notes that Khoi activists argued that there should be "a vertical structure in the ground standing up for people to look up at her instead of looking down and sitting on the space. Indigenous wood should be used". This idea was in fact presented by the Khoi

---

46 See https://www.businesslive.co.za/bd/life/2016-12-11-statues-of-royal-prisoners-unveiled-at-castle-of-good-hope-commemoration/
47 Celebrated every 16 December to commemorate reconciliation in the new South Africa (under apartheid commemorated as 'the Day of the Vow' for the Battle of Blood River of 1838 between the Boers and Afrikaners).
48 Inkatha Freedom Party with its roots in 1920s Zulu nationalist politics, established in 1975.
49 The previous fort and the Castle were Khoi woman interpreter Krotoa's childhood 'homes' during Van Riebeeck's time.

Revivalist Movement to the Castle. "How can we sit on her memory?" Krotoa (also among the first unrecognised political prisoners on Robben Island) is made out to be "the first prostitute of Cape Town, of the Castle, the first Christian, the first noble savage, a high treason traitor by both sides."[50] The bench was unveiled during Women's Month in August 2016, as part of the 60th commemoration of the Women's March to the Union Buildings in 1956.[51] There were protests as the bench was found to be offensive to some members of the movement, who felt it "disrespectful for people to sit on Krotoa's face, which had formed part of the mosaic". The reinterpretation of Krotoa's story (a representation of pre-colonial Khoi history with regards to treatment of women in matrilineal African societies) remains a highly contentious one, as evident in the recent public media debates[52] on the recent film released (Scully 2005). The memory of Krotoa (and that of black women in general) is virtually invisibilised in the contemporary curation at the Castle.

There is the problem of the use of indigenous culture and heritage for commodification purposes. Van Sitters relates the disappointment within the Khoi Revivalist Movement when with the 350-year anniversary in 2016 of the Cape of Good Hope Castle,[53] a "sudden process" transpired where the Indigenous Knowledge System (IKS)[54] Legacy Programme was initially enthusiastically used as a buffer strategy to prevent the then anticipated[55] "#TheCastleMustFall" campaign. Hence there was an initial conscious choice to emphasise indigenous displays, but at the end of the commemorations, the programme was halted. The Khoisan Revivalist Movement felt that this was an ideal opportunity, "in a very tangible Cape colonial space", to "decolonise curation" through a public programme. In this instance, however, the Castle management 'fell back' on visibilising the pre-colonial and chose the public tourist narrative of 'colonial victory' in spite of the site's deep historical contested apartheid past.[56] This occurred even though the movement argued that there was a community of people occupying the site, long before /Ui!arab ('stone kraal'), as referred to by the Khoi in the 1600s. The contemporary Khoi Revivalist

---

[50] Observation by Van Sitters.
[51] http://www.capetalk.co.za/articles/15938/monument-to-the-khoi-woman-krotoa-unveiled-at-castle-of-good-hope
[52] See for instance http://www.huffingtonpost.co.za/2017/08/11/whitewashed-new-krotoa-movie-is-insult-to-heritage-of-khoisa_a_23074394/ [Retrieved 12 December 2017].
[53] Built in 1666 by the Dutch East India Company as of the first and the largest colonial buildings at the Cape.
[54] Indigenous Knowledge Systems, which emerged as an established field in the new South Africa after 1994.
[55] This was happening in the aftermath of the #RhodesMustFall campaign which started in 2015.
[56] It was a much boycotted space during apartheid and was particularly marked with the Three Hundred Years of Van Riebeeck commemorations in 1952.

Movement has decided to call the Castle /Ui!arab as part of its decolonial agenda to rename spaces.

Developing de-colonising epistemologies

Language and new conceptual frameworks

Building on *Ukuhlambulula* – cleansing in historiography – the concept argued by historian Nomathamsanqa Tisani at the conference, Van Sitters noted some further useful Khoi words for new research methodologies and epistemologies, such as *khaoexasib* which means 'humanness' or 'menslikheid' and *naos* for cleansing. Van Sitters also notes that UCT got the spelling of *Hoerikwaggo* for Table Mountain wrong; that the word should be spelled *Huri#oaxa*. *Huri* means 'sea'; *oaxa* means 'rise' and *IIHui!Gaeb* means 'veiled in clouds'. The spelling of *Camissa* is also wrong as the 'c' letter is non-existent in the Khoi alphabet; that it should be *'gammi-isa'*. Clearly, a closer working relationship with communities and transformation of the naming of buildings is required to share knowledge capital in these processes.[57]

Along with the appropriation of Khoi language to position the ongoing presence of the pre-colonial, is the need to challenge 'extinction discourse' in curation practice (as mentioned earlier). As shared by Van Sitters, museums disturbingly prefer to write about the Khoi 'in the past tense' in museums and exhibitions. Any suggestion by the communities of 'present-ness' is dismissed in favour of conventional preferred 'chronological timelines and dates'; also observed as a compulsive curatorial practice in travelling exhibitions of museums ignoring debates and contestations.

Van Sitters also highlights the problem with "colonial methodologies in linguistic research, which invariably relate to curation at some point in the epistemological journey". "The research methodology approach must be indigenous" and not the "question answer response". This is problematic. What is needed are open, equal conversations; the 'us' and 'them' paradigm should be avoided in research approaches and interviews which instil binaries in research methodologies. "Rituals should be observed, and the approach should not be extractive with a list of questions." How do we decolonise research methodologies and disrupt the "power relationship" between the researcher and the community (Smith 2013)?

---

[57] At the time of writing, UCT through CAS is in consultation with descendant indigenous collective KhoiSan communities in the renaming of its campus buildings. This would be historic for the historically white institution.

The Khoi Revivalist Movement is not only reclaiming language, but also looking at the present traces of indigenous languages and cultural expressions in contemporary Afrikaans[58] amongst descendant communities on the Cape Flats. The majority of Cape indigenous groups adopted Afrikaans as the language of communication, apart from a few indigenous people situated in very rural and remote places. The Khoi Revivalists cite that history teaches us that in 1613, Coree c.1580-1626, a local Khoikhoi in Cape Town was kidnapped and taken to England for a year to learn English for bartering purposes. Autshumato c.1625-1665, who was known to the Europeans as Hadah, Adda, or Haddot and after 1652, as Harry, was similarly taken around 1631-32 to the Javanese port of Bantam and taught the essentials of the English language. Krotoa (c.1642- 1674) and Doman (Nommoa) were the first Khoikhoi baptised Christians and during the time of Van Riebeeck there were further instances of Khoikhoi who adopted European languages to facilitate translation and trading.

According to Van Sitters, who has studied Nama at the University of Namibia, "*Afrikaaps*[59] has amazingly encapsulated a lot of the linguistic and cultural manner of pre-colonial expression. A lot of this is vastly overlooked because it was always looked down on. Culturally you would ask #*khaits* go? (male) and #*khais* go? (female); #*khai re* (skrikwakker), literally meaning are you awake?" According to the Khoi Revivalist Movement, many linguists have overlooked this because of the 'colonial approach' to scholarship, avowed of social context and experiential knowledge. "These cultural etiquettes are not European (neither Dutch nor English)." In this regard, one of the works that the Khoi Revivalist Movement draws on is the work of the late Richard Kutela,[60] a widely known linguist and Thembalethu herbalist, former Chair of the George Initiation and Environmental Forum, and chief of the Kai! Koranna Royal House, who tried to show the linguistic connections between Afrikaans and Xhosa. We cannot overlook the connected cultural experiences and knowledges of the communities who experienced language and identity loss. There is also currently the debate that Cape Flats gang language and cultural expression are strongly derivative of Khoi and Xhosa because it infuses Xhosa words such as '*ndoda*'.[61] Related to this, is the notion of the perceived 'ethnic differences' between the Xhosa-speaking and

---

[58] Mahmood Mamdani made the point of the origins of Afrikaans as a multilingual 'decolonial' project (against Dutch colonialism of the 1600s at the Cape as it came from so many languages, including African). TB Davis Lecture, UCT, 22 August 2017.

[59] The local Cape Flats variant of Afrikaans.

[60] Kutela is widely cited amongst Khoi Revivalist communities – as also evident in research by Bam in Mossel Bay in 2015/6.His work is also cited by Environmentalist scientists. See also Zenani 2005.

[61] According to the Khoi revivalists there was a Khoi chief who was highly respected who was called 'ndoda'.

Khoi-descendant communities which also needs to be addressed through studying the pre-colonial more in-depth. Earlier preliminary work in this regard has been done by archaeologists (such as Hammond-Took 1997), but remains publically inaccessible. Van Sitters encountered these tensions in his teaching of 'Africa Day' at the Central Library in Cape Town in 2016 when some of the Xhosa participants were questioning the linguistic connection between Khoi and Xhosa communities: "The colonial experiences were falsification, the retelling of intergenerational lies with the result that Khoi descendent people are seen as a result of the binary between Europe and Africa, not as Africans." "This is because when we insulted people during apartheid, we called them 'Boesman' and 'Hotnot' and the Khoi word *Xam*[62] was of the worst you could imagine." Yet, *u Thixo* for 'God' in Xhosa has the same meaning as the Khoi word *Tsui-//goatse!*, and the two words are connected.

Reinterpreting uMakhulu[63]

There is also a lot still to be researched through *uMakhulu* (using here the research framework coined by feminist scholar Babalwa Magoqwana at the March 2017 conference). In studying Khoi history, this approach would be indispensable as the matrilineal society that was a driving force (with ongoing cultural traces today in descendant communities on the Cape Flats and within rural descendant communities such as those with the ubiquitous use of the word '*ousie*', for the most revered oldest woman of the family, for instance).

Reinterpretation of *uMakhulu* warrants a reinterpretation of public culture today. Attempts to piece together Krotoa's history have been difficult for both historians and organic intellectuals, as we only get to know her through Van Riebeeck's journals. She remains the subject of much debate by lead pre-colonial black feminist scholars such as Yvette Abrahams and public intellectuals such as journalist Sylvia Vollenhoven. Van Sitters has participated in a film project on Krotoa[64] which was released in July 2017, but which has provoked contention and resistance by the Khoi-descendant project partners like himself. In spite of the noble intentions of the

---

62 Denoting those who were wiped out through genocide. Adhikari 2010.
63 Xhosa for elder woman.
64 https://www.facebook.com/pg/Krotoafilm/about/?ref=page_internal; http://www.destinyconnect.com/2017/05/16/local-film-krotoa-bags-eight-awards-release/https://www.youtube.com/watch?v=ARuo-YsVFI4

film, it is widely critiqued by critics like journalist and the writer of *The Keeper of the Kumm*[65] Sylvia Vollenhoven, as having been written by a colonial hand.[66]

Review Research Practice Models

In light of the above discussions, it stands to reason that funding models in support of the 'pre-colonial' may need to be carefully reviewed within the model of de-colonising research practice, including for public culture projects. We need to find a shared new language[67] on 'knowledge' and 'research' as we work with contesting voices and identities at 'sites of memory' in the Cape. Koch reflects on this when she asserts, "The artist and I spoke a different language. Research meant to me hypotheses, methods, results, discussion. To him, it is more diffuse, qualitative. He is not based in an academic structure like I am" (Koch interview, 2016).

This shared language for successful research collaboration, is the necessary condition for epistemological transformation which could ultimately transform and refigure the archive, and de-colonise knowledge frameworks on the 'pre-colonial'. Moreover, it can also contribute to innovation, skills development and building research capacity. "The knowledge of the artist has impacted massively on my thinking as a scientist. I was more technical and focussed; it made me think much more broadly about issues and how they fit into a bigger context, about South Africa and communities; and I learnt how to be a project manager, how to be more efficient, not to panic about small things and about collaboration and respecting another person's way of thinking and doing something – about the world. I had to adapt to diffuse thinking, to the big melting pot of thinking. Three years ago, I was so less efficient ... We are looking at how learners use the space of the project to narrate their daily lives? How do they represent illness?' The findings of this research will be presented at a forthcoming science conference to open up people's minds."[68]

---

[65] See http://www.thejournalist.org.za/art/the-keeper-of-the-kumm-comes-to-cape-town
[66] See https://weekendspecial.co.za/krotoa-movie-review-theresa-smith/ and http://www.huffingtonpost.co.za/2017/08/11/whitewashed-new-krotoa-movie-is-insult-to-heritage-of-khoisa_a_23074394/
[67] Part of the work June Bam has been doing with her Stanford University Sites of Memory classes from 2015-2017 (students include Native Americans).
[68] This integrated approach to decolonial research was highlighted by Mahmood Mamdani, TB Davies Memorial Lecture, UCT, 22 August 2017.

Facilitating multiple and inter-disciplinary skills development strategies

The Khoi Revivalist Movement's 'Aba Te' – 'Carry Me' Education Project focuses on impoverished and marginalised Khoi descendant communities in the Cape (urban and rural youth and farming communities). Through creative activities during the school holidays, the movement engages youth on 'healing' from intergenerational trauma which they view as 'crime news' in popular local media such as *The Voice* and *Die Son*. They make a direct link between gang culture and the loss of pre-colonial identities, knowledge and value systems, citing for example the initiation into manhood through criminalisation in prisons as a response to colonialism. To gang leaders, affiliated to the 'number system', the 'pre-colonial' identity is crucial for identity education in prison as these 'number gang leaders' see themselves as 'Khoi warriors'.[69] The *Aba-Te* Educational project hopes to offer an alternative, as manhood is often linked to going to jail to earn the respect of your peers in contrast to Xhosa communities 'who go to the bush' and whites who 'go to the army'. The educational programmes of *Aba-Te* interrogate the concept of *"Amalawu"* (a Xhosa term depicting people with no culture and no language of their own), which Khoi revivalists argue may have led to 'confused identities' and 'intergenerational inferiority complexes'. The *Aba-Te* project therefore offers a space for intergenerational listening to narratives of connected and interwoven African identities (lost through colonialism and the disavow of knowledge and memories) and their related ancient pre-colonial knowledge.

The *Aba-Te* project demonstrates the role of the inter-disciplinary skilled development strategist as the much needed 'third space' higher education academic professional highlighted in the work of pre-colonial projects and as discussed at the March 2017 catalytic conference at Mandela University. These academics and professionals bring the required application of skills that go beyond the Western-based disciplines and boundaries of history, archaeology, the archive, etc. – very crucial to uncover the invisibilised content knowledge of the pre-colonial. These are skills crafted in public education work and clearly take many years to practise and develop into socially engaged scholarship based on praxis. Skills and knowledges beyond Western scholarship, involving the organic intellectual as an equal, have therefore notably shown to be crucial in forming research partnerships in our work as authors on the 'pre-colonial' over a number of years. This was evident in our respective work on the 'London, Sugar and Slavery' permanent gallery, exhibitions

---

[69] Interview with anonymous Pollsmoor Prison gang leader, Retreat, March 2017. Recent statistics indicate a significant proportion of 'Coloureds' in prison.

and working with collections at Izikc Museums, the public interpretation of the 'Perspectives of and on Africa Map Project' at Parliament, and the creation of the 'pre-colonial' at Freedom Park with renowned poet Bongane Serote, etc.

Addressing equity in partnerships: the land that memory institutions occupy

According to Hill (2004), despite shared commitments to specific geographical places, institutions of higher education and communities are often separated by deep-seated tensions over land and other space issues. Similarly, Hill contends community organisations may want to steer clear of universities that have very negative reputations lest they lose legitimacy with their community constituency (such as we saw with the case of UCT and the national #RhodesMustFall Movement (#RMF)). "The institutional space issue (is said to be) the most difficult aspect of higher-education-community research partnerships and the one over which individual partners have the least control" (Ferman &Hill 2004).

Photo 5: Source: Esa Alexander (Bradley Van Sitters performing a counter narrative at the Castle, The Sowetan, 15 February 2015).

The same can be said of government institutional memory spaces in which the same tensions are prevalent. For instance, the Khoi Revivalist Occupy Movement is in constant battle with the Castle of Good Hope[70] and the Diaz Museum in Mossel Bay[71] with regard to 'occupied land' that obstructs and disrupts partnership building processes around the 'pre-colonial' and contentious social justice issues. Stakeholders, including the #RMF,[72] complain about the lack of acknowledgement of

---

[70] Research June Bam conducted on transformation of museums in 2015-2016.
[71] Research June Bam conducted on transformation of museums in Mossel Bay in 2015-2016.
[72] See mention and reference in the Introduction to this book.

the pre-colonial in 'white appropriated' memory spaces, and until such time that the pre-colonial is dealt with and embraced in an equal dialectic and acknowledgement process, such partnerships can't really materialise. In both the scenarios of the Castle and Mossel Bay, the feelings are that the 'pre-colonial' is not taken seriously and that 'indigenous partners' are relegated to 'song and dance' activities in public programmes. Van Sitters, who leads Khoi language classes at the Castle, speaks of being instructed by fellow black staff at a particular provincial heritage site to "go get your leopard skin and dance and do some Khoi clicks when the tourists arrive".[73]

In these post-1994 spaces, the 'pre-colonial' is interestingly 'othered' in a new internalised way; the 1652 paradigm is entrenched (through predominantly foregrounding the Castle as a military site of the Dutch East India Company (DEIC)) as it is assumed that the Eurocentric approach (with the noon re-enactment of the military parade and the canon) 'keeps tourists happy'. Van Sitters is at pains to present the alternative in an informal way with interested groups, to deconstruct the narrative from long before 1666 (when it was built). These Cape sites of memory on the pre-colonial have therefore now become sites of occupation and counter narrative protests, involving cleansing ceremonies and shouting of the names of Khoi leaders, Krotoa, Autshumato, etc.[74]

Conclusion

Based on our praxis work over many years on the 'pre-colonial' in a variety of contexts, we would like to suggest that higher education institutions rethink and reconfigure their roles in partnership building as memory institutions with communities on the pre-colonial in terms of these 5 key emerging themes that we have discussed in this chapter for going forward. This should be part of the bigger de-colonial and transformation project as institutional transformation (including its *methods* of working with research partners in engaged scholarship) cannot be delinked from content and pedagogical transformation. We believe that the pre-colonial intellectual project can be decisively catalytic in these practical ways as we suggest.

---

73   Interview, Observatory, March 2018.
74   Van Sitters supports June Bam's class sessions at the Castle for Stanford University. His method of problematising the Western narrative of the space is to carry out indigenous rituals and shouting the counter narrative in the physical spaces of the Castle as contestation to the tour guide's Eurocentric tourist script on Lady Anne Barnard, the military parade and Simon van der Stel. Bam employs this pedagogical approach as part of an innovative de-colonial teaching project with public activist intellectuals in colonial spaces.

References

Abrahams, Y. 1996. Was Eva raped? An exercise in speculative history. *Kronos,* 23: 3-21.

Adhikari, M. 2010.*The anatomy of a South African genocide: The extermination of the Cape San peoples.* Cape Town: Juta and Company Ltd.

Arokiasamy, C. 2012. Embedding shared heritage: the cultural heritage rights of London's African and Asian diaspora communities. *International Journal of Heritage Studies,*18(3): 339-345. https://doi.org/10.1080/13527258.2012.651738

Bam-Hutchison, J. 2016. The Public as co-producers: making the London, Sugar and Slavery gallery. In: C.A. Scott (ed.). *Museums and public value: creating sustainable futures.* London and New York: Routledge.

Barrow, J.; Prescod, C.; Qureshi, I.M.; Adi, H.; Bressey, C.; Carty, H.; Casely-Hayford, A.; Dadzie, S.; Dalphinis, M.; D'Mello, M. & Fulton, L.H. 2005. Delivering shared heritage: the Mayor's Commission on African and Asian heritage. London: Report of the Greater London Authority.

Bourdieu, P. 2011. The forms of Capital. In: J.G. Richardson, *Handbook of Theory and Research for Sociology of Education,* 241-258. Wesport: Greenwood Publishing Group.

Doxtater, M.G. 2004. Indigenous knowledge in the decolonial era. *The American Indian Quarterly,* 28(3): 618-633. https://doi.org/10.1353/aiq.2004.0094

Ferman, B. & Hill, T.L. 2004. The challenges of agenda conflict in higher-education-community research partnerships: Views from the community side. *Journal of Urban Affairs,* 26(2):241-257.

Fischman, G.E. & McLaren, P. 2005. Rethinking critical pedagogy and the Gramscian and Freirean legacies: From organic to committed intellectuals or critical pedagogy, commitment, and praxis. *Critical Methodologies,* 5(4), 425-446.

Flick, U. 2004. Triangulation in qualitative research. *A companion to qualitative research,* 3: 178-183.

Flinn, A. 2007. Community histories, community archives: some opportunities and challenges. *Journal of the Society of Archivists,* 28(2):151-176.

Forgacs, D.; Nowell-Smith, G. & Boelhower, W. 2012. *Antonio Gramsci: Selections from cultural writings.* Forgacs, London: Lawrence & Wishart.

Grosfoguel, R. 2013. The structure of knowledge in westernised universities: Epistemic racism/sexism and the four genocides/epistemicides of the long 16th century. *Human architecture,* 11(1), 73-90.

Guillory, J. 2013. Cultural capital: *The problem of literary canon formation.* Chicago: University of Chicago Press.

Hammond-Tooke, W.D. 1997. Whatever happened to/Kaggen?: a note on Khoisan/Cape Nguni borrowing. *The South African Archaeological Bulletin,* 52: 166. https://doi.org/10.2307/3889077

Hoernlé, A.W. 1921. A Hottentot rain ceremony. *Bantu Studies,* 1(1): 20-21.

Hoffmann, A. 2014. Of storying and storing: 'reading'Lichtenecker's voice recordings. *Re-viewing Resistance in Namibian History,* 89-91.

Hoppers, C.A.O. (ed.). 2002. *Indigenous Knowledge and the Integration of Knowledge Systems: Towards a philosophy of articulation.* Cape Town: New Africa Books.

Hoppers, C.A.O. 2001. Indigenous knowledge systems and academic institutions in South Africa. *Perspectives in education*, 19(1): 73-86.

Kaya, H.O. & Seleti, Y.N. 2013. African indigenous knowledge systems and relevance of higher education in South Africa. *International Education Journal: Comparative Perspectives*, 12(1): 30-44.

Koch. 2016. Interview. Cape Town: UCT, Health Sciences, July 2016.

Legassick, M. & Rassool, C. 2000. *Skeletons in the cupboard: South African museums and the trade in human remains 1907-1917*. Cape Town: South African Museum.

Marks, S. 1972. Khoisan resistance to the Dutch in the seventeenth and eighteenth centuries. *The Journal of African History*, 13(1): 55-80. https://doi.org/10.1017/S0021853700000268

Nasson, B., 1990. The Unity Movement: its legacy in historical consciousness. *Radical History Review*, 1990(46-47): 189-211. https://doi.org/10.1215/01636545-1990-46-47-189

Ndlovu-Gatsheni, S.J. 2013. *Coloniality of power in post-colonial Africa: myths of decolonisation*. CODESRIA, Dakar: African Books Collective.

Ngubane, H. 1977. *Body and mind in Zulu medicine. An ethnography of health and disease in Nyuswa-Zulu thought and practice*. London: Academic Press Inc.(London) Ltd.

Ntuli, P.P. 2002. Indigenous knowledge systems and the African renaissance. In: C.A.O. Hoppers (ed.), *Indigenous knowledge and the integration of knowledge systems: Towards a conceptual and methodological framework*, 53-66. Cape Town: New Africa Books.

Peterson, D.R.; Gavua, K. & Rassool, C. (eds.). 2015. *The Politics of Heritage in Africa: economies, histories, and infrastructures* (vol. 48). Cambridge: Cambridge University Press.

Rassool, C. & Hayes, P. 2002. Science and the spectacle: Khanako's South Africa, 1936-1937. *Cross Cultures*, 57: 117-164.

Rassool, C. & Witz, L. 1993. The 1952 Jan van Riebeeck tercentenary festival: constructing and contesting public national history in South Africa. *The Journal of African History*, 34(3): 447-468. https://doi.org/10.1017/S0021853700033752

Raven-Hart, R. 1971. *Cape of Good Hope 1652-1702.The first fifty years of Dutch colonisation as seen by Dutch callers*. Cape Town: Balkema.

Sandell, R. & Nightingale, E. (eds.). 2013. *Museums, equality and social justice*. London: Routledge.

Saunders, C. 1986. Mnguni and Three Hundred Years Revisited. *Kronos*, 11: 74-81.

Scully, P. 2005. Malintzin, Pocahontas, and Krotoa: indigenous women and myth models of the Atlantic world. *Journal of Colonialism and Colonial History*, 6(3).

Shell, R.C.H. 1994. *Children of bondage: A social history of the slave society at the Cape of Good Hope, 1652-1838*. University Press of New England: Wesleyan University Press.

Smith, L.T. 2013. *Decolonizing methodologies: Research and indigenous peoples*. London: Zed Books Ltd.

Spence, D.; Wareham, T.; Bressey, C.; Bam-Hutchison, J. & Anette, D. 2016. The Public as Co-producers: Making the London, Sugar and Slavery Gallery, Museum of London in Docklands. In: *Museums and public value: creating sustainable futures*, C.A. Scott (ed.). London and New York: Routledge.

Spivak, G.C. 1988. Can the subaltern speak? Can the subaltern speak? *Reflections on the history of an idea*, 21-78. Basingstroke: MacMillan.

Tomei, M. & Swepston, L. 1996. *Indigenous and tribal peoples: a guide to ILO Convention (No. 169)*. Geneve: International Labour Office.

Witz, L. & Rassool, C. 2008. Making histories. *Kronos*, 34(1): 6-15.

Wynberg, R. & Chennells, R. 2009. Green diamonds of the South: An overview of the San-Hoodia case. In: *Indigenous Peoples, Consent and Benefit Sharing*. Netherlands: Springer. 89-124.

Wynberg, R.; Schroeder, D. & Chennells, R. 2009. *Indigenous peoples, consent and benefit sharing: lessons from the San-Hoodia case*. London: Springer. https://doi.org/10.1007/978-90-481-3123-5

Zenani, V.J. 2005. Understanding the nature of sacred space from the African traditional religious perspective: challenges of spatial management. Doctoral dissertation. Cape Town: University of Cape Town.

CHAPTER 10

Allegorical Critiques and National Narratives[1]

Mapungubwe in South African history education

Himal Ramji[2]

Brief Background and Introduction

The use of historical novels to support history education in schools is an established global phenomenon (Ogude 1999).[3] This resource could be used to offer rich opportunities for historical learning in South Africa, particularly on the pre-colonial. This chapter explores the potential of the African novel in teaching Mapungubwe.

Mapungubwe is an archaeological site located near the Limpopo river valley, close to the border between South Africa, Botswana and Zimbabwe. This pre-colonial society is often portrayed as the "first state in southern Africa", emerging in the late 10th century, predating such societies as Mutapa and Great Zimbabwe (Chirikure 2013). The ancient state has been embraced into the South African national imagination (Carruthers 2006), with the "Order of Mapungubwe" instituted by government as the highest national honour in December 2002. Soon after this, the network of archaeological dig sites – collectively referred to as the "Mapungubwe Cultural Landscape" – "containing evidence of

---

[1] See also Gallagher 1997.
[2] himalramji@gmail.com
[3] See also Rodwellz 2010; Cromer & Clark 2007; Boerman-Cornell 2015.

interchange of human values that impacted on far reaching cultural and social changes in southern Africa between AD900 and 1300"[4] – was designated a United Nations Educational, Scientific and Cultural Organisation (UNESCO) World Heritage Site in July 2003.

With the adoption of South Africa's new constitution in 1996, then Deputy President of South Africa Thabo Mbeki, was spearheading a drive towards an "African Renaissance" – a rebirth of African culture and politics, requiring, in part, a reconsideration of pre-colonial African histories (Mbeki 1996, 1998a, 1998b).[5]

In line with this African Renaissance project, later under Mbeki's government, former Education Minister Kader Asmal initiated the Values in Education programme in 2000.[6] The History and Archaeology Panel was brought together by Asmal to engage with the required revision of History and Archaeology in a 'values-driven' curriculum for the South African post-apartheid context (Ndebele 2000).[7] A number of 'values-driven' heritage and nation-building projects were then underway in South Africa, including Asmal's South African History Project (SAHP),[8] and the Freedom Park Project (led by novelist Mongane Serote),[9] which aimed at educating South Africans beyond schools in the nation's shared colonial and apartheid history, particularly in the colonial era, but stretching back into the pre-colonial (Bam[10] in Jeppie 2004).

Soon after, when the first revision of the National Curriculum Statement was implemented under the South African History Project (2001-2004),[11] Mapungubwe

---

[4] See https://whc.unesco.org/en/list/1099 [Retrieved 15 June 2018].
[5] See also Mbeki, 1998, 'The African Renaissance, South Africa and the World', 9 April; Mbeki, 1998, 'South Africa, Southern Africa and the African Renaissance', 14 September; African Renaissance conferences were later held in Dakar, Senegal and Salvador, Brazil, documented in Asante 2006. Mbeki also played a major role in the Tombouctou Manuscripts Project, and various African Renaissance Institutes were opened, including a headquarters in Gabarone, Botswana.
[6] See http://www.dhet.gov.za/Reports%20Doc%20Library/Manifesto%20on%20Values,%20Education%20and%20Democracy.pdf [Retrieved 15 June 2018].
[7] The document gives a good idea of the recommendations made towards History content revision.
[8] See https://pmg.org.za/committee-meeting/1217/ [Retrieved 15 June 2018]. Please note the discussion on the inclusion of pre-colonial history. African History is as important for tackling xenophobia as argued by the South African History Project (SAHP). The branding logo of the South African History Project was the Golden Rhino of Mapungubwe.
[9] See https://www.brandsouthafrica.com/south-africa-fast-facts/history-facts/freedompark [Retrieved 15 June 2018].
[10] The South African History project included Ministerial Committee panel members who were pre-colonial history specialists such as Sifisc Ndlovu, Nomathamsanqa Tisani, Yonah Seleti and Jeff Peires. Yonah Seleti was chair of the Ministerial Committee of the SAHP and succeeded to head the Indigenous Knowledge Systems national programme within the Department of Science and Technology after 2004.
[11] The project was ended at the end of the Carnegie funding cycle and Minister Kader Asmal's political tenure. It became embedded within the department to execute the policy and oversee teaching, training and the development of learning and teaching support materials.

appeared alongside Great Zimbabwe and Mutapa. In commemoration of Ten Years of Freedom, the SAHP distributed free copies of the *UNESCO General History of Africa* volumes with an Educator's Guide (Bam & Dyer 2004)[12] to all schools, colleges, universities and libraries. The volumes and Educator's Guide cover Mapungubwe (though in a limited and basic way) focusing on gold and trade in the pre-colonial southern African region (Bam & Dyer 2004:149-157).

Much transpired within the history curriculum development process within the national and provincial education departments since the Carnegie-funded SAHP came to a close in 2004 when Kader Asmal's term as Education Minister ended. The curriculum development, textbook development and commissioning processes were then taken over by the education department to also foreground indigenous knowledge systems and the pre-colonial.[13]

There were a number of revisions to the curriculum since 1995 which impacted on textbook development. The Curriculum and Assessment Policy Statement (CAPS) comes as the most recent revision of the South African curriculum, following a transition curriculum (1995), the revised National Curriculum Statement (NCS, 2002), Curriculum 2005 (1997), and a further revision of that document (2009).

In December 2015 (following on demands for decolonisation of the curriculum by the #RhodesMustFall students since March that same year), Minister of Basic Education, Angie Motshekga, called for a Ministerial Task Team to investigate, centrally, the potential for implementing compulsory history through the grades 10-12 of the Further Education and Training (FET) phase, as well as a review of the grades 1-9 General Education and Training (GET) phase history content. This was the first time since 2002 that there was a call for such review. The Task Team,[14] headed by pre-colonial historian, Sifiso Ndlovu (of the SAHP), released its report on 31 May 2018,[15] making recommendations for history to be a compulsory subject in the FET phase. The report also argues for the embedded values of citizenship and human rights through history education (to replace Life Orientation in the General Education Training phase). These recommendations echo those of the earlier Task

---

[12] Anecdotal evidence suggests that these volumes never reached schools in the poor provinces and rural areas after the SAHP ended. The departments took direct responsibility for distribution.
[13] As related to me by June Bam whose contract as Director also ended then.
[14] Comprising a number of the SAHP members and pre-colonial historians (Sifiso Ndlovu, Amanda Esterhuysen, Gail Weldon and Luli Callinicos) and Nomalanga Mkhize (who is a contributor for this volume). Other members are Sekikaba Lekgoathi and Jabulani Sithole.
[15] See http://www.sahistory.org.za/sites/default/files/file%20uploads%20/report_of_the_history_ministerial_task_team_for_the_department_of_basic_education_final.pdf [Retrieved 18 June 2018].

Team which reported under novelist Njabulo Ndebele in 2001 of which the SAHP was the direct outcome.[16] Whilst the previous report emphasised Africa's history within the context of World History, this recent report calls for an Africa-centred curriculum[17] with the study of Mapungubwe to be upgraded to grade 12. The implementation of these recommendations with its huge new emphasis on pre-colonial African history is to be rolled out from 2023 in grade 10.

While African history content was always present in the various curricula developed since 1995, in some form, prescriptions in earlier formulations were minimal, but very general. The textbook, in CAPS, is at the centre of teaching and learning; and what pre-colonial African history content is presented in textbooks is bound to the prescriptions of the actual CAPS policy statement. CAPS gives topics in history much greater detail, time allocations, and a framework for assessment. However, the biggest critique by the History Ministerial Report of 2018 is the huge pedagogical limitations by CAPS which emerge from recommendations of the Review Committee for the NCS (2009) for 'streamlining' and more 'specific content prescriptions', for 'great communication' of the curriculum.

In trying to find a way to address this problem, this chapter covers specifically the development of textbooks to support the implementation of CAPS in terms of teaching 'Mapungubwe' in the interim to address the limitations as pointed out by various scholars and the current Ministerial Review Committee.

---

[16] See http://www.unisa.ac.za/sites/corporate/default/Colleges/Graduate-Studies/News-&-events/Articles/Report-recommends-SA-to-make-History-compulsory-in-2023 [Retrieved 18 June 2018].

[17] Two question papers are recommended to be written in grade 12: one, African History and the other, General History and World History.

Method

I look specifically at the topic of Mapungubwe (c.900-1300[18]) as prescribed in grade 6 (for average 11-year olds) in CAPS, and compare the interpreted historiography provided in CAPS to the genre of the novel. The case study consists of the treatment of Mapungubwe in each, specifically the prescription of content for grade 6, topic one: 'Mapungubwe', appearing in the 2011 *National Curriculum and Assessment Policy Statement, Intermediate Phase (Grades 4-6) Social Sciences* (p.42) document, provided by the Department of Basic Education (DBE) of the Republic of South Africa.

The textbooks I have selected are:

1. L. Dilley, M. Monteith, A. Proctor and G. Weldon's 2016 edition of the *Oxford Successful Social Sciences Learner's Book Grade 6*, published by Oxford, Cape Town;
2. P. Ranby, B. Johannesson, R. Versfeld, M. Slamang and B. Roberts's 2016 edition of *Platinum Social Sciences Grade 6 Learners Book*, published by Pearson Marang, Cape Town; and
3. G. Clacherty, S. Cohen, F. Dada, A. Joannides and H. Ludlow's 2015 edition of *Day-By-Day*, published by Maskew-Miller-Longman, Cape Town.

These textbooks appear to be relatively popular in both privileged and not so privileged schools. In addition, Gail Weldon (Oxford) and Barbara Johannesson (Pearson Marang) headed the revision of history content for CAPS, and Fathima Dada (Maskew-Miller Longman) had served on the 2009 NCS Final Review Committee.

For the novel, I have opted for Zakes Mda's *The Sculptors of Mapungubwe*[19] (2013) since it offers a creative interpretation of the very history that CAPS endeavours to 'blueprint'.[20] Though there has been critique of Mda's work on its limitation for understanding the pre-colonial in a 'real' sense (Jacobs 2015), I argue that it does offer creative potential for an innovative classroom pedagogy.

---

[18] The Mapungubwe state lasted from about 1220 to 1300. Prior to this, the settlement of Schroda was occupied from about 900, and later at K2 from about 1100.
[19] See also Sewlall 2016.
[20] Zanemvula Kizito Mda is a prominent South African playwright, novelist and poet, whose published writing career began in the late 1970s. Much of his early writing is political, reflecting his involvement in both the ANC and Pan Africanist Congress (PAC). In his later works, particularly *Heart of Redness* (2000) and *The Sculptors of Mapungubwe*, Mda experiments with the possibilities of telling African histories in narrative form. The former, concerned with the tale of Nongqawuse and the Xhosa cattle killings of the 1850s, attempts to give life to a fraught historiography, drawing heavily on previous historical works, like those of Jeff Peires (particularly his work, *The Dead Will Arise*, 1989).

Mda tells the story of Chata, a man born of a !Kung mother, but brought up in the town of Mapungubwe. The tale shifts in its engagements, Mda fluidly recreating an historiography of the ancient state, while dealing with issues of power and politics, gender and sexuality, aesthetics, economics, and alienation.

This comparison between the institutionalised prescription and the creative interpretation does not emerge from a vacuum. Creative interpretations of southern African history have been produced at varying rates since at least the early 1900s, including the works of Herbert Isaac Ernest Dhlomo, Rolfes Robert Reginald Dhlomo, Thomas Mofolo, and Sol Plaatje. Analyses, particularly those by Bheki Peterson of HIE Dhlomo's work,[21] propose an argument for the historiographical power of the creative interpretations of hfistory, particularly in this age of necessary and demanded decolonial and interdisciplinary history production.[22]

An Allegorical Critique

It is useful to first draw up some sort of analytical framework. Bheki Peterson provides a useful analysis of the work of HIE Dhlomo, utilising German theorist Walter Benjamin's application of the concept of *allegory* to illuminate the depth of meaning in Dhlomo's plays.[23] Benjamin had, in the 1920s, engaged a theory of allegory, particularly in *Ursprung des deutschen Trauerspiels* (*Origin of the German Mourning-Play*, 1928, Verso), in which he explored allegory in German tragic

---

[21] Bhekisizwe Peterson is Professor and Head of African Literature at Wits University. His work stretches from academia into the public sphere, having worked on a number of dramatic productions, including, collaborations with filmmaker Ramadan Suleman on *Zulu Loveletter* (2009) and *Zwelidumile, Natives at Large* (2010). His published works include: *Black Writers and the Historical Novel: 1910-1948* in David Attridge and Dav d Atwell (eds.) The Cambridge History of South African Literature, Cambridge: Cambridge University Press (2012) and, alongside Suleman, *Dignity, memory and the future under siege: Reconciliation and nation-building in post-apartheid South Africa* in Michael J. Shapiro and Samson Opondo (eds.) *The New Violent Cartography: Geo-Analysis after the Aesthetic Turn*, London: Routledge (2012).

[22] Since 2015, and the rise to prominence of such university student movements as #RhodesMustFall and #FeesMustFall, there has been a growing public call for the decolonisation of university syllabi. Quickly, this spread to secondary schools in particular. However, it must be said the decolonisation of history, and the decolonisation of education both emerge from a far longer history, stemming through the times of such thinkers as WEB Du Bois, CLR James, and Chiekh Anta Diop who have written for the *UNESCO General History of Africa* distributed to schools and universities by the SAHP.

[23] Herbert Isaac Ernest Dhlomo was a prominent literary figure in Black intellectual circles in the early 1900s. He was the brother of fellow writer, Rolfes Reginald Robert Dhlomo. Their father was a close affiliate of Bambatha, leader of the Bambatha Rebellion, and both brothers later became ANC members. Most of HIE Dhlomo's work consists of plays, and journalistic commentaries. Arguably, his most famous works are his fantastical re-mythologising of the tales of Zulu kings Dingane and Cetshwayo, and Basotho king, Moshoeshoe in a series of independently published works collectively known as *The Black Bulls*, which were later compiled by Nick Visser and Tim Couzens in 1986, published as *H.I.E. Dhlomo: Collected Works* by Ravan Press. Dhlomo's concerns are often with the relations between the courts of these kings, and colonial officials. As Peterson notes in his analysis, Dhlomo foregrounds in the text his struggles to reconcile his Christian orthodoxy with his African nationalism.

dramas (Knaller 2010). His work contributed to a rethinking of the relation between allegory and symbol, arguing for a reciprocal, dialectical relation between the two, rather than conferring upon either a hegemony in meaning-making. Allegory, as a concept, was, over years, disparaged as an analytic tool and literary method by writers like Jorge Luis Borges in 1976, Benedetto Croce in 1965, and Samuel Taylor Coleridge in 1853 (Knaller 2010:83).[24] There has, in the past two decades, been a resurgence of interest in allegorical studies, and in the work of Walter Benjamin (Wilkens 2006:285).

In his analysis, Peterson articulates the contribution to the political by the creative historiography. For him, "allegory posits parallel frames of reference" goes beyond "simple metaphorical significations" (Peterson 1991:30). For Benjamin, the meaning bred into the symbol is not merely that of signification, but a reciprocal derivation of meaning between the frames of reference (Peterson 1991:30). The meaning of the symbol is always *constitutive of* and *constituted in* the meaning of other symbols. As Peterson reiterates, it "is not merely a sign of what is to be known but is itself an object worthy of knowledge" (Peterson 1991:30). Rather than simply focusing on a single metaphorical level, study of the allegorical allows the analytic gaze to venture through the numerous levels of meaning in the text.

In his exploration of HIE Dhlomo's anthology of plays, *The Black Bulls* (compiled in N. Visser and T. Couzens [eds.], 1986, *H.I.E. Dhlomo: Collected Works*, Ravan Press), Peterson outlines some of the layers of meaning through which Dhlomo interacts. While the representation of pre-colonial African societies in the plays is an allegorical critique of the politics of 1930s South Africa, they also serve as "powerful cultural reconstructions" (Peterson 1991:31) of the African past. For Peterson, the allegorical methodology of Dhlomo's writing allows the author to write along two temporalities: firstly, as a critique of present-day politics; and secondly, as an attempt to reconstruct the past for oneself and one's audience. It is a challenge to the existing truth discourses of the day by reimagining the proposed historical foundations of that moment. However, these critiques always emerge from a specific context. That Dhlomo's critiques often emerge from a westernised and very Christian point of analysis is not unimportant to the allegorical critique he levels. Peterson

---

[24] According to Knaller, Borges referred to allegorical art as "dumb and frivolous", during a speech in which he cited Croce's attitudes. Similarly, for Coleridge, there was always a polarisation of symbol and allegory. Knaller (2010:83) cites Coleridge: "allegory is but a translation of abstract notions into picture language, which is itself nothing but an abstraction from objects of senses," but the symbol "always partakes of the reality which it renders intelligible; and while it enunciates the whole, abides itself as a living part in that unity of which it is the representative".

reflects upon the inevitable imposition of the self into the critique, arguing that the allegorical critique is not simply reflective of the reality of an historical moment, but rather that the narrative is mediated by the socio-political concerns of the author (Peterson 1991:31-32).

For HIE Dhlomo, that moment was the pre-apartheid moment of the 1930s, at the time of these early plays, including *Dingane, Cetshwayo and Moshoeshoe* (Visser & Couzens 1986). In 1926, Dhlomo's brother, Rolphes Reginald Robert, published *An African Tragedy* (Lovedale Press), the first English-language novel to be published by a Black author. In 1930, Plaatje's *Mhudi* (Negro Universities Press) was published.[25] During the early 1930s, Reverend John Henderson Soga had published *The South Eastern Bantu* (1930, Lovedale Press), and *The amaXhosa, Life and Customs* (1932, Lovedale Press).[26] Around this time, Cornelis de Kiewiet had been active in historicising same periods as HIE Dhlomo in South Africa, publishing *British Colonial Policy and the South African Republics, 1848-1872* (1929, Longman: London) and *The Imperial Factor in South Africa; a Study in Politics and Economics* (1937, Russell & Russell: New York).

Meanwhile, Thomas Mofolo had been writing in southern Sotho, against the stream of English literature written by Black intellectuals, producing *Moeti oa bochabela* (originally written in 1919, later republished by Morija Sesuto Book Depot, 1980), *Chaka* (published in Sesotho in 1925, translated into English by FH Dutton and published by Oxford University Press in 1931), and *Pitseng* (written in 1910, later translated by DP Kunene and published by Morija Archives and Mission: Lesotho). Despite Mofolo writing in seSotho, the concerns arising from his work in the focal relations between colonised and coloniser, and the mythicisation of the African past, are remarkably similar to Dhlomo's.

For Peterson, the allegorist is responsive to the context in which he writes by *wandering*, "in his fascination with alienation, through the ruins that are his historical inheritance, seizing fragments, emblems, and subjecting them to a scrutiny

---

[25] Plaatje had written it years before, during which time he had translated four of William Shakespeare's plays into Setswana, including *Julius Caesar* and *The Comedy of Errors*. During this time (1910s-20s), he also published *Native Life in South Africa*, (PS King & Son: London, 1921), *Sechuana Proverbs, with Literal Translations and their European Equivalents...* (K. Paul, Trench, Trubner & Co., 1916), and co-authored with linguist, Daniel Jones, *A Sechuana Reader: In international Phonetic Orthography, With English Translations* (Arts & Culture Trust, 1916).

[26] JH Soga was a missionary – and later Scottish-educated theologist, translator, and historian. While spreading colonial education and religion, he also endeavoured to record the Xhosa culture and history, which he recognised to be receding against the spread of Christianity. See: Christopher C. Lowe 1995.

that will reveal their hidden truth and knowledge" (1991:31). By taking hold of the fragment and imparting into it certain meanings, the allegorist is able to critique existing interpretations of the past *and* the politics of the present by writing into the text "continuities and divergences between the past and present" (1991:31). For thinkers like Benjamin, Peterson, Dhlomo and Mda, the allegorical opens the way for grasping of the fragments of the past which are visible, which have already been 'found', and to seriously think about the possibilities of meaning of this thing in the distant past, as well as in the present.

For 'pre-colonial' histories, there is a significant power and agency involved in creatively reimagining a past that has either been silenced, banalised, or bastardised. Contemporarily, it allows the post-colonial author to take hold of these histories, and to reinvent a past, always in relation to the present. Of course, these could come to critique existing politics, or to affirm them. The allegorical could reach into the near past, or deep into the distant past – or both, simultaneously, as Mda (2000) does so deftly with the character of Camagu in *Heart of Redness*, through whom he could work through contemporary cultural debates, alongside academic historical discourses. Mda could re-create an image of the distant past – according to his own readings, ideologies, proclivities, interests – while musing over contemporary understandings.

The pre-colonial in CAPS

In the revised CAPS, Mapungubwe became the central focus of the first term of grade 6, while Great Zimbabwe was shifted to the end of the topic, and Mutapa removed (Department of Basic Education, 2011, *Curriculum and Assessment Policy Statement Intermediate Phase Social Sciences*, 42)(Hoadley 2011).

Even before this, Mapungubwe had flitted in and out of academic archaeological and historical discourses, first emerging in the 1930s, at which stage colonial social scientists believed the ruins to be the making of European or Arab groups; certainly not the work of Africans (Carruthers 2006). In the 1970s, as new discoveries were made in nearby dig sites, and new methods of interpretation employed, with new links made, the reading of Mapungubwe shifted towards the ancient state as an African construction (Carruthers 2006).

The pre-colonial in CAPS occupies most of the intermediate phase (grades 4 to 6), and gradually recedes through the Senior Phase (grades 7 to 9) and is virtually absent from the FET phase (grades 10 to 12). There are only three dedicated topics on pre-colonial histories: 1) "Hunter-gatherers and herders in southern Africa"; 2) "The first farmers in southern Africa"; 3) "Mapungubwe". Just prior to this, Mapungubwe enters the curriculum as "Heritage in objects" at the end of grade 5, comprising a study of the "Golden objects at Mapungubwe: Limpopo". Mapungubwe, like the San rock art of the Drakensberg, is a national and world heritage site. The historic state reappears at the beginning of grade 6, titled as "An African kingdom long ago in southern Africa", under its own dedicated topic. It is what is prescribed here that I wish to take as the textual excerpt for analysis.[27]

There are two main categories under which I will compare the interpretations of the distant past of CAPS history and Mda's *Sculptors of Mapungubwe*: 1) the context afforded to Mapungubwe history within the world, and 2) the internal socio-political differentiation modes inscribed into Mapungubwe, which head towards an analysis of the presentation of a Mapungubwe aesthetic in both pieces of literature. Here I refer to the specific authority and norms (or normative values) which are infused into the historiography of Mapungubwe to categorise its classes, etc. – those categories which are inscribed into the complexities of the Mapungubwe state. Simply put, I am asking how socio-political differentiation is described or studied, or is manifested differently in CAPS and Mda's novel as two pieces of literature?

Mapungubuwe in a Global Context

What world does Mapungubwe exist in according to each literature? This I will deal with systematically, describing and comparing curriculum and novel interpretations in turn. I will also look at what information is afforded in describing the relations between the people of Mapungubwe as well as with other groupings or societies in southern Africa.

---

[27] In the previous revisions of curriculum – the NCS of 2002, revised in 2009 – the pre-colonial appeared in all phases, although *southern African* pre-colonial history has been, since 2002, included in grades 5 and 6. CAPS does include histories of the Ashanti (Ghana, 1700s-1800s), in the first term of grade 8), as well as the Mughal Empire, China, the Songhay, and Europe before 1600 (in the first term of grade 10). Mali and Timbuktu in the 14th century appear in grade 7, and ancient Egypt appears in grade 5. These were all present in the NCS. The only major reframing occurs in grade 10, with the revision of topics on southern Africa from 1750 until the early 1900s, moving to include the academic debates around the Mfecane – see Cobbing and also Hamilton. What has occurred, from CAPS to the NCS, is a streamlining of the content (deletion of what was considered excess), with greater prescription of what was included.

Mapungubwe in Global Context in CAPS

In CAPS, we encounter the K2 (Bambandyanalo; called 'K2' by arhaeologists) and the Schroda area (east of Mapugubwe) – before we encounter 'Mapungubwe'. The state of Mapungubwe is presented as a progression from these earlier societies, although no absolute link is made. Other sites around the Leopard's Kopje/Zhizo area, such as Mapela Hill or Leokwe are not considered in the CAPS-prescribed content.[28] Once we enter Mapungubwe itself, it is only with 'trade' that Mapungubwe seems to interact with the world beyond its own boundaries. As an analytic category, 'trade' is broken up in CAPS, appearing as several separate bullet-points. Under the six-hour main section on Mapungubwe, there are three noteworthy references to trade which appear consecutively:

1. "Trade across Africa and across the Indian Ocean and beyond (globalisation)";
2. "Goods traded";[29]
3. "People's journeys on foot: routes, dangers, finding the way".[30]

After this body section, an hour is dedicated to a prescription that simply reads: "Change and continuity in East Coast trade with settlements inland". No further detail is given, and so the onus falls upon the textbook author(s) and educators to interpret these stipulations into workable history textbook content and classroom pedagogy.[31]

The historicisation of 'Swahili' is an illustrative example of the different meanings constructed in textbooks. After a short explanation of the sea routes, religion and materials of the traders,[32] Ranby 2016:109) reads: "African groups living on the East Coast of Africa absorbed the culture and Muslim religion of the Arabs. These people became known as the Swahili. The Swahili language is a mix of African languages and Arabi". Dilley (2016:30) follows a somewhat different approach. After introducing

---

[28] Shadreck Chirikure (see papers from 2013 and 2014) has argued for a more nuanced and open-ended reading of the archaeological sites, inferring the possibility that Mapela Hill bears evidence of similar statehood. The dig sites in the area number over 400, according to Carruthers (2006), and include K2, Schroda, and Mapela (which all predate Mapungubwe).
[29] This section, in all textbooks analysed, becomes a repetition of earlier sections, on glass beads, etc.
[30] This will be dealt with later in the chapter, as it is the uncertainty of the creative piece which brings into question the certainty with which the textbooks regard this section.
[31] CAPS has strict time allocations. Generally, each topic prior to the FET phase is afforded one term, or 15 hours. Generally, three of these hours are reserved for revision and assessment, leaving 12 hours for teaching and learning. In the first topic of grade 5, for example, the San are allocated eight hours, and the Khoi only two, with two hours spent on general archaeological concepts. Similarly, in the Mapungubwe topic in grade 6, three of the 12 hours are allocated to a study of Marco Polo, while Great Zimbabwe receives only one.
[32] A section problematically begins: "The people who live in North Africa and the Middle East are called Arabs. Most Arabs are Muslims".

Arabs and Islam from the 700s and their own settlement on the East Coast of Africa, the text reads:

> Many Africans in these coastal towns converted to Islam and began to practise the Muslim religion. The language on the East Coast soon changed. African and Arab languages got mixed together to form a new language called Swahili. Swahili means 'people who live along the coast'. The Swahili way of life was a mixture of Arab and African languages, culture and customs.

Neither Swahili nor the Arab culture is mentioned in CAPS. Rather, these are inferences made by the textbook authors. The sections are also extremely short with simplistic and often repetitive text, dealt with in two pages in Dilley *et al.* and Ranby *et al.* and in one page in Clacherty 2015.[33]

The revised curriculum has been criticised for its complexity of the content, the sheer workload required to cover all the content, and the required quick pace of teaching and learning because of this.[34] Even at this early stage, learners are expected to engage with complex concepts like 'the state', 'democracy', and 'citizenship' (DBE 2011a:42), which are often oversimplified and unproblematised towards a certain ideological understanding of the concept. In other words, at this level, in grade 6, there is no real scope, practically speaking, for engaging the complexity and contestation of these concepts, as considered from Hobbes and Rousseau to Mbembe and Mamdani.

What is engaged with in greater depth in CAPS are the journeys of Marco Polo towards the east. Mapungubwe was not of interest to Polo (and vice versa), and so the study of his travels merely sets Mapungubwe within the same temporality as Polo. It reads, in part, as a plea for historical equality with European 'discoverers', but also as a thought towards 'globalisation' – a concept specifically mentioned in the CAPS prescription for the topic (DBE, 2011a:42). More emphasis is placed on the geographically distant journeys of Polo than on the relations between Mapungubwe and its neighbours and so, in CAPS, then, Mapungubwe comes to exist in a hazy context, vaguely inhabited by traders to the east while Polo scours distant lands in search of *something*. Similarly, a much more wholesome picture is drawn of the relations between Mapungubwe's King and Arab and Swahili traders, than internal or regional relations.

---

[33] Perhaps this is due to the relatively low level of the topic (grade 6).

[34] Kros and Harrop-Allin (2014) deal with the complexity of concepts and language in Mapungubwe in CAPS directly. In general, Peter Kallaway (2012) has criticised the curriculum for often being too much of a political science course, particularly in FET dealings with concepts of nationalism, communism and capitalism. Rob Sieborger (2012) quickly responded to Kallaway, citing generally the requirements stipulated in the Final Review of the NCS (2009).

When compared to other sections in CAPS, the erasure and banalisation of southern African history *outside of South Africa* is striking, particularly in the case of the San (where the study of the San in Namibia and Botswana is refused in a CAPS endnote),[35] as well as in the refusal to follow Ndebele history with Mzilikazi into what is now Zimbabwe.[36] A similar case occurs later in the Mapungubwe topic, where Mapungubwe and Great Zimbabwe are simplistically compared across textbooks, rather than perhaps engaging the history of Great Zimbabwe (DBE 2011a:42).

What, then, might the novel, the creative interpretation, offer to supplement, complement or refute the iterations of CAPS? What absences, if any, might be made visible through the creative allegorical critique?

Mapungubwe in Global Context in Mda's writing

While Marco Polo and other Europeans make no appearance in the novel, Swahili traders play particularly prominent roles. Still, it is only on rare occasions that these traders enter Mapungubwe, and it is even less frequently that Mapungubweans venture out to meet these traders. Only with Chata do we encounter any real will to venture out; but this "wanderlust" is solidly rooted in his cultural heritage. A will to travel, adventure, or discover, in Mda, is presented as almost alien to the people of Mapungubwe. In fact, Chata's wanderlust becomes part of his wide range of *mbisili*, which become taboo in Mapungubwe, but which the narrator inscribes as essential to San communities of the time (Mda 2013:208).[37]

But these relations between Arab and Swahili traders and the people of Mapungubwe are more nuanced than a simple trade relationship. Mda creates for the reader a richness of relations, which allows the protagonist to engage in his travels with the help of a Swahili trader. It is also with this trader that the pivotal moment of Rendani's downfall occurs (Mda 2013:211) which results in Rendani's expulsion from the elite enclave on top of Mapungubwe Hill, as well as the trader's flight from the village. In Mda's Mapungubwe, social mobility could work in both ways; one could progress to become a greatly respected authority, but should one contravene the rules of society, then that perceived cause of disorder must necessarily be expelled.

---

35   "LTSM writers should not include detail on modern San in the Kgalagadi or in Namibia" (CAPS, IP:38). LTSM refers to Learning Teaching and Support Materials.
36   In grade 10's fourth and fifth topics, "Transformations in southern Africa after 1750", and "Colonial expansion after 1750".
37   Eccentricities which are perceived as a threat to the social order of Mapungubwe. "When he (Chata) asked what it meant exactly he got no clear answer... If it did not satisfy their aesthetic tastes it was *mbisili*".

Internal Socio-Political Differentiation

Socio-Political Differentiation in CAPS

The content prescribed for the Mapungubwe *state* begins with "King and sacred leadership" (DBE 2011a:42). All the analytic categories which follow are centred around this figure of the King. This unfolds into the King's "first stone-walled palace", built for him by his subjects on top of Mapungubwe hill. All the textbooks emphasise that the walls were built to keep the King "separated" (Dilley *et al.* 2016:26) or "hidden" (Ranby *et al.* 2016:105) from the ordinary people, or to "screen off" (Clacherty *et al.* 2015:96) his homestead. Similarly, discussion on the significance of Mapungubwe hill centres around the King rather than a whole elite class.

It is only a bit later (after a uniformly short discussion on the 'First town') that class differentiation in Mapungubwe is engaged with, as per the CAPS prescription ('Distinct social classes'). Following Pearson's *Platinum*, this warrants only a brief revision of what has already been discussed: "The rulers of Mapungubwe lived on top of the hill and the ordinary people lived in the valley below. The social hierarchy was physically obvious as ordinary people lived at the bottom of the hill" (Ranby *et al.* 2016:106). Dilley *et al.* (2016:28) goes a bit further, mentioning that:

> When we compare what archaeologists have found on top of the hill with what they find in the valley, we can see that the people on top of the hill lived very differently from the ordinary people. Their huts were much bigger and finely decorated. They were built on large flat terraces that had been made by hundreds of people carrying stone and soil to the top of the hill for their kings. This shows that Mapungubwe was not an equal society. The king and his relatives were richer than other people and had great power over them. They were a ruling class.

Clacherty *et al.* (2015:98) delivers even more certainty: "There were different classes of people in the kingdom of Mapungubwe. The royal family was the most elite group. Then the religious leaders followed. The king's sister was probably the chief diviner". As in the case of the Oxford publication, no evidence is provided for these claims –

they simply appear as interpretations or examples of personalised flair on the part of the textbook author(s).[38]

Socio-Political Differentiation in Mda

Mda complicates things for contemporary ideas about gender, sexuality and marriage in the distant past. According to Peterson, allegory can be used as a critique of contemporary political conditions. In this sense, Mda takes up actual undefined issues such as gender and sexuality in Mapungubwe, and imparts highly specified meaning into his fictionalised state. Mda here posits *historical possibility* (possible because of historiographical and ethnographical uncertainty) as a critique of contemporary popular and public ideas and attitudes about indigenous concepts and norms of gender and sexuality in the distant past.[39]

Right at the beginning of the book Chata's exquisitely polished floor is explained: "... he did it with his own hands even though it was regarded as women's work" (Mda 2013:4). In Mda's Mapungubwe, it is men who hunt, sculpt and serve as soldiers; it is women who cook, clean and tend to children. While Chata does pose a challenge to contemporary ideas of gender in the distant past, Mda does parallel CAPS in making the rules of later Bantu societies the rule for Mapungubwe and, by proxy, its predecessors. It is, in his narrative, always the outsider who challenges the norm; the challenge very rarely emanates from 'purer' Mapungubweans.[40]

In fact, it is only with the character of Marubini that we encounter a Mapungubwean who is willing to challenge the norms of the society. She refuses the advances of

---

[38] What becomes most intriguing here in the case of the school history textbook in South Africa at present is that there is no requirement explicitly stated, citations or sourcing of the text – this is only required for photographs. There is zero disclosure of the textbook's sources for their own narrativised text, and so it is curious as to where such interpretations actually come from. How does the writer of the Oxford text know that "hundreds of people" helped build the terraces and houses of the elite? Upon what information does the writer of *Day-By-Day* muse over the probability of the king's sister being the chief diviner? Such are the curiously obvious examples of the subjectivity of the interpretations of the textbook genre. Mda discloses his sources in his acknowledgements at the beginning of the novel: "The setting – place and period – of this novel is imagined and re-imagined from the various oral traditions of the peoples of the region and from the sterling scholarship of Thomas N Huffman, McEdward Murimbika, G Pwiti, A Meyer, C E Cloete, A G Schutte, Maryna Steyn, Duncan Miller, Nirdev Desai, Julia Lee-Thorp, Innocent Pikirayi, Gail Sinton Schoettler, T G O' Connor, G A Kiker, Mark Horton, John Middleton, Edward Eastwood and Cathelijne Eastwood."

[39] CAPS makes no reference to gender in Mapungubwe; the sole mode of differentiation in the curriculum is a dichotomised understanding of *class*. However, gender *roles* are discussed under the "First Farmers" topic in the previous year. Problematically, though, these concretise as the informal 'rule' for Mapungubwe gender dynamics.

[40] The claim to purity is not Mda's, but rather that of the people of Mapungubwe in Mda's story, who themselves regard Chata as an outsider because of his maternal heritage. Mda's push appears to be towards culture as something fluid, using Chata as the vehicle for his critique of histories of essential and stagnant African cultures.

Rendani, to which her relatives respond that no woman has ever refused marriage in Mapungubwe, certainly not when the marriage was offered by a man of such status and wealth as Rendani. In Mda's Mapungubwe, men are polygamous. The author does, however, throw into the fold the complications of hierarchy among wives, where the first and last wives have the highest authority, and so authority shifts when a new wife is married. Of course, for Rendani, this means that him marrying Marubini would mean the demotion of Princess Dova (his current youngest wife), something which Dova and Chata attempt to address. This is all simply to say that Mda creatively inserts some nuance into his idea of Mapungubwe.

Eventually we reach a point where Chata's house has been broken down, and his unfinished gold and ivory masterpiece is exposed. This attracts a group who call themselves the "Community of Gapers". This group is led by spiritual leaders from different sects, including two noted by Mda's narration: Anotida and Lutendo. While Anotida is of a lower class (or caste, rather), Lutendo comes down from the Hill to join the Gapers. Mda describes the norms of marriage described for these blue-blooded priests and priestesses in Mapungubwe: "The young men who salivated whenever they saw her said hers was wasted beauty because she would never marry any man, as was the tradition in her order of diviners. She could only marry other women, in the same way that male diviners of that order married other men" (Mda 2013:179).

Similarly, the nuances of the political are allowed the literary space to be imagined in Mda's work. The King, regarded as a sacred being, never appears before the people, apart from his performance of the rain-making ritual. Thus, it is up to the "Young Father", Baba-Munene, and his Council of Elders, to deliberate over political matters (Mda 2013:12). It is repeated that Baba-Munene is the voice of the King, and often it is Munene's decision that is taken as the King's decision. The King is symbolic, while the Young Father is agential.

In Lieu of a Conclusion: Heritage

When Mapungubwe is presented in CAPS, it is presented as an unproblematised World Heritage Site, then stretched towards a discussion on the Order of Mapungubwe, as per CAPS prescriptions. The grade 6 section on Mapungubwe as heritage is repetition of the discussion which occurs in the previous year. In none of the textbooks is the rise of Mapungubwe to Heritage Site status problematised or even historicised. Dilley *et al.* (2016:31) gives a brief explanation of what it means for a site to be declared a world heritage site and ends there. Clacherty *et al.* (2015:100) follows a similar (but more succinct) angle, but adds that "Mapungubwe reminds us that there were large, organised kingdoms in Africa many hundreds of years ago". Unlike the other two textbooks, Clacherty *et al.* make note of the links between heritage site status and the tourist industry, a point which is taken up strongly in the work of Jane Carruthers (2006). This link, however, is not stipulated in CAPS, but emerges from authorial flair. Ranby *et al.* (2016) takes an even more determined stance: "Today, no-one lives at Mapungubwe," which is fairly true, although there are nearby settlements, some of the Venda people from whom much of Mapungubwe ethnography appears to have been drawn. The rest of Ranby *et al.* (2016:111) follows much the same tack as Clacherty *et al.*, concluding that "World Heritage Sites recognise and protect areas of outstanding natural, historical and cultural value".

While bringing in the idea of Mapungubwe as a symbol[41] – as heritage site and award – does engage with Mapungubwe in the present, it does obfuscate or ignore at least two other contentious issues surrounding Mapungubwe. These are issues of tourism, and issues of mining interests.[42] These are fundamentally material concerns. The first is related to heritage, and is brought up in at least one textbook, but is absent from the actual CAPS prescription. The second is completely absent from any textbook consulted, and is absent from CAPS. Mining interests and wealth play a central role in *Sculptors*.

My argument here is that allegorical critiques and other creative representations of the past before colonial times can be used (specifically by educators, rather than learners, unless these learners are at the Senior or FET phase of their school education) to expand upon the national(ist) curriculum prescriptions, so as to produce in teachers a capacity to teach a nuanced history of Mapungubwe (and other such historic instances). Mda's piece illuminates some contemporary contestations, bringing into question, with creative flair, the unknown of Mapungubwe. More than imposing rules upon the past, he converts the history of Mapungubwe into an allegorical critique of present-day politics and attitudes about the past and cultural traditions.

Mda's work (and the work of other African novelists) can innovatively be used to make visible the absences in the curriculum and can, through creative teaching,

---

[41] Discussion on the Order of Mapungubwe – the highest symbol of achievement in South Africa – is generally extremely thin and not historicised. It is merely stated, in all cases, that the order reflects great achievement. In some cases recipients are mentioned (in Dilley *et al.* 2016 and Ranby *et al.* 2016) and/or pictured; in other cases the award medal is pictured (Clacherty *et al.* 2015).

[42] Both of these are referred to by Carruthers 2006.

supplement CAPS historiography and open up new possible approaches in a critical pedagogy on the pre-colonial.

References

Asante, M.K. African Renaissance Conferences of the 21st Century: Dakar and Salvador in Perspective. *Journal of Black Studies*, 37, (2): 169-176. https://doi.org/10.1177/0021934706293281

Bam, J. & Dyer, C. (eds.). 2004. *Educator's Guide to the UNESCO General History of Africa for the FET curriculum*. Cape Town: New Africa Books.

Benjamin, W. 1998 (1963). *The Origin of German Tragic Drama*. Translated by J. Osbourne. London/New York: Verso.

Boerman-Cornell, W. 2015. Using historical graphic novels in high school history classes: Potential for contextualization, sourcing, and corroborating. *The History Teacher*, 48(2): 209-224.

Carruthers, J. 2006. Mapungubwe: An historical and contemporary analysis of a World Heritage cultural landscape. *Koedoe*, 49(1): 1-13. https://doi.org/10.4102/koedoe.v49i1.89

Chirikure, S.; Manyanga, M.; Pikirayi, I. & Pollard, M. 2013. New Pathways of Sociopolitical Complexity in Southern Africa. *African Archaeological Review*, 30: 339-366. https://doi.org/10.1007/s10437-013-9142-3

Chirikure, S.; Manyanga M.; Pollard, A.M.; Bandama, F.; Mahachi, G. & Pikirayi, I. 2014. Zimbabwe Culture before Mapungubwe: New evidence from Mapela Hill, South-Western Zimbabwe. *Plos One*, 9 (10). https://doi.org/10.1371/journal.pone.0111224

Chisholm, L. 2004. *Changing Class: Education and social change in post-apartheid South Africa*. Cape Town: Zed Books/HSRC Press.

Christie, P. 2006. Changing regimes: Governmentality and education policy in post-apartheid South Africa. *International Journal of Educational Development*, 26: 373-381. https://doi.org/10.1016/j.ijedudev.2005.09.006

Clacherty, G.; Cohen, S.; Dada, F.; Joannides, A. & Ludlow, H. 2015. *Day-By-Day*. Cape Town: Maskew-Miller-Longman.

Cromer, M. & Clark, P. 2007. Getting graphic with the past: Graphic novels and the teaching of history. *Theory & Research in Social Education*, 35(4): 574-591. https://doi.org/10.1080/00933104.2007.10473351

Dada, F.; Dipholo, T.; Hoadley, U.; Khembo E.; Muller S. & Volmink, J. 2009. Report of the Task Team for the Review of the Implementation of the *National Curriculum Statement*: Final Report. Presented to the Minister of Education: Ms. Angela Motshekga. Pretoria: Department of Basic Education.

De Kiewiet, C. 1937. *The Imperial Factor in South Africa; a Study in Politics and Economics*. New York: Russell & Russell.

De Kiewiet, C. 1929. *British Colonial Policy and the South African Republics, 1848-1872*. London: Longman.

Department of Basic Education, Republic of South Africa. 2018. *Report of the History Ministerial Task Team*. Pretoria.

Department of Basic Education, Republic of South Africa. 2011a. *National Curriculum Statement (NCS) Curriculum and Assessment Policy Statement (CAPS), Intermediate Phase (Grades 4-6) Social Sciences*. Pretoria.

Department of Basic Education, Republic of South Africa. 2011b. *National Curriculum Statement (NCS) Curriculum and Assessment Policy Statement (CAPS), Senior Phase (Grades 7-9) Social Sciences*. Pretoria.

Department of Basic Education, Republic of South Africa. 2011c. *National Curriculum Statement (NCS) Curriculum and Assessment Policy Statement (CAPS), Further Education and Training Phase (Grades 10-12) History*. Pretoria.

Dhlomo. R.R.R. 1926. *An African Tragedy*. Alice: Lovedale Press.

Dilley, L.; Monteith, M.; Proctor, A. & Weldon, G. 2016. *Oxford Successful Social Sciences Learner's Book, Grade 6*. Cape Town: Oxford.

Elfasi, M. (ed.). 2003. *UNESCO General History of Africa: Africa from the seventh to the eleventh century. Abridged edition*. Cape Town: New Africa Books.

Gallagher, S.V. 1997. The backward glance: history and the novel in post-apartheid South Africa. *Studies in the Novel*, 29(3): 376-395.

Hamilton, C.; Mbenga, B. & Ross, R. 2012. The Production of pre-industrial South African History. In: C. Hamilton; B. Mbenga & R, Ross (eds.). *The Cambridge History of South Africa. Volume I: From Early Times to 1885*. USA: Cambridge University Press.

Hoadley, U. 2011. Knowledge, knowers and knowing: Curriculum reform in South Africa. In: L. Yates & M. Grumet (eds.), *Curriculum in Today's World: configuring knowledge, identities, work and politics*, 139-154. New York: Routledge.

Jacobs, J.U. 2015. Performing the Pre-colonial: Zakes Mda's The Sculptors of Mapungubwe. *Current Writing: Text and Reception in Southern Africa*, 27(1): 13-25. https://doi.org/10.1080/1013929X.2015.1037567

Jeppie, S. (ed.). 2004. *Toward New Histories for South Africa*. Lansdowne: Juta-Gariep.

Kallaway, P. 2012. History in senior secondary school CAPS 2012 and beyond: A comment. *Yesterday & Today*, 7.

Knaller, S. 2010. A theory of allegory beyond Walter Benjamin and Paul de Man; with some remarks on allegory and memory. *The Germanic Review: Literature, Culture and Theory*, 77(2): 83-101.

Kros, C. & Harrop-Allin, S. 2014. The C Major scale as index of 'back to basics' in South African education: A critique of the curriculum assessment policy statement. *South African Review of Education*, 20(1).

Lowe, C.C. 1995. In: K. Irvine (ed.), *The Encyclopaedia Africana Dictionary of African Biography (In 20 Volumes), Volume Three: South Africa- Botswana-Lesotho-Swaziland*. Michigan: Reference Publications.

Mbeki, T. 1998a. The African Renaissance, South Africa and the World. Speech delivered at the United Nations University, Japan, 9 April 1998.

Mbeki, T. 1998b. South Africa, Southern Africa and the African Renaissance. Speech delivered at the Paasviki Society, Helsinki Finland, 14 September 1998.

Mbeki, T. 1996. I am an African. Speech delivered at the inauguration of the 1996 Constitution of the Republic of South Africa, Cape Town, 8 May 1996.

Mda, Z. 2013. *The Sculptors of Mapungubwe*. Cape Town: Kwela Books.

Mda, Z. 2000. *Heart of Redness*. Oxford: Oxford University Press.

Ministry of Education. 2001. *Manifesto on Values, Education and Democracy*. Pretoria.

Mofolo, T. 1980 (1919). *Moeti oa bochabela*. Morija, Lesotho: Morija Sesuto Book Depot.

Mofolo, T. 1931 (1925) *Chaka*, translated into English by F.H. Dutton. Oxford: Oxford University Press.

Mofolo, T. 1910. *Pitseng*, translated by D.P. Kunene. Lesotho: Morija Archives and Mission.

Ndebele, N.S.; Odendaal, A.; Mesthrie, U.; Jordan, P.; Nasson, B.; Esterhuyzen, M.; Van Onselen, C.; Callinicos, L.; Maloka, E.; Bashe, T. & Kallaway, P. 2000. *Report of the History and Archaeology Panel to the Minister of Education*. Pretoria: Department of Education.

Ogude, J., 1999. *Ngugi's novels and African history: narrating the nation*. London: Pluto Press.

Peires, J. 1989. *The Dead Will Arise. Nongqawuse and the Great Xhosa Cattle-Killing Movement of 1856-7*. Johannesburg: Ravan Press.

Peterson, B. 1991. The Black Bulls of H.I.E. Dhlomo: Ordering history out of nonsense. *English in Africa*, 18(1).

Peterson, B. & Suleman, R. 2009. *Zulu Love Letter: A screenplay.* Johannesburg: Wits University Press.

Plaatje, S. 2014. *Mhudi*. Long Grove, Illinois: Waveland Press.

Ranby, P.; Johannesson, B.; Versfeld, R.; Slamang, M. & Roberts, B. 2016. *Platinum Social Sciences Grade 6 Learners Book*. Cape Town: Pearson Marang.

Rodwell, G. 2010. Historical novels: engaging student teachers in k-10 history pre-service units. *Australian Journal of Teacher Education (Online)*, 35(7): 15. https://doi.org/10.14221/ajte.2010v35n7.2

Sewlall, H. 2016. Love in the time of mirrors: the real and the imaginary in Zakes Mda's The Sculptors of Mapungubwe. *English Academy Review*, 33(1): 24-37. https://doi.org/10.1080/10131752.2016.1153571

Sieborger, R. 2012. *A reply to Peter Kallaway: History in High School 2012: A comment. Curriculum and Assessment Policy Statement. History Grades 10-12*. School of Education, University of Cape Town, Seminar, 9 May 2012.

Soga, J.H. 1932. *The AmaXhosa, Life and Customs*. Alice: Lovedale Press.

Soga, J.H. 1930. *The South Eastern Bantu*. Alice: Lovedale Press.

Visser, N. & Couzens, T. (eds.). 1986. In: H.I.E. Dhlomo, *Collected Works by H.I.E. Dhlomo*. Johannesburg: Ravan Press.

Wilkens, M. 2006. Towards a Benjaminian Theory of Dialectical Allegory. *New Literary History*, 37(2): 285-298.

CHAPTER 11

Whose History Counts?

A Conclusion

June Bam[1] & Allan Zinn[2]

The 2017 conference which led to this book grappled with three broad framing questions relating to how we decolonise historiography in South Africa:

- How to reconceptualise the 'pre-colonial'?
- What would new interdisciplinary methods look like that would be groundbreaking, inclusive and different from existing methodologies in pre-colonial studies?
- What is it that society wants us to teach?

As is shown in the introduction, attempts to decolonise African historiography are not new. The post-independent period in Africa in the 1950s and 1960s was accompanied by the rewriting of Africa's history as an essential precondition for decolonising education and culture, very clearly articulated by Nkrumah and others. The result in education of these Pan-African movements was the eight-volume *UNESCO General History of Africa*, first developed in the 1960s and 1970s and published later through a number of reprints (KI-Zerbo 1981; Mokhtar 1981; Fasi & Hrbek 1988; Niane 1984, Ogot 1992, Ajayi 1989). South Africa's democracy, which came in 1994, almost 30 years after the *UNESCO* volumes, also made its own attempts of decolonising

---

[1] june.bam-hutchison@uct.ac.za and june.hutchison@gmail.com
[2] allan.zinn@mandela.ac.za

historiography through initiatives such as the South African History Project in the Education Ministry under Kader Asmal (2001-2004), which also included a reprint of the *UNESCO* volumes.[3] However, as has been demonstrated in this book, its historiographical framework remained within the Eurocentric conceptual framework, working within the existing canons of "disciplines" within universities and therefore remaining far removed from the people themselves (no matter how well intended). This book has shown that, on the whole, much of the written oppositional texts of the last century (those which were not novels or other literary works) were a form of "nationalist histories" of heroes in pre-colonial history. One could call this "reactive historiography" (Picaudou 2008),[4] which tried to show that Africa had political systems, ancient civilisations, etc. in relation to European history and development. Some of the oppositional histories tried to show Africa as part of world history. Yet, as is evident in especially the first part of the book, the gap in African historical writing is as much about decolonising content as it is about decolonising *method*.

By drawing on and also moving beyond the various seminal theories, diverse scholarship and debates on "decolonisation" in epistemology – of what it is and what it is not or what it could be (Spivak, 1988; wa Thiong'o, 1986; Mbembe, 2015; Mamdani, 2016) – this volume has attempted to take on the difficult task of *illustrating* what an interdisciplinary "decolonial historiography of South Africa" could look like. We hope we have offered something *methodological* in historiography, rather than simply new content. This volume tried to critique and problematise the major African historiographical paradigms that have been manufactured in Europe.

Though this volume has shown that decolonising historiography has a long-established tradition within black intellectual thought in South Africa, it has also shown how it is scattered and found in different forms of literature and archives, including in ritual. In a sense, it has started to grapple with Falola's notion of the "ritual archive" (2017), but further work and research in this new and vast field in Africa (and in the Global South) is required.

---

[3] These were Special Editions of each of the UNESCO volumes which were published in 2003 for the South African History Project (to support teacher training). The books were published by New Africa Books (Cape Town) under licence from UNESCO. See also discussion in chapter 10.
[4] This term has been used within the Palestinian historiographical context in response to Israeli historiography. The Historiography of the 1948 War, *Online Encyclopedia of Mass Violence*, https://www.sciencespo.fr/mass-violence-war-massacre-resistance/en/document/historiography-1948 [Retrieved 22 June 2018]
See also Wolfe & Huneman 2016.

Another pertinent point this book highlights is that the indigenous people have become invisibilised as knowledge keepers and partners. In this, South Africa is not alone. For instance, George Manuel speaks of the 'fourth world' in Canada, of leaving the indigenous people out of the post-colonial intellectual decolonial discources (Veracini 2007). The historiography of decolonisation has forgotten the very people that are central to the project. This volume attempts not to merely include this "fourth world" at the margins (which often happens in liberal scholarship), but to put it at the very centre of epistemology, in decolonising historiography in South Africa.

We believe this volume is timely and that some chapters are, respectively, useful on the continent, within the Global South and within the African Diaspora, where decolonising historiography is long overdue.

The Way Forward

In debating the three key questions raised at the outset of this chapter, delegates identified six emergent questions for further research. Some of these are addressed to some degree in the chapters presented in this book, while others still need further research engagement in the next phase of the project. The six emergent research questions were:

1. *The problem of the concept 'pre-colonial'*: The Eurocentric concept 'pre-colonial' was problematised in various papers and panel discussions. Should the term be used at all? Does it provide a useful and sufficient framework for understanding the *longue duree* (long term) of history? It was argued that African history and African systems should allow us to speak in a different language on the 'pre-colonial', as we must endeavour to understand the African imagination. For instance, what are the folktales of the San and how do they help us to decolonise pre-colonial historiography and our understanding of time and space?

2. *The problem of periodisation and time*: Related to the conceptual revisiting of time, how do we theoretically frame our understanding of this past; how do we structure periodisation in southern Africa? Can we speak of a Classical Age in Africa between the 1100s and 1300s? Equally, can we speak of a Late Independent Period between 1600 and 1700? There are regional differences in southern Africa and how could we enable ourselves as scholars to tell these histories regionally, as similarity does not imply uniformity? We also engaged with debates on time. Presenting African history in

"linear" time has not always been helpful, and we may need to look at African History in thematic ways.

3. *Repositioning history before 'remembered history'*: In order to study African History properly, one has to grapple with African concepts, with the linguistic idiomatic elements of ancient African culture – "the myth of historical era" (tales and legends) (Tisani 2017). It was argued that this rethinking is foundational and should be a point of departure for historical thinking and for forming 'historical consciousness'. For example, in studying Greek History, one has to deal with Greek concepts such as *demos*, etc. Similarly, one cannot study African History properly, without studying its foundations in African Mythology. In understanding the African imagination, we will be capacitated as scholars and researchers to feel comfortable to teach the myth of 'historical era'.

4. *An Africa-centred Interdisciplinary Methodology*: Izithakazelo (e.g. how clans define themselves through ancestral oral history as they settle, disperse and migrate) helps us to move between disciplines such as Archaeology (the material) and others such as Linguistics. *Izithakazelo* helps us to understand that the hunter-gatherer moves through different modes of living and that the static archaeological frames of understanding are not useful. If we were to write a southern African textbook, we should deliberately bring in concepts such as *Izithakazelo*. The concept of the 'ritual archive', explained at the conference by eminent African scholar, Toyin Falola (2017), gives us an understanding of how we accumulate data such as words, texts, ideas and symbols, in which we can understand a vast and diverse African world. Such interdisciplinary methods (*Izithakazelo* and the 'ritual archive') are new in Africa and decidedly different from existing disciplinary methodologies and Eurocentric canons with regard to pre-colonial studies.

5. *Ukuhlambulula*, meaning 'cleansing' in Xhosa, would be a useful philosophical approach to decolonising language as we are currently taking the language of the 'colonial' into the 'pre-colonial', e.g. using the term *uMakhulu* as a source of indigenous knowledge, as discussed in chapter 5. One of the recommendations at the conference was that we develop a multilingual keywords guide for the next conference in 2019.

6. *Secrets, confidentiality and ethics*: At the conference, the question was asked: How can we stop ourselves from using exploitative research methods? How do we ensure that we conduct research on the 'researched people's' terms? The question on research ethics in working with indigenous communities is a vexing one in the Global South. What would 'equal authorship' with research participants look like? How do we ensure that the rightful sources of knowledge get the credit they deserve? How do

we develop a framework for the ethics of research on sacred sites and joint research? These questions are central to decolonising research on the pre-colonial.

There was recognition that the practice of decolonising historiography could not be achieved merely on an epistemological level (method, language, concepts, content, etc.), but needed an operational context, within the establishment of strategic networks. In this regard, delegates proposed the establishment of Research Committee Networks to, among others, conduct checks and balances on 'community research'. This arose out of a concern that what we are teaching right now, is probably not what is needed by society in general, something that was evident in the recent student led campaigns and protests. Typical questions that came up included the following: What is it that society wants us to teach and what research and learning can we engage to assist us in decolonising historiography in ways that matter and are relevant? How can we partner with 'organic intellectuals' to help us arrive at new and enriched insights?

In the final analysis, four working groups were established, focusing on: Education; Public History & Heritage Preservation Management; Ethics; and Organic Intellectuals & Universities.

The Education Working Group has been tasked with developing education materials for southern Africa within a decolonising framework, and possibly organising a '*Future* Teachers Conference' to prepare future history teachers. The Public History & Heritage Preservation Management Working Group will investigate ancient and memorial sites that are being bulldozed, vandalised, neglected and not being conserved. There is also the issue of human remains, and the development of a relevant and informed framework for repatriation, which would include working with the 'ritual archive'.

The Ethics Working Group will research policies and legal frameworks on working with indigenous communities, while the Organic Intellectuals & Universities Working Group will pay attention to the need to research, for incorporation into the curriculum, knowledge that is developed by 'organic' intellectuals outside formal educational institutions, including universities. There was a strong view among delegates that there are many organic intellectuals out there, not only those who were/are trained in Western education and go on to adopt a critical stance of Eurocentrism outside formal educational structures, but also indigenous knowledge practitioners such as *uMakhulu*. How do we bring their knowledge into the university, and how do we take the university back to the community?

It is hoped that these groups will present their findings and ongoing research on the above matters in the next conference of the catalytic project on pre-colonial historiography whose proceedings, as with the first conference, will be published in the *Rethinking Africa* series.

References

Ajayi, J.F.A. (ed.). 1989. *General History of Africa, Volume VI, Africa in the Nineteenth Century until the 1880s*. Paris: UNESCO.

Adu Boahen, A. (ed.). 1985. *General History of Africa, Volume VII, Africa under Foreign Domination 1880-1935*. Paris: UNESCO.

Fasi, E. & Hrbek, I. (eds.). 1988. *General History of Africa, Volume III, Africa from the Seventh to the Eleventh Century*. Paris: UNESCO.

Falola, T. 2017. Ritual Archives. In: *The Palgrave Handbook of African Philosophy*, 703-728. New York: Palgrave Macmillan. https://doi.org/10.1057/978-1-137-59291-0_45

Ki-Zerbo, J. (ed.). 1981. *General History of Africa, Volume I, Methodology and African Prehistory*. Paris: UNESCO.

Mamdani, M. 2016. Between the public intellectual and the scholar: Decolonization and some post-independence initiatives in African higher education. *Inter-Asia Cultural Studies*, 17(1): 68-83. https://doi.org/10.1080/14649373.2016.1140260

Mazrui, A.A. & Wondji, C. (eds.). 1993. *General History of Africa, Volume VIII, Africa since 1935*. Paris: UNESCO.

Mbembe, A. 2015. Decolonizing Knowledge and the Question of the Archive. Unpublished Wiser paper: Aula magistral proferida.

Mbembe, A. 2010. Fifty Years of African Decolonisation. *Chimurenga Magazine*, 25.

Mokhtar, G. (ed.). 1981. *General History of Africa, Volume II, Ancient Civilisations of Africa*. Paris: UNESCO.

Niane, D.T. (ed.). 1984. *General History of Africa, Volume IV, Africa from the Twelfth to Sixteenth Century*. Paris: UNESCO.

Ogot, B.A. (ed.). 1992. *Africa from the Sixteenth to Eighteenth Century, General History of Africa, Volume V*. Paris: UNESCO.

Spivak, G.C. 1988. Can the subaltern speak? *Reflections on the history of an idea*, 21-78.

Veracini, L. 2007. Settler colonialism and decolonisation. *Borderlands e-journal*, 6:2.

Wa Thiong'o, N. 1986. *Decolonising the mind: The politics of language in African literature*. Nairobi: East African Publishers.

Wolfe, C.T. & Huneman, P. 2016. Man-Machines and Embodiment: From Cartesian Physiology to Claude Bernard's 'Living Machine'. In: J.E.H. Smith. Forthcoming. *Embodiment, Oxford Philosophical Concepts*. Oxford University Press.

APPENDIX 1

Conference Closing Remarks and Thanks (transcribed)

Denise Zinn[1]

I always consider it a great privilege to be able to do closing remarks and thanks, because it gives me an opportunity to express gratitude, and the impact that an event like this has had on us. It is a moment where in our giving thanks, we also acknowledge how this coming together takes us all forward.

I want to express gratitude for this conference. It has been imbued with a spirit of huge generosity; the spirit in this space has almost been poetic and aesthetic. I think it captures and embraces that notion about all that we are, and I want to borrow from sis'Tisani, and from Reverend Soga that saying, 'We ARE the earth'. I think that is what we've embraced in this conference. I think this is what the poet Rumi also says, when he wrote in the 13th century:

> "You are not a drop in the ocean. You are the entire ocean in a drop."

That is part of the spirit that has come through in this conference. I want to acknowledge and recognise the important words with which Lungisile Ntsebeza started this conference, which have been echoed by many people in the course of this conference, and that is that we are taking part in this *at this moment*. It is a special moment. It is the moment when the student movement

---

[1] denise.zinn@mandela.ac.za

has taken us to a new beginning. I am echoing the words that have come from this conference, and I think it is again the words from sis'Tisani, about the cyclical nature of things. So it is a momentous and significant conference. It has brought home again my gratitude for the student movement at this particular time (young people at this particular time). One story I want to relate is how during #FeesMustFall, during the early part of the year, when there was a sit-in at the Dean of Arts' offices, we got a message from the students who addressed us as follows, they wrote to us: 'Dear colonial administrator'. I had a shock because anyone who has a little bit of knowledge about my history and the history of my generation would know that part of our struggle was an anti-colonial struggle; so to be addressed by students calling us 'colonial administrators' was a huge shock to me. But it was a reality shock, because I had to recognise that what they were saying was true. We exist in an edifice, in an administration, that is largely colonial. And another student said to me, pointing her finger at me, 'You don't know your job; because we don't want to hear about your years as a student activist or as a person who was engaged in the struggle. We want to know what you are doing NOW as the Deputy Vice Chancellor'. And again I had to swallow hard, very hard, and think about the truth of what she was saying. So, I say all of this with gratitude.

I think what moments like these bring to us, is a recognition not just of where we have come from, but where we are now, and what that then asks of us in this moment, for these new beginnings, for these new cycles that are starting. What is it that is being asked of us? And so I am grateful even for those challenges, even for those lumps in my throat, even for what one is experiencing emotionally under these kinds of conditions. In terms of this conference, we have drawn on the humanities and social sciences. We have drawn on music, language and poetry, images, and to a great extent, on *imagination*. We have drawn on education and we have drawn on *alternative sources of knowledge*. We have also drawn on the natural, the physical and life sciences. For example, last night's exhibition and discussion on palaeontology, archaeology and architecture, and what all of that brings together.

What I give gratitude for in this conference is that we have taken back our right to be fully authoritative experts and scientists; *to own and possess, to produce, to create that from which we were dispossessed. That is what we are taking back in this conference. And so, through this, to enrich and to heal.*

Sis'Tisani, we have to give you an honorary position because I've quoted you three times now. This concept that takes us even further (I actually had to get her to write it for me so that I can say it right), Ukuhlambulula – not just to heal, but also *to cleanse and heal who we are, so we can fully embrace the idea that 'we are the earth.'*

So, more formally and specifically, let us share our gratitude with those who have made all this possible. Firstly, the delegates, the participants, all of you, from far and wide; Mozambique, for example, and from all across different institutions in South Africa, from the north and south, from all directions, – the movement has come. To be here, to present from your different disciplines, from education, art, music, archaeology, architecture, history (most particularly), philosophy, sociology, all these different knowledges have come together in this conference. So, I thank all you for being here. Secondly, I thank all the presenters who with courage (I know for some of you it took great courage) put forward their ideas here. As Lungisile Ntsebeza says, this is an academic conference, and we know that academics can come from all different walks of life and all different levels. The generosity with which you put forward your ideas, your research, your tentative thoughts, your works in progress before us – to stimulate us, to provoke us, to help us think, ponder, imagine and to contest an exciting range of concepts, indeed to catalyse, to speed up (that is what a catalyst does; it does not only start up, but it *speeds* up) towards a future that we want to contribute to creating. Thanks to the session chairs who did a great job. Simphiwe (Sesanti) set a high standard for discipline in the chair. To the conference teams, CAS – June Bam[2] and Lungisile Ntsebeza, for your inspiration, your dedication and hard work that went into this. And CANRAD for the particular excellence in the way they organise things. They think of everything (transport, food etc.). They make sure that there are children who participate, that there is music, and a spirit that imbues what we do; that it is inclusive not only in terms of the different disciplines in our institutions, but also from our communities. I thank the community members who are here. I thank the way they have come, the way CANRAD organises to ensure that that happens. Lungisile Ntsebeza has already named and thanked the interns in CANRAD. I can't wait for them to be in these positions; to not be called 'colonial administrators' but something else as facilitators of *a new way forward* for us all. Thank you for giving your energy, your life force. No matter how long the night, the day will come.

Thank you, everyone.

---

2   Also known as June Bam-Hutchison.

INDEX

Symbols
#FeesMustFall 4, 5, 8, 36, 184, 206
#RhodesMustFall 4, 168, 174, 181, 184

A
abaMbo 62-65, 67-72
abaThwa 130, 132-133
African Renaissance 30, 180
amaGcina 124, 128, 135
amaHlubi 64-65, 69-72, 124, 128, 166
amaKalanga 64, 72
amaLala 64, 67
amaMfengu 62-66, 70, 135
amaMpondomise 124, 128, 132-133, 135
amaNguni 3, 95
amasiko 66-68
ancestors 21, 25, 45, 68, 83-84, 94, 99, 108, 110
archaeology 9, 35, 92, 96-98, 101-102, 104, 107, 111, 173, 180, 202, 206-207
archive 61, 77, 84-85, 91-92, 94, 95-97, 101, 103-105, 107-109, 111-112, 121, 146, 155-158, 172-173, 186, 200, 202-203
Autshumato 167, 170, 175

B
Biko 82
bodies 60, 76, 79, 80-82, 85-87, 100, 160-161
Bushmen 101, 161

C
Cabral, Amilcar 17
CALUSA 120-121, 122, 124-125, 127, 136, 147
Castle of Good Hope 162-163, 174
catalytic 1, 15, 24, 92, 112, 120, 130, 145, 155-156, 161, 173, 175, 204
ceremonies 21, 164-165, 167, 175
chieftainess 44, 49-50
clans 7, 8, 21, 25, 30, 57-59, 62-69, 71, 84, 93-94, 98, 129, 132, 202
class 3, 141, 175, 192-194
community 9, 10, 17, 23, 25, 37, 45, 48, 75, 76, 80, 81, 82, 85, 95, 119-125, 127, 130, 135-136, 140, 143, 145, 147-150, 155-162, 165-166, 168-169, 170-175, 191, 194, 202-203, 207
conceptions 2, 8, 47, 58, 76, 79-80, 86, 139
conflict 63, 146, 157
conservation 143, 147, 149
Coree 170
cosmology 18, 23, 25-26, 28, 30, 37, 101
curriculum 4-6, 10, 18-19, 30-31, 36, 83, 87, 93, 111, 128, 180-183, 187-188, 190, 193, 195, 203
customs 46, 67, 99, 162, 186, 190

D
decolonial 155-156, 162, 169, 170, 172, 184, 200-201
Dhlomo 184-187
digital 77, 87, 158, 159

209

Diop, CA 16, 184
Doman 167, 170
domestication 16

E

early travellers 102
education 1, 4-7, 10, 18-19, 39-41, 43, 46, 51, 82-84, 86, 92, 120, 128, 136, 147, 155, -158, 161-162, 165, 173-175, 179-181, 183-184, 186-187, 195, 199-200, 203, 206-207
embodiment 78, 80, 87
epistemicide 160
epistemology 11, 17, 19, 40, 44, 66, 200-201
erasure 20, 44, 191
ethics 86, 161-162, 202-203
ethnicity 66, 94, 107
ethnography 97-98, 100, 104, 108, 195
etymology 35, 43, 50-51, 53
Eurocentric 6, 17, 19, 31, 47, 60, 175, 200-202
evidence 8, 35-36, 38, 40, 43, 45-48, 52-53, 67, 98, 101, 106-107, 120, 127, 133, 149, 179, 181, 189, 192
exclusion 23, 61, 65, 78, 86
extinction 21, 24, 169

F

family histories 7, 21, 29, 84, 93, 127
feminism 40
FHYA 156, 158
Fingo 20, 21, 28, 64
folktales. See iintsomi (folktales)
food 133, 135, 159, 207
funding 18, 92, 157, 172, 180

G

Gcaleka 65, 69-70, 146
gender 8, 36-38, 40, 47-53, 76, 77, 84-86, 107, 123, 141, 148, 184, 193
General History of Africa 181, 184, 199

genocide 159, 160-161, 171
Ghana 30, 188
globalisation 189, 190
Global South 92, 97, 155, 200-202
Gqoba, William 40-43, 47-49, 58, 63, 64, 146

H

headman 124, 128-130
healing 17-18, 31, 76, 156, 162, 164, 173
hegemonic 155
heritage 10, 47, 53, 77, 86, 87, 93-95, 139-144, 147, 150, 156-157, 161-162, 164-166, 168, 172, 175, 180, 188, 191, 193-195, 203
Hintsa 30, 69-70, 77 147
historians 7, 18, 58, 60-62, 65-68, 72, 92-93, 95, 97, 99-100, 101, 104-105, 108, 143, 161, 169, 171, 181, 186
historical consciousness 22, 59, 202
historical studies 59
historicise 75, 77
historiography 1-3, 7-8, 10, 13, 57-58, 60, 61-65, 68, 72, 139, 146, 164, 169, 183-185, 188, 196, 199-201, 203, 204
Hlubi 64-66, 72, 95
households 8, 75-82, 83, 85, 86, 87, 128, 161
human remains 149, 161, 203
Huri#oaxa 169

I

identity 21, 28-29, 35-37, 39, 44, 46-49, 51, 62-63, 66-68, 93, 107, 108, 141, 170, 172-173
ideology 37, 43, 86, 105-106, 187
idiom 42, 57, 59, 62-63, 67, 71-72, 78
llHui!Gaeb 169
iintsomi (folktales) 8, 76, 83
IKS (Indigenous Knowledge System) 77, 168, 181

Indian Ocean   25, 92, 110, 189
inkosi   28, 50
intellectuals   3, 7, 11, 20, 47, 51, 53, 94-95, 141, 157-158, 171, 175, 186, 203
interconnectedness   18, 67
interdisciplinary   76, 104, 158, 184, 199, 200, 202
interlocutors   61, 102, 105, 106
invisibilised   48, 79, 162, 168, 173, 201
isazela   76-77, 85
/Ui!arab   162, 168, 169
izibongo   21, 59, 62, 67
iziduko   21, 30, 59, 62, 65-66, 68, 84
izithakazelo   21, 30, 59, 67-68, 94, 111, 202

J
Jordan, AC   3, 5, 6, 42, 46-49, 51-52

K
khaoexasib   169
Khoikhoi   24, 146, 149, 170
Khoikhoi of Queen Hoho   146
Khoisan   93, 123, 141, 149, 165, 167-168
King Shaka   94, 101
kinship   50, 94, 107
Klasies River   147
Krotoa   166-168, 170-171, 175

L
labour   63, 65, 77, 80-83, 85, 101, 128, 133
land   3, 16, 20, 23-24, 28, 30, 39, 65-66, 69-70, 120, 123-125, 128-130, 135, 146, 149, 156-157, 164-165, 174
landscape   16, 110, 160-161, 179
language   7-8, 17, 18, 21-24, 35-38, 40-49, 51-53, 57, 59-60, 62, 65-70, 76, 77, 78, 81, 83, 87, 96, 105, 107, 111, 133, 156, 161, 169-170, 172-173, 175, 185-186, 189-190, 201-203, 206
lexicon   35, 40, 43, 48-49, 51-53
liberal   60-61, 164, 201
lineage   94

literature   36, 43, 46, 48, 51-52, 130, 132-134, 184, 186, 188, 200
Lovedale   18, 46-47, 186

M
Mafeje, A   6, 7, 41, 43, 59-60, 66
Mamdani, Mahmood   6, 7, 11, 16, 19, 20, 23, 99, 158, 170, 172, 190, 200
maps   27, 28, 31, 105, 125, 126
Mapungubwe   10, 179-184, 187-195
marriage   50, 52, 81, 83, 133, 193-194
Marxist   60-61, 100
Matanzima   123, 127
matriarchal   77-78, 86-87
matrilineal   168, 171
Mbembe, Achille   16, 23, 25-26, 190, 200
Mda   10, 183-184, 187-188, 191, 193-195
memory   35, 43, 44, 46, 53, 68, 157, 160, 168, 172-175, 184
Mfecane   62-63, 65-67, 69, 188
Mfengu   21, 64-65, 66, 68, 70
Mhlehle   28, 29
migrant labour   82, 128
mining   71-72, 105, 195
missionaries   3, 39, 43-46, 50-51, 58, 62, 69, 98, 102
Mkhize   8, 57, 67-68, 84-85, 93, 146, 181
morpheme   38, 48-50, 52, 53
Mossel Bay   147, 156, 170, 174-175
Mozambique   2, 16, 207
Mpondoland   148
Mpondomise   51
Mpumalanga   93, 143
Mqhayi, SEK   18, 21, 37, 47, 58, 146, 147
Mudimbe, VY   15, 17, 20, 22-23
multilingualism   157
multiversalism   19
museums   10, 95, 103, 107, 142, 150, 156, 161-162, 166, 169, 174
myths   20, 26, 42, 102, 202

N

naming 15, 21, 31, 38, 52, 67-68, 98, 169
narratives 8, 16, 27, 37, 76, 94, 105-106, 111, 139-142, 147-150, 158, 168, 173-175, 179, 183, 186, 193
native 21, 23, 30, 38, 43, 45-46, 61, 172, 186
natives 184
neo-traditionalism 75
newspapers 21, 42, 46-47, 57, 64-65, 69, 95, 141
nomenclature 71, 98
Nongqawuse 77, 144, 183
North Africa 132, 189

O

ontology 21, 40, 67, 76
Opland, J 46, 58-59, 60, 146
oracy 38, 42
oral history 58-59, 77, 82, 84, 121, 202
oral traditions 46, 57-60, 62, 63-65, 67, 69, 99, 100, 105, 109-110, 146, 161, 193
Oyewumi, O 36, 75-76, 79-81, 85-87

P

palaeontological 10, 92, 139, 142, 144
patent 159-160, 162
patriarchal 75, 77
Pedi 93, 100
Peires, Jeff 3, 58, 63, 65, 68, 77, 100, 133, 134, 143, 145, 147, 161, 180, 183
periodisation 15-16, 18, 97, 111, 145, 201
philosophy 15, 17, 22, 25, 37, 207
Plaatje, Sol 184, 186
plants 20-21, 82, 133-135, 159-162, 165
policies 5, 10, 28, 30, 94, 181, 183, 186-187, 203
political 7-8, 16, 20, 23-24, 43, 45, 59, 63, 67-68, 76, 78, 85, 93, 96-99, 101, 103, 105-108, 140-142, 148, 157, 162, 165, 168, 180, 183, 185-186, 188, 190, 192-194, 200

polyepistemic 19
post-apartheid 9, 17, 111, 156, 160, 166, 180, 184
post-colonial 15-19, 27, 31, 77, 102, 187, 201
praise poems 59, 69
pre-colonial 1-4, 7, 8, 10-11, 15-16, 18-19, 22, 31, 35-36, 38, 40, 44-45, 47-48, 51-53, 68-69, 71, 75-76, 77-79, 82, 84, 87, 92-93, 97-98, 101, 111, 128, 139, 140-150, 155-163, 165-166, 168-175, 179-183, 185, 187-188, 196, 199, 200-204
public 3, 8, 10, 59, 69, 76, 85-87, 93-98, 102, 104, 108, 112, 140-143, 149, 155-156, 158-160, 164-166, 168, 171-175, 184, 193, 203

R

reconciliation 17, 165, 167, 184
religion 7, 22-25, 75, 121, 136, 186, 189-190
research 1-3, 6-7, 9-11, 15, 17, 24, 27, 31, 37, 39, 48, 92, 94-98, 101-102, 104, 106, 108-109, 112, 120-123, 125-127, 136, 139-142, 144-145, 147-148, 150, 155-159, 161-162, 169-175, 200-204, 207
resistance 17, 27, 141, 171, 200
Rharhabe 77, 146, 147
rituals 24, 66-68, 108, 128, 134-135, 165, 169, 175, 194, 200, 202-203
rock paintings 101, 121-122, 124-127, 130-131, 133-136, 160

S

SAHP 180-182, 184, 200
San 130, 146, 149, 159-160, 162, 188, 189, 191, 201
secrecy 157, 160-162
skills 9, 38, 41, 122, 136, 157, 172, 173

slavery 16, 22, 156, 173
social cohesion 18, 44, 141
social justice 141, 144, 174
social stratification 38, 47, 50, 53
sociolinguistic 37, 38, 45
Socwatsha kaPhaphu 102
Soga, JH 58, 64, 72, 146, 186
Soga, Tiyo 28, 205
sources 8-9, 17, 20, 35-36, 38, 41, 43-46, 53, 59, 61-62, 64-66, 69, 72, 76, 82, 86-87, 95, 99- 105, 108-110, 121, 125, 130, 133-134, 146, 163-164, 174, 193, 202, 206
SS Mendi 21
Stewart, James 46
storytelling 82, 87, 128
Stuart, James 95, 99-103, 105-106
Swahili 189-191
Swaziland 105
Swazis 70-71, 100

T

Tabata, IB 7
teachers 65, 130, 195, 200, 203
temporal complications 91
temporalities 26, 111, 185, 190
terminological problems 91
textbooks 10, 181-183, 189-195, 202
time 2, 4, 15-16, 18, 23-29, 31, 43, 45-47, 58, 68, 71, 78, 81, 91-94, 96, 98-101, 103, 105, 107-111, 123, 128-129, 133-134, 143, 145, 158, 165, 167, 169-170, 175, 181-182, 186, 189, 191, 201, 202, 206
totemic 68
tourism 135, 140, 142-143, 157, 162, 164, 195
trade 25, 70-71, 110, 162, 181, 189, 191
traditional leaders 94, 135, 145
tribe; tribal 20, 64, 95, 103, 107, 111, 123, 128, 159
Tsui-||goatse! 171

U

ukuhlambulula 18-19, 27, 31, 169, 202, 207
universities 2, 4-5, 19, 29, 60-61, 87, 92, 120, 161, 174, 181, 184, 186, 200, 203

V

values 8, 18, 29, 37, 41-42, 46, 48, 53, 76, 78, 86-87, 140, 143, 159, 173, 180-181, 188, 195
vernacular 58, 62, 65-66, 85, 105

W

women 3, 7, 30, 35, 37, 39-40, 46, 48, 51-53, 75-82, 86-87, 103, 124, 146, 166, 168, 193, 194
workers 4, 5, 80, 95, 129
world history 110, 200
worldview 21-23, 25-27, 30-31, 76

X

Xhosa polity 18, 77

Y

Yoruba 20, 36, 80-81
youth 9, 30, 41, 82-83, 120, 122, 125-127, 134, 136, 147, 158, 165, 173

Z

Zimbabwe 16, 70-72, 179, 181, 187, 189, 191
Zulu 37, 62-63, 67-68, 78, 82, 93-94, 99, 101-103, 166-167, 184

www.ingramcontent.com/pod-product-compliance
Lightning Source LLC
Chambersburg PA
CBHW071114160426
43196CB00013B/2569